Courtesy of salon.com

A Second Life

Also by Dan Gerber

A Second Life

A Collected Nonfiction

Dan Gerber

Michigan State University Press

East Lansing

♾ The paper used in this publication meets the minimum requirements
of ANSI/NISO Z39.48–1992 (R 1997) (Permanence of Paper).

Michigan State University Press
East Lansing, Michigan 48823-5202

Printed and bound in the United States of America.

07 06 05 04 03 02 01   1 2 3 4 5 6 7 8 9 10

LIBRARY OF CONGRESS CATALOGING-IN-PUBLICATION DATA
Gerber, Dan, 1940–
A second life : a collected nonfiction / Dan Gerber.
p. cm.
ISBN 0-87013-589-9 (cloth : alk. paper)
I. Title.
PS3557.E66 S4 2001
814'.54–dc21
2001003698

Some of these essays originally appeared in *Gray's Sporting Journal, Men's Journal, Motor Boating
& Sailing, Outside, Playboy, Sports Afield, Fly Fishing in Salt Waters, Fourth Genre,* and *Sports
Illustrated;* as well as the following anthologies: *Seasons of the Angler,* ed. David Seybold (N.Y.:
Weidenfeld and Nicholson, 1988); *Boats,* ed. David Seybold (N.Y.: Atlantic Monthly Press, 1990);
Fathers and Sons, ed. David Seybold (N.Y.: Grove Weidenfeld, 1992); *Road Trips, Head Trips, and
Other Car-Crazed Writings,* ed. Jean Lindamood (N.Y.: Atlantic Monthly Press, 1996); and *On
Killing,* ed. Robert F. Jones (N.Y.: Lyons Press, 2001).

Cover artwork is detail from "March Evening, Spring Hill Road"
by Carol Peek, used courtesy of the artist.

Cover design is by Ariana Grabec-Dingman, Harriman, NY
Book design in by Sharp Des!gns, Inc., Lansing, MI

Visit Michigan State University Press on the World Wide Web at:
www.msupress.msu.edu

for Deb

Ah, not to be cut off,
not through the slightest partition
shut out from the law of the stars.
The inner—what is it?
if not intensified sky,
hurled through with birds and deep
with the winds of homecoming.

—Rainer Maria Rilke

Contents

Introduction

A frowning Thistle implores my stay.
What to others a trifle appears
Fills me full of smiles and tears;
For a double vision my Eyes do see,
And a double vision is always with me.
With my inward Eye 'tis an old Man grey;
With my outward a Thistle across my way.
                              —William Blake

THE STORIES IN this collection, set in places with names as exotic and prosaic as the Kaisut Desert, the Dry Tortugas, Mackinac Island, and Indianapolis, come from what I think of as my second life, the time-and-space life of outward adventure, as opposed—if indeed they *are* opposed—to that inward life from which poems come. Of course, which is first and which second depends on your focus and where you happen to be looking at the moment, the important point being, as Blake reminds us, not to be limited by *single vision and Newton's sleep*. Our truest lives must be imagined.

The first conscious realization that there could be another kind of life, a kind I hadn't yet envisioned, came to me through two discoveries I made the year I was twelve years old: the discovery of the power of a poem, and the discovery that I could find solace, even in what seemed my life's darkest moments, by paying close attention to the natural world.

THROUGH PEOPLE I'VE encountered as an adult, people who also knew me as a child, I learned that I was thought of then primarily as a loner, not because I didn't have friends, but because, unlike my friends, I was part of no particular group. I was sent away to northern Michigan for six weeks of summer camp when I was five, and to the first in a series of boarding schools at twelve. Being the youngest of five, I came along at at time when my parents were tired, and being the only male child, they wanted to ensure that I wouldn't be a mama's boy, though my exiles, I believe, had the reverse effect. I cried myself to sleep most nights and obsessed on ideas of escape. I befriended inanimate objects. When I was six, a small white plastic human skull on a key chain became my most intimate companion and confidant because I could rely on it to be there in my pocket through a long summer of homesickness. I talked to animals, even, and perhaps especially, while they were absent. At boarding school when I was twelve, I communed through the medium of a stuffed toy Scottie with my real dog, Skipper, two hundred miles away. And I think that for me the primary attraction of poetry was that of a reliable being to whom I could listen and with whom I could speak.

These empowered objects which became my companions were a primitive way of escaping my miserable little self. They weren't terribly satisfying, but they were what I made do with, until one October morning when I opened a literature textbook and began reading a poem which so absorbed me in its sense of mystery that I completely forgot about the unhappy boy I had conceived to be me. It was a poem called "The Highwayman," by Alfred Noyes, and it transported me to a world of mystery, tragedy, and romance through its chiaroscuro imagery and the galloping rhythm of its lines. I'm sure that I also fell in love with "the landlord's dark-eyed, red-lipped daughter, Bess,/plaiting a dark red love knot into her long black hair." But that was incidental.

I didn't know exactly what it was that had taken possession of me, but I knew that I needed it as surely as I needed water and air. At that moment, the poem seemed more tangible than the book that contained it. I knew that those words, arranged as they were, had awakened someone in me I hadn't known, and that more than anything else I might do, I knew that I, too, needed to do something with words and images to recreate the kind of larger experience I'd received from the poem.

The second discovery occurred the following spring and seems to me now inseparable from the first. Still miserable, though now in a different school, in St. Louis, Missouri, I had built a world of hope around a long-anticipated visit from my mother. For weeks I had taken comfort looking forward to a Saturday in April, and as the day approached I could already feel my loneliness beginning to dissolve in her embrace. I knew, of course, that I would plead with her to take me along when it came time for her to leave, and she also may have known this. But after breakfast on that long-awaited Saturday, my dorm master, a dour and soberly religious Brit who seemed wanly resigned to his tenure among the children of rude colonials, handed me a blue envelope redolent of my mother's perfume and addressed to me in her hand. Along with a note of apology and an explanation that she had been called to the bedside of a stricken friend, I found a crisp twenty-dollar bill. The note went on to express her hopes that the money might somehow compensate for her absence and brighten what she knew must be a great disappointment.

I had never possessed a twenty-dollar bill, and although it struck me as an amazingly unsatisfying piece of paper, I realized that it could readily be converted into something else. And the something else I most wanted right then was to be some*where* else—if not at home with my mother, then at least somewhere far away from the harsh and stultifying atmosphere of the school. I don't remember exactly how the idea occurred to me (though I had been reading *Huckleberry Finn* at the time), that I was not very far from the great Mississippi River. I pulled on the white duck trousers I'd laid out for my mother's visit, a white T-shirt, and a blue cotton windbreaker, walked out of the school grounds, hailed a taxi, and asked the driver to take me to the river, someplace where I could rent a boat.

I had grown up in and around water and felt quite at home in the green wooden rowboat with rusty oarlocks I managed to rent for three dollars and my Bulova watch, which I left as collateral with the somewhat skeptical liveryman, whose name, I remember, for reasons beyond reason, was Fred. I shoved off across the muddy current and rowed out to a small island where I found a rotting dock, a sagging tar paper and green shingle shack, herons, ducks, songbirds, turtles, and a garden hose-sized water snake which I watched as it unhinged its jaw and swallowed a remarkably indifferent frog.

It was so quiet on the island I could hear the purling of the river, and it seemed to me, as I lay with my belly against the dock planks in my now very gray and grass-stained white trousers, that it was the island, not the river, that was moving, and that it might be a great ship pulling me upriver toward home.

I stayed on the island all day, watching the shadows of clouds sweep the water and listening to the familiar reedy call of the blackbirds. I didn't think about my mother or my unhappiness at school or what might be waiting for me when I returned, believing then, as I do now, that it was one of the most satisfying days of my life, that if my mother had appeared as promised I would have simply been more miserable when she left and that the eighteen dollars I paid for two taxi rides, the boat rental, and a ham sandwich was holy money and the best I ever spent.

That day alone on the river confirmed something in me, something discovered and reaffirmed through the years, that, as Rilke tells us, "It is our task to imprint this temporary, perishable earth into ourselves so deeply, so painfully and passionately, that its essence can rise again invisibly inside us."

Ten years later, on the chilly, overcast afternoon of August 20, 1962, out of college and working at a job I hated, feeling listless and forlorn about my existence, I took a walk down an abandoned road, a road through a swamp, and sat on the trunk of a tree that had been uprooted in a storm. There I took a vow, as if to a religious order, that I would devote my life to watching and listening to the world around me and to making poems, as best I could, out of my experience, because, along with and in spite of everything else that would be required of me, it was what I had to do.

A POET-FRIEND ONCE commented that the tough thing about being a poet is to figure out what to do between poems. Of course, the real work a poet does *is* what he or she does in the times between, the poems themselves being only the fruition. There are, in addition to the demands the poem makes of constant attention to life and to language, the demands of ordinary living, of getting and spending and regarding the needs of others.

In those times between poems I taught, worked in various businesses, raised a family, wrote novels and short stories—not unrelated to the poems themselves—and gave in to the fascination of a world of adventures, partly, I suppose, because I lacked the inner resources to simply sit and wait, and because the world itself is fascinating.

This collection is, for the most part, a record of those experiences that have filled the gaps between poems and, most particularly, the ones the editors of various magazines found interesting enough to present to their readers.

John Ruskin tells us that the greatest thing a human soul can do is to see something and to tell about it in a plain way. If we were truly awake, each day would be a great adventure and each day would be a poem. But we're not. We get tired and we get bored. Our experiences wear us down and we fall into habit. Or, our experiences seem dull to us because of our habits. Your choice.

Fortunately, however, there are breaks in the clouds. Our lives transcend our routines. Sometimes a breakthrough comes as a gift. When that happens to me and I'm lucky and manage to stick with it, it may become a poem. But, as Wallace Stevens noted, this sort of thing doesn't happen every day. So I've gone out to find ways to occupy myself between lightning strikes. Often the search for adventure is fun and gets the heart going, and frequently it has paid well enough to at least cover the trip. In any case, the experiences I've collected here have been important to me, both in themselves and in the stories I've made of them. They have been my second life.

My beloved Rilke, in this translation by Robert Bly, expresses the idea of a second kind of life more beautifully than I can explain.

I love the dark hours of my being
in which my senses drop into the deep.
I have found in them, as in old letters,
my private life, that is already lived through,
and become wide and powerful now, like legends.
Then I know that there is room in me
for a second huge and timeless life.

But sometimes I am like a tree that stands
over a grave, a leafy tree, fully grown,
who has lived out that particular dream, that the dead boy
(around whom its warm roots are pressing)
lost through his sad moods and his poems.

As you can see, I love to quote poets who have already said what I, more or less, might be trying to say. It's like using magic to illuminate a text, and it comes from the not altogether forlorn hope that some of that magic will adhere to me. Of course, "the second huge and timeless life" of the poem *is* the poem. But here, in this book, it's what I've tried to get into these stories.

At Speed

from *Out of Control*

This first piece isn't nonfiction at all; it's the introductory chapter from my second novel. As it fairly well captures the experience of driving a racing car, and thus rounds out that avenue of experience, I've included it.

EVERYTHING WORKED. He was driving to win and nothing could intrude. He had a feeling he was slightly out of control, never absolutely sure the car wouldn't fly off the road at each corner or soar at the crest of each hill. He'd had a nightmare in which the car became an airplane and he had no way to land it, exhilaration going up and terror knowing he must come down. The forces on his body were like movements in a dance danced in a space no larger than his body so it became more a dance of the mind, the road rushing into his car, the dips and bends and rises, the vibrations from the engine behind him, choreography for his toes in asbestos ballet slippers and the quick slight movements of his hands from the wheel to the shift lever and back.

The scream of the engine was behind him, pushing him as if he were trying to escape it. He imagined the twisting force, the flywheels and gears trying to drill through the firewall into the small of his back. He was more aware of vibration than sound. The fuel vapor rose from his injector stacks where the engine sucked in the air and shot it out the exhaust pipes as sound. But now it was all one, movement, vibration, sound and the smell of heat on brake pads, rubber and oil. The sign from his pit told him there was no one ahead and twelve seconds of vacuum behind. Three laps to go. In plain English this meant that if the car held together he'd won the race.

He didn't have a sense of it being a race anymore; he was simply trying to hold the car together, watching the oil pressure dial he'd ignored during most of the race and listening for the engine to falter. He silently apologized to the car for the abuse he'd given it and begged it not to die. He passed slower cars. He passed the pits again. Two laps to go. He braked for the left-hand bend and downshifted for the carousel right that followed. He feathered the car through the carousel and fed the accelerator on the way out. The long straight began to rush up on him. It was like driving into a green funnel. He spotted a red jacket and knew it was Frank. The red jacket was gone now and he set up for the bend in the straight.

It was the most perilous spot on the course, an almost imperceptible crick in the long straight when you passed over at highway speed, but at 163 miles per hour it became a thrill. He had to place the car on the right-hand edge of the asphalt and let it drift to the left, hoping that he ran out of bend before he ran out of road. Each year the cars went a little faster and each year each driver had to find out for himself if the bend could still be taken without letting up on the gas. It could. But each time he took it, the bend was an adventure. Would there be oil on the road? Would the tar be soft? The car weighed seven pounds when it got to the bend. Seven pounds distributed to four patches of rubber about a foot square each. He didn't like to think about that. He couldn't think about that when he drove. He watched the road slide from left to right under the silver of his car. He watched the green rush by and the specks of color that were the spectators. He picked his spot to shut off for the tight right-hander and anticipated the bumps in the asphalt that would make the car jump as he braked.

IT SEEMED AS if the cars were driving themselves because the drivers were barely visible, a plastic or metallic-looking bubble of helmet protruding from the sleek wedge of the car, most of them a distinctive color or design contrasting with the body of the car; and then Roger's helmet passed, a deep metallic blue, looking really more black than blue above the silver body of the car; and nothing but the color and his name on the side of the car which he knew was there but couldn't read as the car hissed by in its pocket of air followed by the scream of exhaust as if the twin megaphone exhaust pipes were actual megaphones through which the engine was begging to be left alone. It seemed to be always on the edge of exploding, and when he had looked at it in the garage and listened to the mechanics warming it up and checking the timing he regarded it more as a bomb than a vehicle and wanted to stand clear in case it should explode and fill the air with shrapnel. The red blur on the side of the car that was Roger's name against the silver blur that was the car itself and the furtive helmet that was Roger were now gone, leaving only the scream from the black void of the megaphones rising and falling, rising and falling like a baby alternately screaming in a tantrum and pausing to catch its breath, then the steady rising pitch as he picked his apex and accelerated through the unseen corner and into the unseen straight, then lost in the sound of the other engines and erased by the cars now passing the spot where he stood.

The cars were spread out so that it seemed there was really no race, simply an undetermined number of cars amusing themselves with speed and sound, as if hurtling their unseen drivers past the crowd in an attempt to disguise them, to smuggle them past without notice as a child might scream about pain or injustice to obscure the fact that he was stealing cookies. It somehow wasn't Roger in that car, at least not the same man he had seen that morning absorbed in his own thoughts, whatever thoughts he might have before becoming anonymous in silver plastic and traffic and the stew of sound punctuated by the mention of his name from a loudspeaker as if it were the only word he could recognize in a foreign tongue, the same Roger who had eaten a rare steak and salad and drunk over half a bottle of wine the night before and over-tipped the waitress because she was pretty and certainly not the same Roger who read T. S. Eliot aloud to no one who wanted to hear it and drank straight tequila when he drank it at all, which wasn't very often, and had actually claimed he didn't want to screw his fiancee until after they were married. And suddenly it was quiet as if everything in the world had been switched off except the katydids or crickets or whatever kind of bugs that hum on a summer afternoon, now overcast and looking as if it might rain, the grass and trees a deeper green against the gray sky, dense and still and the crackle of the loudspeaker and the sound of engines like toys passing the official's pagoda where the announcer stood. Maybe it was Roger's car he was hearing through the speaker like a sound effect on a radio drama he remembered as a child or a Memorial Day broadcast of the Indianapolis 500 he'd heard years ago while driving to a beach on Lake Michigan.

THE MAN WAS standing on the apron of the track in front of the pit wall. He was a small man in a lavender suit. He seemed contemptuous of the cars passing a few feet from the crease in his trousers. He chewed an unlighted cigar and held a long stick in his hands. There was a piece of cheap muslin, dyed black and white, stapled to the stick and furled around it. He was looking down the track in the direction from which the cars were coming, watching for a silver car with the number 7 on the nose. Actually the car was so low that he wouldn't be able to see the number on the wedge-shaped nose from the level of the track, but the men in the tower would be able to see it and would announce it over the public address system. The man on the track would see a thin silver wedge with a dark blue helmet growing out of it. He unfurled the flag and held the loose end of it in his left hand. He began shaking the stick, still holding on to the loose end, a quick up and down motion, a motion of excitement. He was about to perform. Now he could see the silver car. It appeared out of a mirage, vague and shimmering at first, then distinct, then it was past him and he felt the vibrations in the ground beneath his feet. He continued to wave the flag and to leap into the air again and again. To the spectators he looked like a Milanese flag dancer. To Roger he was a blur of black and white that meant he could slow down, that meant he didn't have to listen to the engine anymore, that it didn't matter if it faltered now, that meant he'd won the biggest race of his life.

He'd won many races in the seven years he'd been driving, but never a Can-Am. The win would open a lot of doors for him. His picture would be in all the newspapers and magazines that regularly covered racing and he'd appear in advertisements endorsing tires, oil, brake pads, spark plugs, gasoline and maybe even a certain brand of sport shirt. Years ago racing drivers had endorsed hair tonic, but not many drivers used hair tonic anymore. When his helmet was off, Roger's dark hair hung almost to his shoulders. He couldn't imagine himself endorsing shampoo.

Now the man with the black and white checkered flag was behind him. Roger let off on the gas and coasted the remainder of the straightaway. He lifted his right hand from the steering wheel and waved to the spectators and corner workers who cheered back. Roger couldn't hear the cheers, he could only hear the engine popping and sputtering as it loafed through the carousel and began to smooth out as he picked up speed down the back straight.

He cut the engine and coasted to a stop at the start-finish line. Sam Dandy, his crew chief (everybody kidded him about his name), was waiting there, so was Walter Ellison, the car owner, a flock of photographers and race officials and the man in the purple suit who was the first to congratulate him and handed him the checkered flag. Roger pulled off his helmet and the flameproof balaclava he wore under it and accepted the paper cup of tepid water from Sam Dandy.

"God damn, boss-man, you did it. You sure as hell did it," Sam said. He said it again and again. Sam Dandy was from South Carolina. Walter Ellison came over and shook his hand, then turned and shook Sam Dandy's hand. Walter Ellison was happy. His car had won an important race and the Armstrong Tobacco Company would be happy because they sponsored the car which carried advertising for Sylvan cigarettes, and photographs of the car with their advertising would be in all those magazines and on the 11:00 P.M. sports roundup on all those television stations. Walter Ellison bent down and said something to Roger, but Roger couldn't hear what it was. He was looking for a face he couldn't find. He motioned to Sam and Sam bent down to him. "Carrie?" he shouted in Sam's ear.

"I haven't seen her, boss-man."

Carrie was Roger's wife. He'd left her at the motel that morning. She didn't come to the races anymore; at least she was never there for the start of the race, not since Roger's accident. She'd seen Roger's car stall on the grid at the start of a race several years before. There was always a lot of dust and smoke at the start, and always a lot of confusion. She'd seen one of the cars from the back of the grid crash into Roger's car and seen both cars explode into flames. Roger got out with a whiplashed neck and a few minor burns, but the man in the car that had hit him died. The safety crew got to him quickly and put out the fire, but he'd inhaled the flames and there was nothing they could do for him. His body wouldn't hold water. They took him to the hospital and kept him alive for three days, but they knew they couldn't save him. He was in the room next to Roger's when he died and his wife and his father were there. After that Carrie never came to the track until after the race had started. Usually she never came at all.

A Second Life

$\mathbf{I}$N A PENTHOUSE apartment on the Upper West Side, a woman in a black Oleg Cassini dress and a discreet strand of pearls asked me what it was that had drawn me to racing. "You, with so much to lose," she said, "money, talent, your obvious enjoyment of life?" She didn't mention my wife and children. "Why would you want to risk all that for something so mindless and brutal?"

"Racing *was* my enjoyment of life." That's what I told her, though of course it wouldn't suffice. I couldn't tell her how it felt when you broke through the tension and anxiety and something beyond your own conscious sense of control took over, how you were carried along on something ineffable, and how it almost brought tears to your eyes. I couldn't tell her it was the heat and vibration and G forces, the glare of the low sun refracted through oil-coated goggles, the terror of racing nearly blind through the rain, your tires feeling for the track somewhere under the layers of water, or that it was the masked joy of seeing a competitor spinning ahead of you, knowing you were going to make it through, that you had been given a gift that might just as easily have been taken from you, or that it was the feeling of omnipotence when everything was working and there was music in your head and you had become, in that moment, the hero of your own childhood, or that it was the abject despair of taking second in a race you should have won but for that single irrevocable mistake, or the euphoria of winning the race that seemed beyond hope because someone else made the mistake or because something unaccountably broke through inside you and you were able to drive faster than you, or anyone else, thought possible. I couldn't tell her how it felt to see the expression on the face of a woman behind the catch fence as you passed at over 100 miles an hour and to share a moment of inviolable intimacy, or how it felt to have simply survived a day of dire premonitions and terrifying frustrations, and the savor it gave to the sky and to laughter and to the wine you had that night with dinner, how it could make you forget, for a short time at least, that you and the confusion of the world even existed. I couldn't convince her that any of it mattered.

"I did it because it was what I wanted to do," I told her.

She raised an eyebrow and tilted her head skeptically. "Do you always do what you want to?" she asked.

"No. Unfortunately, I don't."

OF COURSE, I hadn't been completely honest. I could have told her it was the glory, the deification of victory when you took the flag and lapped to the cheers of the spectators and the exuberant gestures of the corner workers, or the looks you got when you walked along the pits in your driving suit. I could have told her I wanted to be like those men whose lives, and deaths, I had lived through as a child, that I wanted the attention I could only get by being conspicuously brave.

I could have told her it was because I loved the beauty of the cars, their menacing sounds and acrid smells, and how watching them at speed frightened me, and that I had to race them to know for myself that I could. I could have told her I did it because I wanted to be a hero, and that too many men I knew had died doing it, and that finally, after so many funerals, it wasn't as much fun as it was supposed to be. But I still wouldn't have answered her question.

IT WAS OVERCAST, a raw wind off the desert, threatening rain. November 27, 1966, a date I remember vividly, and on the fourth lap I outbraked another car at the end of the long back straight at Riverside, California, and dove into turn nine inside of him to take third place. We were running close, coming off the turn, when he nudged the right rear corner of my car, and I was sliding sideways, my concentration broken, suddenly aware how fast I was actually going, the world slipping away past my windshield. I tried to correct, but at over one hundred miles an hour, my tires were making blue smoke. I felt the momentary exhilaration that comes with being out of control, and then the butt end of the pit wall zoomed in on me. I remember very distinctly exclaiming those words most often recovered from the cockpit recorder, and I felt a deep sense of resignation. I didn't really know if I was going into the wall head-on or sideways. I only knew that the concrete was porous and those tiny little holes were coming at me like moon craters to a meteor before impact. And then something big knocked the life out of me. I watched the windshield crystallize and disintegrate. I noticed the fleeing postures and terrified expressions of the people behind the pit wall. I ripped the steering wheel off its spokes and bent the column down with my face. I watched the engine push through the fire wall and come to rest against my shoulder, my bones popping like automatic weapon fire. A large man in a red jacket was running for his life, and I was on fire. I was on fire, and I had to get out of the car. I reached for the seat belt release as I ricocheted back off the wall. I felt the impact of another car broadsiding me, and I was spinning sideways again down the straight. Then another car spun me back in the opposite direction and I came to rest on the start-finish line. I had the belt undone, and all I could think of was getting out of the fire. I crawled through the window and took a couple of steps, not yet aware that my legs were broken. I was lying beside the burning car, hoping it was finally all over, when the car was hit again and skidded over on top of me. I watched it all as if it were a movie, and I was drowning in my own blood.

My mechanic was the first one over the wall. He dragged me out from under the car and lifted my head up so that I could breathe. Then a doctor arrived and was telling him to put my head down. They were arguing about what to do with my head, and, though I wasn't able to voice an opinion, I was desperate for air. I could hear Peggy Lee singing "Is That All There Is?" and it echoed the relative indifference I felt at that moment. It all seemed kind of sad. Nothing more dramatic than that. I remember thinking it was a dumb way to die and that I had thought I would live to be older than twenty-six. I remember the grim faces of the doctors looking down at me in the emergency room. I remember throwing up most of the blood I had swallowed as they wheeled me into surgery. And I remember waking up the next day to see NASCAR legends Paul Goldsmith and David Pearson standing by my bed, inscribing my casts. I had pretty well broken every bone I possessed: both arms, both legs, all my ribs, displaced my spine, and fractured my skull, along with numerous lacerations, contusions, and burns, and one dramatically broken nose. If I had been having second thoughts about racing, my body had made up my mind for me.

After my crash everything seemed to be more vivid, more beautiful, because everything was more clearly transient, more fleeting. Things kept that hallowed aura for a month or two, and then began to fade back into habit, self-judgment, worry, and self-indulgence. But I'd had a glimpse of life without filters, when only living itself mattered, a vision, through crisis, of William Blake's: *If the doors of perception were cleansed, everything would appear to man as it is, infinite.*

WHEN MY BODY had healed enough that it could be moved, Carroll Shelby sent his plane down to Riverside, and at LAX I was transferred on a stretcher to TWA and flown back to my home in Michigan. Racing had ceased to be a part of my life, almost as abruptly as I had stopped against that wall in California. I hadn't wanted to end my career like that, but I knew it would be a long time before I could drive again, and I also knew it would be like starting over, only this time with a lot less self-confidence. But most importantly, I had chosen another life.

Seven years later I began writing about racing for *Sports Illustrated,* and subsequently for a number of other magazines. I spent a succession of Mays in Indianapolis, wrote a book about the 500, and became reacquainted with a number of old friends. But now I was only a spectator. I was on the outside of the fence, and while it made me feel a bit ambivalent, that was okay. It had been my choice, the new life I had made, and yet some part of me still wanted to be out there. And then I remembered how, in those nervous hours of waiting before the start of a race, part of me had wanted to be in the grandstand, enjoying the prerace excitement, maybe having a bratwurst and a couple of beers, rather than trying to settle my stomach while projecting a confident demeanor. *We live our lives forever taking leave,* Rilke said. I'm always longing for the desert when I'm living by the sea.

Over the years I'd often been asked if I missed racing, and the answer had always been yes. But I would go on to explain that racing isn't something you can play at casually now and then when the mood strikes you, like golf. The consequences of an off day are far greater. You are either given to it or you're not. You can't be any good at it without dedication, and if I couldn't be running up front, I wasn't interested.

WHAT I MISSED more than the racing itself, however, was the life. I missed the people with whom I had shared the excitement, the risks, and the intensity of focus that had bound us together, that had made us different. Racing drivers are a largely undemonstrative lot. They like to give the impression that they don't think there's anything special about what they do. They strive to be nonchalant, but usually they are churning inside. They are decompressing the balloon, as Jackie Stewart has described it, but all that forcibly expelled emotion has to go somewhere.

We raced against each other in a very public way, but what went on between us and within us was another matter. We were friends, and it wouldn't be going too far to say that we loved each other, in the way of soldiers who have been through combat together, though given the times, and who we were, love wasn't a word freely used. And yet, of course, we were adversaries—enemies almost. We didn't want the other guy to know what we were thinking. We wanted our beloved adversaries to believe we were a good bit more confident than we actually were. And we wanted them to believe that beating them wasn't quite as important to us as it actually was. We wanted to keep them off guard. We wanted them to respect us, but we also usually wanted them to underestimate us a little, so that at a crucial moment, we might take them by surprise.

The man in the other car was a visible personality, and you tried to know his strengths and his vulnerabilities. You laughed at his stories over dinner on Saturday night and tried to run him out of road on Sunday afternoon. Week after week after week.

Some drivers could be rattled if you rode their tail and filled their mirrors long enough, while others were able to convince themselves that they enjoyed the close company as well as the dry mouth, pounding heart, and shallow breathing that came with close-in fighting, dicing, it's called. It was often like a dogfight, in World War II–era terms. At least that's how I thought of it. You waited for the other guy to make a slight mistake, to lose his concentration, and you did what you could to make that happen, without losing your own.

There were desperate moments. And there were treasured ones when you triumphed, and also, though somewhat sardonically, when you didn't. But you lived more intensely, that was certain. You created new time. You multiplied your life. You tested each other, playing a high-stakes game, and you admired the other guy who played it hard and well. You desperately wanted to beat him, though you usually gained something more valuable, something you could use another day, when you failed. If, as psychologists tell us, the opposite of love isn't hate but, rather, indifference, then you could say you loved the guy you were trying to beat. You may have hated him at times, but you certainly weren't indifferent. Carroll Shelby, who has been an unyielding competitor all his life and projects the image of a kind of hard-bitten cowboy, just recently, at seventy-five, told me that he loved me. This is something he never could or would have said back when I was driving his cars, though I'm sure he must have felt something like that then, as I know I did and do now. People spend their lives trying to figure out what they mean by that word.

When someone died, though, someone like Ken Miles or Dave McDonald, someone for whom you felt that kind of love and admiration, you couldn't talk about it, because you had to stay focused. You couldn't indulge your grief and still take the kinds of risks you had to take to be competitive. To an observer, privileged to the intimate conversation among racers, or to the lack of it, it would seem a fairly callous society. But it wasn't. And this was often manifested in the occasionally outrageous behavior that accompanied our traveling circus.

There was another Cobra driver named Tom Payne who could be counted on for displays of hutzpah of the "let's piss on their leg and tell them it's raining" school. I watched him successfully impersonate race officials, Ford executives, and police detectives, and several times, facing a long wait in a crowded restaurant, I saw him drape a napkin over his arm in the manner of a maitre d' and motion us to the first available table. More often than not, he got away with it. In Canada, where we were paid appearance money predicated on the organizer's estimate of our individual worth in drawing spectators, Payne drove his races attired in a red and white seersucker sport coat, white shirt, and tie, and the fans loved it. He had them chanting his name each lap as he passed, and no doubt doubled his fee.

As an up-and-coming twenty-three-year-old, I was paid $3,000 just to cross the starting line, the price of a new pickup truck at that time, and it wasn't hard to interpolate what drivers like A. J. Foyt, Jimmy Clark, and Dan Gurney were getting. It was an era when drivers were more like barnstormers than the test pilots they resemble today, and big appearance money often led to a liberal interpretation of the rules.

Having had fuel injection problems in the first 100-mile heat of the Player's 200 at Mosport, the great Foyt had finished last and was accordingly gridded at the back of the field for the start of the second heat. When the flag dropped, he swerved over into the pit lane and floored it, sending crews, officials, and journalists scattering for their lives, and dove back into the field in third place going into turn one. It was a maneuver that would have gotten me disqualified, at the very least, but perhaps because of the investment the organizers had in his being there, they didn't seem to notice.

IN THE PADDOCK at Elkhart Lake, a driver named Rutherford asked me if I would like to see his King Cobra. Assuming he was referring to a racing car commonly called a King Cobra–a Cooper chassis with a Cobra engine–I politely assented, supposing this car had some unique modification. I followed him to a Buick station wagon, from which he pulled a long green wooden box. He lifted a burlap bag from the box and dumped an honest to God king cobra, a living and very angry snake about nine feet long, on the grass of the infield, and that beautiful Wisconsin summer afternoon grew noticeably cooler. The snake was molting, he explained, and consequently a bit pissed off. It reared its hood a good three feet off the ground and came at me without hesitation, until Rutherford grabbed it and pulled it back with his special snake-handling stick.

An hour later I was in the pits, getting ready to go out for qualifying. I was telling Carroll Shelby about my startling encounter with the snake when we heard the siren of the ambulance. The driver named Rutherford did not make the race. He'd been nailed by his testy pet, though with prompt medical attention he survived. The incident prompted Carroll to order Al Dowd, our team manager, to get rid of the pet cobra he kept in an aquarium in the racing shop back in L.A., though this ultimately proved unnecessary as the Shelby team mascot was bitten on the nose by a mouse that was supposed to have been its dinner, and it died of infectious pneumonia.

THERE WERE OTHER memories though, far less fond, like watching my friend, Dave McDonald, perhaps the fastest and certainly the bravest Cobra driver in the country, burn to death in a raging gasoline fire coming out of turn four at Indianapolis. We had all been thrilled about Dave's big break, but on the second lap our excitement turned to horror. "Yeah, too bad about Davie," is what we said a week later at Mosport, where I had been given the starting spot that would have been his, a big break for me, but a bitter one. What we said in no way expressed what we felt; it expressed only as much as we could afford to let ourselves think of it while we were still racing. Any true expression of grief would have been met with an embarrassed silence. But the feelings didn't go away. They often came back in dreams the night before a race and in a vividly enhanced sense of our own mortality.

There was also a rainy afternoon in Bruce and Pat McLaren's motel room near Watkins Glen a few days before the U.S. Grand Prix. Bruce had just begun developing the first McLaren racing car and had finished second, inches behind Jim Hall's Chaparral, the previous weekend at Mosport. I had won the G.T. race in a Cobra (which Bruce pronounced, *Coobra*), and Bruce had invited Tom Payne and me to watch the race from his pits. Tom and I were there for a prerace ceremony in recognition of Ford's World's Manufacturer's Championship, in which I drove Ferrari Formula One driver Lorenzo Bandini around the track in a Cobra Daytona Coupe. Bruce introduced us to his teammate, a young Austrian driver named Jochen Rindt, whom Bruce called Jo. Bruce, Pat, Jochen, Tom, and I had dinner with Jimmy Clark that evening. I don't remember what we talked about, except that Bruce was explaining "Coobras" to Jochen and telling Jimmy Clark how Jim Hall had developed into a first-rate driver. I remember thinking that these three men had reached a level of expertise so great that they really didn't have to take chances anymore, that they were beyond making mistakes. And I was almost right. Then, two years later, word came of Jimmy Clark's death in a crash in Germany, apparently caused by a blown tire. In June of 1970 Bruce was killed while testing one of his cars at Goodwood when a body section came loose, and the following September Jochen Rindt died in a crash, undoubtedly caused by a mechanical failure while he was practicing for the Italian Grand Prix at Monza. Jochen won the World Driver's Championship that year, the first man to win it posthumously. In 1971, Bandini died in a fiery crash in the Grand Prix of Monaco. Bruce was the only one of these men I knew at all well, but I took each death almost as if it were a death in the family.

Racing has become safer now. The tracks are equipped with compression barriers, the trees and ditches screened out with walls, corners bordered with sand-filled catch basins. The cars have been designed to break up, absorbing the impact of a crash rather than passing it on to the driver, who is sheltered in a carbon fiber tub or a steel cage, strapped in by a five-point harness and sheathed in flame-proof Nomex. The horror of fire has been effectively eliminated by fuel tank cells and onboard Halon extinguishing systems. A fatality in racing today has become an aberration and, as a result, the drivers themselves have become dangerous. Survival used to be an important factor for them; now it's almost taken for granted.

FROM THE AGE of twelve I wanted to be a racing driver. My heroes were drivers like Fangio, the Marquis de Portago, and Billy Vukovich, Carroll Shelby, Phil Hill, and Peter Collins, and though half of them had been killed by the time I drove my first race, I had coached myself so thoroughly in my imagination, listening to the Indy 500 on the radio, reading every book and magazine story on racing that I could acquire, and imagining I was driving in the Mille Miglia every time I took corners flat out on the back roads of western Michigan, that when I finally could begin racing at twenty-one, I actually believed that nothing bad could happen to me and that with a little honing of my skills, I could drive as fast as anyone out there, and maybe even faster. That foolish belief, though it faded into wisdom through experience and through the deaths of far too many friends, served me well in the beginning, because, in addition to being a young fool, I was lucky. I drove way over my head and got away with it more often than not. I won my first four races, won an award as the outstanding novice driver of 1961, and finished my first year of racing second in my class in championship points.

But as I moved into faster cars and bigger races, I came up against other former young fools grown wise and discovered that a number of them believed they were faster than I was, and demonstrated it with some regularity. And one or two of these became mentors.

BOB JOHNSON WAS an established master when, in my second year of racing, I switched from Austin Healeys and two-litre Ferraris to the far more powerful and demanding Cobras. Johnson was fourteen years older than I, and for some reason he took me under his wing. He could see I was dedicated, that I was a bit green, and that I was struggling with spotty equipment. He generously allowed his mechanic to lend advice in setting up the car. He lent tools and even, occasionally, hard-to-come-by parts, and he was forthcoming with driving advice, allowing me to follow him to pick up the fast line around an unfamiliar circuit. Johnson was straight with me, as far as I could tell, though so-called mentors have occasionally been known to present very Zen-like lessons to their understudies. When the young Roger Penske was trailing Bob Holbert to pick up his braking points, Holbert severed their student-teacher relationship quite dramatically by switching off his brake lights going into a tight turn at Elkhart Lake, suckering Penske in way too deep, so that as Holbert powered smoothly out of the corner, Penske went skidding off into the weeds.

When I made a brief foray into driving super-modifieds on a half-mile dirt oval, I asked a grizzled veteran if he would give me a few pointers about the track. "Sure," he said. He put his arm across my shoulders, walked me over to the rail, and pointed downtrack. "See that there," he said. "That's the first turn. When you get to it, turn left, and hurry every chance you get."

MY TUTORIAL RELATIONSHIP with Bob Johnson lasted just shy of a year. There came a race where I passed him twice before he finally regained the lead and edged me out in a finish that had to be decided by a photograph. I felt I had arrived, and apparently he felt it too. After the smiles and handshakes on the podium, he put his hand on my shoulder and looked me in the eye. "Okay. That's it," he said. "No more Mr. Nice Guy." My goal and my gauge of transcendence thereafter was to beat him, which I did only once, though, ironically, it was at Mid-Ohio Raceway, his home track. I became a good driver, though not a great one. People said I was a natural, and I was a charger, usually running at or near the front of the pack. But there was something missing, something it took me about five years to discover. And I learned what it was by watching two of my contemporaries.

Mark Donahue and Peter Revson started racing at the same time I did, and in our first several years on the circuit, when I came up against them, I came out ahead as often as not. Based purely on ability, I was as good as they were, though before they were killed in separate Formula One crashes, Donahue in Germany and Revson in South Africa, Donahue had won the Indianapolis 500 and they were both ranked among the best drivers in the world.

There was another calling in my life, and, as all callings do, it required sacrifice. At about the same time in my childhood that I discovered racing, I also discovered poetry. I didn't think about wanting to become a poet in the way that I knew I wanted to become a racer, but I began to realize that writing was something I needed to do. I needed to do it to make sense out of my experience. I needed to write about or tell about the things that happened to me in order to make them seem real. I discovered that, for me, life was barren without stories and poems. As inept as my early writing was, I couldn't feel as if I really had a life here on earth if I didn't try to get at least some essence of it down on paper.

So I found myself conflicted, torn between two seemingly opposed passions. Racing required a certain set of blinders, a monomaniacal focus and a suspension of the imagination which seemed inimical to *the poet's eye in fine frenzy rolling*. And they say dreamers don't make good astronauts or test pilots. Or racing drivers, it seems.

HENRY MILLER WROTE a wonderful and quirky book called *The Time of the Assassins*, a book that spoke directly to me about these two seemingly opposed aspects of my life. Miller compares his own life to that of the great and mercurial French poet, Arthur Rimbaud, who had produced an extraordinary body of work by the time he was nineteen years old and then quit writing to go off and make his fortune, he supposed, as a slave trader and gunrunner in North Africa. Miller sees his own life and Rimbaud's as mirror images with the poles reversed. Miller's study of these two lives, with which he was so intimately familiar, is played out against the backdrop of two differing universes: The Being and The Doing. While Miller spent the first forty years of his life creating Henry Miller, establishing himself in the literary worlds of New York and Paris as Henry Miller the novelist (though he had not actually written a novel), Rimbaud spent the first half of his life in the realm of being, plumbing the depths of his dream-fed consciousness and writing some of the most unanticipated and brilliant poems in French, or in world, literature, including *The Drunken Boat, Illuminations,* and an autobiography, at nineteen, called, *A Season in Hell.*

But then Rimbaud decided he needed fifty thousand francs to secure his future and allow himself the freedom to pursue his art unimpeded by financial concerns, and he embarked on a second life of perversion and adventure. And he fell into the maw of the God called security. When he'd made his fifty thousand francs, he decided he needed one hundred, then two hundred thousand, and he died in the Ethiopian desert without ever writing another line of poetry. Miller examines Rimbaud's letters from this dissolute, doing, period of his life and comments, "What adventure. And what boredom."

Miller, in what turned out to be quantitatively as well as qualitatively the second half of his life, undertook to fulfill the image he had created for himself as a novelist, by living in the being universe, the universe of the examined life, and by actually writing novels.

The *being* and the *doing* aspects of my life manifested themselves in what seemed to be the diametrically opposed worlds of poetry and sports car racing. A poet filters his inward experience and his perceptions of the world around him through his imagination and works to make some *thing*–in this case a poem–which will have a more vivid, distinct, and enduring reality than the objects and experiences that inspired it. Racing, on the other hand, requires an arbitrary and practiced suspension of the imagination. If a racer allows himself to entertain images of what might happen to him if something goes terribly wrong, he won't have the stomach to drive just that little bit beyond what he thinks he can do.

In 1966, at the age of twenty-six, I left the world of racing behind because the *being* aspect of my life was making ever increasing demands on my consciousness, and I wanted to devote myself to it. My heart just wasn't in racing anymore. I also had some increasingly pressing business responsibilities and a wife and two children I wasn't seeing nearly often enough. I was feeling torn and conflicted when my nearly fatal crash decided the issue for me. Hitting the wall knocked me off the fence, to make a bad pun of it. Later I discovered a statement by Johannes de Silento, one of the many pen names used by Kierkegaard, which seemed to me to define my dilemma: *As God created man and woman, so too He fashioned the hero and the poet, or orator. The poet cannot do what the other does; he can only admire, love and rejoice in the hero. Yet he too is happy, and not less so, for the hero is as it were his better Nature, with which he is in love. . . .*

OVER THE NEXT thirty years I taught high school English, beginning in a wheelchair, and taught writing at a number of colleges. I looked after business interests. I lectured. I wrote sixteen books, novels, poetry, short stories, and nonfiction, and published ten of them. I wrote about racing for *Sports Illustrated* and *Playboy* and undertook adventures, from safaris in Africa to being an L.A. cop, and wrote about them for several dozen other magazines. I lost a wife through divorce and then through death, moved to Key West and then to southeastern Idaho, and found a kind of sanity in an almost maniacal devotion to fly-fishing. I met a woman who became my wife as well as my best friend, a combination in one person I hadn't thought possible. And the light I believed I had lost at the end of the tunnel began rising in the east every morning.

THEN, ABOUT TWO years ago, an old familiar and almost forgotten ache reasserted itself and began growing in me. I began to think about racing again, and not just as a spectator or journalist. I began to think about driving. Maybe it's a manifestation of some complex compulsion to recapture my youth. But why, when so much I wouldn't want to repeat seems to be behind me and so much I cherish each day lies ahead, would I want to revisit a part of my life that holds so many tragic memories?

If it's a syndrome, it does seem to have some precedent in classical mythology. Odysseus, after his arduous twenty-year voyage home from the Trojan wars, after slaying his wife's suitors, restoring his kingdom, and living in it peacefully for a number of years, unaccountably sets off once again on a final voyage. Meister Eckhart speaks of *the wayless way, where the sons of God lose themselves and, at the same time, find themselves.* And Bruce Chatwin writes that *Sluggish and sedentary people, such as the ancient Egyptians, project on the next world the journeys they failed to make in this one.* These allusions are useful guides, but they don't quite answer my question. And as regards Chatwin and his Egyptians, I'm going back to a journey I have already taken once.

I suppose that all I can say about that earlier part of my life is that if it holds tragic memories, it also holds moments that, in memory at least, transcend all the hours and years surrounding them.

So I WENT back to race-driving school to see if I could still do it. Bob Bondurant, a former Shelby American teammate, runs the best racing school in the country, and he arranged for me to take a three-day, one-on-one course designed for current racing drivers who want to sharpen their road-racing skills. I felt that I still had it, but of course I wouldn't really know until I got back behind the wheel.

My instructor was a young NASCAR hopeful named Chris Cook, who, it turned out, was born a year and a half after I had stopped racing. Chris got behind the wheel to show me a few things about the school track. It was my first time as a passenger in a racing car at speed, and the first couple of laps were a thrill bordering on terror. In the right-hand seat everything seems faster because you don't have the level of concentration that driving enforces. You have the leisure to glance off to the side and to notice just how rapidly the scenery disappears. By the second lap, though, I felt confident in Chris, and we could carry on a conversation through the G forces, the howl of the exhaust, and the screaming tires. "Brake lightly here. Carry your speed into the turn," Chris instructed. "Trail brake here. Ride the brake through and wait on your apex. Now feed the throttle gently, all it will take, use up the whole track. Now here put the wheel up on the curbing, hit the apex, and stand on it. This is a real launching pad into the next short straight." That sort of thing.

We switched seats, and I found Chris to be a very composed passenger. He was direct and still tactful in his observations. He told me he couldn't believe I hadn't been racing in thirty-two years, and that I hadn't lost much. "You're on the throttle too hard and too early," he said. "I can see you're used to cars with lots of horsepower and not much traction." These cars were more sophisticated, and the tires and brakes were worlds better than what I'd been used to.

"Easy on the gas," Chris prompted. "Okay, stay on the brakes a little deeper here. You're trying too hard. You want to be back where you were when you left off, and that might take a day or two."

Each time I went out I vowed I was going to ease off a little, to work on getting smoother and ultimately faster. But when I came up behind another car, or saw another car in my mirrors, I couldn't stifle the impulse to race. I would regularly put too much right foot in it and scrub off speed with throttle-induced understeer. In the less sophisticated cars of the sixties, when we were turning hot laps, we spent a lot of time hanging the rear end out and sliding sideways. Today, though, as Chris pointed out, when you're sideways you're losing time. "Lift off a little later and ride the brakes into the turn," Chris reminded me.

The real problem I was having was ego. I had been a professional racer, not world-class, but a definite front-runner and fairly often a winner. Thirty years ago, that is. So why wasn't I running away and hiding from my classmates, mostly Porsche Club racers who had taken the basic Bondurant racing course the year before? The obvious answer was that these guys were pretty good drivers. They had been racing just lately, while I had been dreaming.

A LOT OF old familiar feelings and sensations came back: the smell of burning castor oil; glowing manifolds; scorched tires and brake pads; the engine and tire sounds riding with me; the quickly reversing G forces (the strain of which I had forgotten); the crisp, sharp, and slightly threatening rack of the exhaust as I sit revving the engine before going out; the nervous attention to detail and the slight edge of apprehension, getting under way on an unfamiliar track, and the easing of it as the turns begin to fall into place and a rhythm develops; and finally the sensation of flying as it all comes together and the seams of each lap disappear.

What had been a series of turns began to become one linked maneuver, like a bird banking and rolling all in one motion. I didn't remember working so hard and with such intensity, or being so thirsty, drinking so much water and having it taste so good. I scared myself a little at first. I didn't feel quite as invincible as I had at twenty-one, but I loved the way I was feeling, *wide and powerful now, like legends.*

I had a significant moment on the second day when we moved to the longer and faster circuit at Firebird Raceway. I hadn't slid up close to concrete since my collision with the wall at Riverside. When you are turning hot laps at Firebird, you drift out to within about a foot of the wall, coming out of the last turn onto the main straightaway. The turn is a tight one, and you're doing only about fifty miles an hour at that point, but speed becomes relative with proximity. I took note of it on the warm-up laps, but after the first time past at full speed, it became just another part of the scenery.

I spent time in a computer car wired to record my performance at every braking point and apex on the track. Chris downloaded the data and printed out a graph so we could analyze my driving and see just exactly where I was picking up or losing speed on each lap. We could overlay my graphs on his, and by the third day, I was registering some pretty competitive lap times. After three days of training and a race against the newly fledged graduates of Bondurant's basic four-day Grand Prix course, which I won fairly easily, I had my SCCA license back, and I was ready to race.

ON SUNDAY, JULY 25, 1999, at Road America near Elkhart Lake, Wisconsin, I drove my first real race in thirty-three years, in the Merrill Lynch/Brian Redman International Challenge. It seemed fitting for this to happen at Road America, where I saw my first race when I was four-teen and where, at twenty-one, I drove my first national race. It was definitely a homecoming, and I was welcomed back by fans with long memories, by drivers with whom I had raced in the sixties, and by younger men who had watched me drive when they were kids and had subsequently become racers themselves.

I drove a 1964 USRRC (United States Road Racing Championship) Shelby Cobra, a sister car to the Cobra I had last driven in the 24 hours of Daytona in 1966. I was a bit nervous before the first practice on Thursday, wondering just how I would handle the high speeds down Elkhart's long straights and how it would feel to dive into turn five in a pack of cars, braking from 170 to fifty miles per hour and then sliding through the corner to rocket up the steep hill, cresting into the tricky reverse-camber turn six. I discovered that, after settling in for a couple of laps, it felt just fine. By the end of qualifying I was gridded sixth out of a field of fifty-five cars for Sunday's race.

On Saturday night I experienced the familiar half-sleep, a sort of restful drifting, a continuous film of each turn, apex, shifting, braking and throttle point playing involuntarily on my eyelids. I fought the uncontrollable nervous yawning in the final hour before the start while I suited up and made final equipment adjustments, worked to compress the tension into concentration, and waited on the grid, tightly strapped into my five-point harness, baking in the 105-degree heat in my Nomex driving suit.

Then we were off on the pace lap, zigging and zagging our cars sharply left and right to bring the tires up to temperature before the start, and then finally pulling into formation coming onto the front straight. I lost several positions avoiding spinning cars in the first two turns, and then managed to work my way up near the front of the pack by lap number four. I had a good tight race with a big block Corvette and a Trans Am Mustang Boss 302 and counted a dozen crashed cars by the time I took the checkered flag to finish in third place. On the cool-off lap, the drivers of the Corvette and the Boss 302 pulled alongside and made applauding gestures, and when I pulled into the pits, my old friend and boyhood racing hero, Augie Pabst, was there, full of smiles, to tell me I drove a great race. "Just beautiful," he said. "You did everything just like you're supposed to." After more than three decades of nothing but memories and dreams, I was back. And it felt good. It felt very, very good.

THE RACING I'M doing now in late middle age isn't cutting-edge, career-building stuff. It's racing purely for fun, though I intend to drive to win and at speeds most people can only imagine. It's called vintage racing, racing cars that were legends of an earlier time. It's nostalgia, history, and art. Still, racing is racing, and the signed waivers acknowledging the risk, the helmets, flameproof suits, Halon systems, and roll bars, the ambulances and medical staff present, enforce the realization that danger is a more imposing presence than in other spectator sports or in most other aspects of one's life.

If the skeptical woman in the black dress and pearls were to ask me now why I am taking up racing again at almost sixty, I would tell her it's nostalgia, it's being a historic relic, my reputation enhanced by the filter of time, it's because I have fewer years to lose now. And finally, to return to that place where we began, I'm doing it because I still can do it. And because I want to.

Indy—The World's Fastest Carnival Ride

In the fall of 1974, Geoffery Norman, then articles editor at Playboy, *asked me to write a story about the Indianapolis 500, not only as a race, but also more broadly as a Midwestern American cultural phenomenon. The experience opened the floodgates of memory and childhood dreams, and the proposed magazine article grew into a book. Though the speeds and the dollars have changed, as they inevitably will, and the Indianapolis 500, through the greed and the politics of the organizers and organizations that control open-wheel racing in the United States, has lost the status it had enjoyed since 1911 as the great race that mirrored the historical development of the automobile, its importance as a uniquely American institution remains.*

Nothing is ever quite what it was, as the old bromide goes. But then, maybe it never was.

IN THE EARLY fifties it was a movie starring Clark Gable, titled *To Please a Lady,* with actual race footage and the faces of real drivers like Mauri Rose and Wilbur Shaw and huge ferocious cars resembling U-boats on wheels.

The tires were absurdly narrow and grooved with tread only on the right half of the running surface. The movie was my first glimpse of a world that had previously enthralled me purely with sound. I was ten years old and had already decided that to become a racing driver and to drive at Indianapolis was the only thing worth growing up for. Each Memorial Day was spent with engine sounds and the voice of Sid Collins. It didn't matter much what he said; it was just the sound of his voice, the switching to his reporters around the track, the roar of the cars in the background, and the litany of what were, for me, almost holy names: Troy Ruttman, Tony Bettenhausen, Jimmy Bryan, Sam Hanks, Johnnie Parsons, Pat O'Conner, and, most holy of all, Billy Vukovich. It meant school was getting out and I could get sunburned and go fishing and spend three months on Lake Michigan trying to let the magic names fade into some kind of perspective. Whenever I wasn't in a bathing suit, I wore slightly grimy white duck trousers and a grease-smudged white T-shirt, because that's what "Vuky" had been wearing in the one photo I'd seen of him, sitting on a workbench, barefooted, his knees pulled up to his chest, exhausted and dejected after leading the 1952 race for 191 laps until a fifty-cent steering part let go and put him into the northeast wall. "The tough little driver from Fresno," the papers called him, using his standard quote, "Just don't get in my way."

Then Vuky won in 1953 and again in '54. It was the way it had to be. Speeds had climbed past the 140-mph barrier and everybody wondered if they hadn't reached the limit. "We're going too fast out there," Vuky said. "Well, Vuky," the interviewer reflected, "you're the only one who can slow it down." But he didn't slow it down. He qualified for the 1955 race at 141.071 mph, led the race for fifty-six laps, then crashed and was killed attempting to avoid a pileup on the back straight. I saw the newsreel and the photograph of the now-primitive-looking Hopkins Special lying upside down, the hand of my boyhood hero protruding from the cockpit as if waving good-bye. I remember feeling somehow responsible for Vuky's death. It was the first time I hadn't listened to the race. My father had taken me fishing in Ontario, and on Memorial Day we were flying down from Saddle Lake in a floatplane when the bush pilot tuned in the race on his radio and told us that Vukovich had been killed. I asked him to turn it off. I didn't want to hear the cars or Sid Collins and the magic names if Vuky wasn't among them anymore.

Another year went by and my aversion to racing cooled. But it would never be quite the same without Vuky. My interest turned to road racing and more exotic, if somehow less personally awesome names, like Juan Fangio, Stirling Moss, Phil Hill, and the Marquis de Portago. It was more intricate and interesting racing, and I learned to pronounce Le Mans like the French, and Sebring and the Mille Miglia and Nurburgring. Yet as much as I pontificated that it was dumb to turn left all the time, Indy and Sid Collins and Tony Hulman orating "Gentlemen, start your engines," was still where the magic was.

The day I got my driver's license, I borrowed, without permission, a 1955 Thunderbird and pushed the speedometer needle up over 100 to see what it felt like to be Vuky; speed is always in the present tense. I raced motorcycles and an assortment of cars and pickup trucks on Michigan back roads, and two weeks after my twenty-first birthday, drove my first real race on a dirt track in an Austin Healey, and won. A boyhood friend who, with skepticism and boredom, had endured years of my racing dreams, now regarded me with a certain reverence and said, "Well, Vuky, you really did it." It was a far-fetched comparison, but at that moment I was God's gift to racing, and Indianapolis seemed only a short step away.

I never drove at Indianapolis, never even came close. I raced sports cars for five years, with moderate success, then stuffed one into the end of the pit wall at Riverside, broke every bone in my body, and quit. For seven years I stayed away from racing, not wishing to taunt myself with failed aspirations. Then, two years ago, at the invitation of Bob Jones, a friend who covers racing for *Sports Illustrated,* I went to Indianapolis to watch qualifying and the race. Somehow I always knew that sooner or later I'd have to confront this track, if not as a driver then at least as a spectator.

It wasn't quite the way it had been in *To Please a Lady.* The bricks had been covered with asphalt, the great wooden pagoda replaced by a glass and steel tower, and most of the names had changed. There was a Bettenhausen, a Parsons, and a Vukovich; and though they were a new generation of drivers, the sons of the men I had idolized, the names retained their fascination. There were newer names that had acquired their own aura—Foyt, Ruby, Unser, and Andretti—and several, like Donahue and Revson, I'd competed with on road courses ten years earlier. I remember being a little awed by the realization that those men I'd learned to race with, and sometimes beaten, were driving and even winning at Indianapolis. Of course, they weren't the same men, and neither was I. But Indianapolis was the same track (at least it was in the same place), and coming to it finally was like visiting a historic battleground, with one important exception. Another battle would soon be fought here, and another and another. New monuments would be built over the old. Racing drivers must perforce live totally in the present and pay no more than a token deference to last year's winner or last year's dead.

That was in 1973, and it proved a bad year to reacquaint myself with racing. During the final practice session before qualifying began, I had just come through the Sixteenth Street tunnel on my way to the pits when I heard a loud *wuump* and turned to see Art Pollard's car, both right wheels broken off on impact with the wall, sliding sideways through the short chute. About one hundred feet in front of me, the axle stubs dug into the infield grass and the car began flipping. Upside down, it skidded back onto the track, flipped right side up and came to rest in the middle of turn two. Pollard sat motionless amid the alcohol flames, visible only as heat vapor rising from the car, and at that moment a strange thing happened. Looking back on it, it seems improbable, but I could have sworn I heard the crowd in the bleachers on the far side of the track, in unison, scream "Save him!"

It was a full thirty seconds before the crash truck arrived, put out the flames, and extracted Pollard from the car. The two disembodied wheels rolled together in formation and came to rest in the infield as neatly as if they'd been stacked there for future use. Several hours later, in an interval between qualification attempts, they announced that Pollard was dead. A fat woman in the bleachers behind the pits broke into tears. There was an official minute of silence, then qualifying resumed. The announcer announced a new one-lap record. The fat lady was cheering.

Two weeks later I came back, waited through the tension of two days of race-delaying rain and two aborted starts, one of them catastrophic, and went home. I watched the carnage on television, Salt Walther's legs protruding from the wreckage of his burning, spinning car, Swede Savage's fatal crash in turn four, and the STP crewman hit and killed by an emergency truck speeding to the rescue. It seemed a more macabre spectacle couldn't have been planned. Indy had lived up to its reputation, and anyone who'd paid his five dollars hoping he might see blood got his money's worth.

The rules were changed in the interests of safety. The fuel capacity of the car was halved, to diminish fire hazard. The size of the airfoils was cut, and pop-off valves installed on the turbochargers to limit boost, all in hopes of slowing the cars down. The track facility was improved, spectator barriers strengthened, the pit entrance widened, and the inside wall in turn four, the one that had killed Savage, was eliminated. The 1974 race was one of the safest in the Speedway's history, no fatalities and no serious injuries. *Maybe I would go back to Indianapolis,* I thought. After all, it's the possibility of an accident that is racing's fascination, the risk, without which racing would be sterile and pointless; but it was the almost historical certainty that sometime during the month of May someone would be killed there that had tended to make Indy seem more like a Roman circus than a twentieth-century sporting event.

MAY 2, 1975. The day before the track opens and I've got nothing to do but pick up my credentials and have a look around. It's quiet—almost eerie—like visiting an amusement park closed for the winter. Nothing seems to be moving, and the only sound is the grandstand-muffled traffic passing on Sixteenth Street. Two men are painting new Coca-Cola and Sprite billboards on the scoring tower at the north end of the infield. In Gasoline Alley a dilapidated golf cart sits outside locked garage doors near the pit entrance, Jim Hurtubise—#56—Miller High Life, in oxidized red letters. It has two flat tires and looks as if it hasn't been touched since last May. Strange to think of this huge arena empty all but one month a year. The seasons change, the pits, the track, and the grandstands covered with snow, but in everyone's mind—save a few maintenance men and administrators—this place has no existence apart from the month of May. And to those for whom racing is a way of life, it *is* the month of May. I stand in the middle of the front straight, where, tomorrow, highly specialized machines will be traveling at over

220 miles an hour. Heat waves rise from the track and the huge tier of grandstands above turn four. Now there's one sound, a regularly sequenced rachidic burst. I walk back into Gasoline Alley and around the rows of ancient wooden garages till I find its source, a mechanic with bulletproof thick bifocals, an oil-soaked cowboy hat, and a patch on the back of his shirt that says: *Smokey's—Best Damn Garage in Town.* He's sitting on what looks like a railway baggage cart, polishing the ports of an intake manifold with an air-powered buffer, the first indication that someone's got in mind to go racing here.

To kill time, I take the fifty-cent track tour in a Chevrolet minibus. Once around the Speedway while the driver, with marginal accuracy, relays the speed the racers will be traveling, swings the van high on the nine-degree banking to show us how close the cars come to the wall, and points out the prices of various grandstand and tower terrace seats and the locations of the most recent notable crashes: "Salt Walther ended up here, and he'll be racing again this year. Swede Savage hit the wall right there where there used to be a wall, and the part of the car with him in it ended up way down here." I find myself silently augmenting his list with the names of heroes and friends: Pollard in the south chute, Pat O'Connor in turn two, Vukovich on the back straight, Jim Malloy in turn three, Eddie Sachs and Dave MacDonald coming out of turn four—their names now eclipsed by Swede Savage's.

At first reflection, this catalog of crash locations—both the minibus driver's and my own—seems a morbid preoccupation with tragedy, but these are places of history (like the location of Pickett's charge at Gettysburg or the box at Ford's Theater in Washington), important to us for the violently abbreviated lives with which we have identified our own. What seems morbid to me is the propensity of most racing people and sports journalists to pretend those deaths never occurred. I remember that I was fishing in Key West with Bob Jones when we heard the news that Peter Revson had been killed while practicing for the South African Grand Prix. I had known Revson and raced against him back in the early sixties. Jones had done a personality piece on Revson for *Sports Illustrated* and spent many evenings with him in the course of five years covering major races. The news came over the radio, and for what seemed like almost an hour, neither of us had anything to say. Finally, when so much time had elapsed that it seemed to come almost out of context, Jones said, "You realize that for the next six months now, nobody will mention his name."

"Yeah," I reflected, "and when they do it'll be as if he had lived twenty years ago."

It is easy to understand this sense of detachment among the drivers. If they were to ponder too deeply the dangers to themselves or the deaths of their competitors, their imaginations would take control and make it impossible for them to continue. Physical courage relies, to a great extent, on the ability to suspend the imagination, and sometimes this kind of control is transmitted to the outsider as callousness. I was standing a few feet away when Johnny Rutherford was interviewed shortly after the death of his close friend Art Pollard. "It's too bad that you can't turn back the clock," he said matter-of-factly. "Art was doing what he loved to do, and there's a risk we all take." His statement seemed to echo Faulkner's that "The irrevocability of action is tragic." A few minutes later, Rutherford went back out on the track, qualified for the pole, and set a new one-lap record of 199.071 mph, a heroic effort that would have been impossible for any man whose mind hadn't been totally on his business.

The tour bus pauses in front of the pits and the driver explains how the names of the drivers qualifying for the race will be painted: "Right between them various red marks you see along that wall there." The teenage girl sitting next to me spots a driver with long frizzy hair and a flowered Hawaiian shirt. "There's Rick Muther. Hey, Rick! Rick, can I have your autograph?" Muther is talking with another girl and seems not to hear the request.

Saturday, May 3. The track is supposed to officially open for practice, but the sky is overcast and threatens rain. Nobody expects any really hot laps the first day out, and with qualifications still a week away, most of the top drivers haven't shown up. There are several rookies (highly experienced racers, but new to Indianapolis) who must learn the track and turn twenty observed laps within each of several speed brackets to pass their driver's test, and a few veterans, anxious to get back in the groove and check out their cars. The only real question on anyone's mind is who will be the first driver on the track. Being first out has no effect on qualifying or on the race, but, like everything else here, it is part of a tradition. It's supposed to be a coup. It generates a good deal of publicity, and publicity is what attracts sponsors and sells their products. It's why Gatorade and Surfine Foods and Jorgensen Steel invest up to three hundred thousand dollars to run this race, the hope that their sponsorship will generate millions of dollars worth of publicity, maybe even get a picture of their car, their billboard on wheels, on the cover of a national magazine, the kind of advertising money alone can't buy.

Dick Simon, a forty-one-year-old retired insurance executive from Salt Lake City, wheels his car to the end of the pit lane, ready to go. Then a few drops of rain fall and his crew covers the car with a plastic sheet. A band of Scottish pipers march onto the track, and the absurdly elaborate pageantry of May in Indianapolis has begun. Every flower show, car wash, and tea party will append the label "500 Festival." Today's official events include a radio-controlled model-car race, a bridge tournament, a Dress Up Like Mom parade, a Look Like Your Favorite Television Personality contest, a bubble-gum blowing contest, and the mayor's breakfast, at which 1,665 paying guests will hear Jimmy "The Greek" Snyder pick A. J. Foyt as the race winner, meet the 500 Festival Queen, and then adjourn to the track for opening ceremonies, where each of those attending the breakfast will be permitted to make one lap of the track in their Corvette or Cadillac.

The thirty-three official Buick pace cars stream by, bearing celebrities. I'm leaning on the pit fence, eavesdropping on two Speedway guards, sad-faced old men with the perennial look of small boys who got what they wanted for Christmas and then discovered it didn't make any difference. "Who was that boy got his head cut off down in Dayton? Shit, that 'as a good track till they ruined it with blacktop. You could come outta turn one, aim'er at the grandstand, pour the coals to it and slide 'er all the way round. I remember when Mel Kenyon slid . . ." The Speedway, Indiana, High School Band plays "The Eyes of Texas" for Johnny Rutherford, last year's winner. A few more drops of rain.

The Festival Queen accepts her crown and steps up to the microphone: "I wanna reckanize the twenty-eight princesses behind me." Now it's pouring. The band marches off, the crowd scatters for cover, and Dick Simon's car sits abandoned, fogging its plastic shroud in the pit lane. The rain pools up all afternoon, discouraging everyone but the golfers on the Speedway golf course, their official black and white umbrellas dotting the fairways.

THE BAR AT the Speedway Motel has the atmosphere of a neighborhood tavern. Everybody knows everybody, and if you don't know everybody, everybody knows you don't. But the waitress will flirt with you all the same, and you're invited to listen in on any stories you like. It's fairly quiet this evening and as I sip my gin and tonic I remember sitting there the evening after Art Pollard's crash, overhearing a large man with ruptured capillaries tell how once in Korea he'd put a forty-five to the head of his "moose," when he'd come back to his "hooch," and found her "shackin' up with a nigger supply sergeant."

"Whad you do?" his companion asked.

"I shot 'er head off."

"Really?"

"Yeah, but I missed and shot off her foot instead." The scalp beneath his silver flattop flared with laughter and, still laughing, he turned toward me. "Say, you don't know what happened to that fella crashed in turn one, do ya?"

"He's dead." I didn't want to discuss Pollard in this context, but it was the only straight answer to his question.

"Aw, shit, I'm sorry," he said, as if apologizing to me.

"You really shot her in the foot, huh?" His companion was intrigued.

"Naw, I never hit her at all. I just shot the bed full of holes." He leaned toward the bar and covered his face with his hand. "Aw, Jesus," he said and began weeping. Something bumped my leg, and I noticed seat belts dangling from each of the bar stools.

It was getting dark and the rain still hadn't let up. A man well decorated with official badges and patches introduced himself. "Everybody knows everybody here."

"So I noticed."

"These paintings, see these paintings on the walls?" He swept his hand in a slow circle indicating a half dozen pictures by Leroy Neiman, impressions of the 1963 race. "They're valued at more than a million dollars, and they don't even have a guard here to watch 'em. Like I said, everybody knows everybody here, and they're good people." I raised my glass and we drank to the good people. "I'm the weighmaster here."

"Pardon me?"

"I'm the weighmaster. I weigh the cars. My company's got twenty-five thousand invested in the scales, and we can't afford to have anything go wrong." I raised my glass again and we drank to his scales.

THE NEXT MORNING a rookie named Billy Scott beats Dick Simon to the track. Scott passes his driver's test with no problems. "A cakewalk," he says to me as he steps out of his car. But Jigger Sirols, who in six years at the Speedway has yet to make the race, is having trouble again. He takes four or five laps to warm his engine, then stands on it coming past the pits. I am standing next to a track photographer when we hear the engine noise fade in the first turn, the horrible scrubbing of tires, an instant of silence, and the dull, grinding thud of rubber, steel, and fiberglass embracing concrete. "Oh, goddam Jigger"–the photographer slaps his thigh–"he done it again." Now the track is officially open. A middle-aged lady with ultramarine blue wings painted on her eyelids walks by. The wing tips extend to her temples. No cars are moving now, and she's leaning on the pit fence, casting a spell on the empty grandstands across the track. The infield bleachers are three-quarters full of spectators, yawning and turning pink. They respond like a chorus each time they hear the putter of a wheel horse or the pit-gate guard blow his whistle, stretching their spines to see whose car is being pushed into the pits, then collapsing again in the shade of their newspapers, swatting flies and occasionally each other. The guards drag off a streaker.

With the exception of the two qualifying weekends and the race itself, it'll go on this way most of the month. Already there is gossip about cheating, and Foyt, as everyone's nemesis, is the center of attention. George Bignotti, who for years had been Foyt's crew chief, has publicly accused Foyt of carrying more fuel than the rules allow. Foyt won the California 500 in a walkaway, and Bignotti has suggested he did it carrying an extra five gallons of methanol in the canister of his fire extinguisher. The controversy rages all month, and though the concerns are genuine, I sense a certain patina of showmanship.

When and if he finally gets around to it, no one, even those with the most peripheral interest in racing, seriously entertains the possibility that anyone could go faster than A. J. The hitchhikers I picked up last night had no doubt about it.

"We come up here with a couple a cunts, but they dropped us," said one. He was wearing the first honest-to-God duck's-ass hairdo I'd seen since 1961. "'Course we was drunk, I'll give 'em that. But you can bet your ass I'll be straddling my B.M.W. the next time I hit this town." He leaned forward from the backseat and tapped me on the shoulder. "Say, you an Elk?"

"No."

"You ain't even from around here, is you?" The one beside me had tattoos on his arms.

"No."

"Well, if you was, you'd be an Elk too. We're from Greencastle. Ever hear of it?"

"Something about Dillinger. He robbed a bank there, didn't he?"

"He sure did." The tattooed one seemed to point to it as a matter of civic pride. "Everybody knows that, I guess."

The D.A. laid his arm across my shoulder and pointed to an overpass about a mile ahead. "You can just drop us off on my bridge up there."

"Your bridge?" I was being set up.

"I laid every inch of concrete in that sucker and sloped the banks with a dozer. I 'as the first one to drive across it, too."

In the rearview mirror, I could see I was being regarded with suspicion, a foreigner, not even an Elk. "What're you doin' here anyway?"

"I'm here for the race."

"Well, I don't give much of a shit about that, but I know Foyt's got a few more miles in his pocket. You wait an' see."

"Can I quote you?"

"Hell, I said it, didn't I?"

ON THE FIRST day of qualifying, Foyt pulls in after one lap at 189.195. It is the fastest lap turned in during the first half hour of qualifications, but not close to the 192-plus laps he's been turning in practice. He rants around the pits, ostentatiously complaining about his tires, then storms off to his garage and locks the doors. The story goes around that he was so pissed off he took a screwdriver and punctured all four tires on his car. "That'd be a good trick," he says later, "I'd like to see somebody try it." There is also some speculation that the tire tantrum is a ploy to get his car back into the garage so he can tamper with the turbocharger pop-off valve installed by the United States Auto Club (USAC) and illegally increase its pressure.

Late in the afternoon when the track is cooler and three other cars have qualified at over 190, A. J. tries again. The first time he goes by, everyone knows that, if he survives, the pole position will be his. I watch him power through turn two, using every inch of the track. I can feel everyone around me holding their breath, with A. J.'s engine screaming at full power as he slides up to the back straight wall till there isn't an inch of daylight between his right rear tire and the unimpressionable concrete. I can feel his engine vibrate all the way down the back straight and into turn three. No one is really surprised when they announce his first lap speed of 195.313 mph, and we know we were watching something so frivolously momentous, so ethereally and courageously executed and yet so seemingly pointless: A man, unquestionably the best in the world at what he does, transcending even his own abilities, extending himself to the mercy of intricately overstressed steel and rubber and any stray speck of dirt on the track, to go nowhere faster than anyone else possibly could. For three minutes and five and a half seconds all the allegations of cheating seem pointless. A. J. Foyt owns the track and no one will dispute it. "I thrilled the hell outta myself three or four times out there," he says, just to let everyone know it hasn't been quite as easy or predetermined as it looks.

Apart from Foyt's run, the greatest spectator interest on the front straight is generated by a rabbit. Qualifying is stopped and several spectators chase the rabbit up and down the track in front of the pits, the crowd cheering, as in the lion feeding scenes from *Quo Vadis*. The rabbit has strayed into a jungle without cover, nothing but asphalt, concrete walls, and four pairs of Adidas track shoes pursuing him. Five minutes later he is strung from the infield fence, dead from an apparent heart attack.

In the bleachers behind the pit fence, I notice a cheering section of thirty or forty men in orange T-shirts. I'm attracted by the wry, subtle wit of the posters they've hung from the railing in front of their seats: *Fire Up Go Nuts, Super Tits, Take I-69 to the 500, Give Harlen the Fengler,* and *I'll Bet My Ass on Loydd's Rubys.* One sign, *Sandy Lovelace* (with a phone number), they disclaim but admit they've rented the space to a new girl in town and that they've "all been behind her 1,000 percent." Their P.R. man insists I have a Coors with him before he'll answer any questions. It's a hot day and I hadn't realized how thirsty I was. "You're okay," he tells me. "We like the way you drink your beer."

The Classics were founded by "fifteen men of like vision" in 1963 and have had the same block of seats each year since. They even have a special Speedway guard assigned to protect and contain them. "For years it was Pops Middleton, but when he died we acquired ole Larry here." The P.R. man puts his arm around the porcine and obviously pleased track attendant, who beams deferentially from under his pith helmet. "We got our own hospitality suite at the Mayfair Motel and our own clubhouse here under the stands. That's where we have our Rookie of the Year Contest."

Their number has grown from the original fifteen to thirty-five, and each year any member may sponsor a rookie, who becomes a probationary member until he distinguishes himself with a bold and forthright act such as mooning the sheriff, entering the topless go-go contest at Mother Tucker's, or jumping onto the stage at the Red Carpet Lounge and stealing the entertainer's hat, as one desperate rookie did last night. "Oh, we got lawyers, accountants, factory workers, salesmen, bartenders, a heterogeneous mixing of fine fellows. We come from all over the country, Washington, Oregon, Davenport, Tallahassee."

I ask him about their uniform beer hats and sunglasses. "Oh, we all wear these so our families won't recognize us when they see us on TV."

I finish my beer and I thank the P.R. man for his time. "All part of the service," he says. "Here, have one of these." He hands me a cigar with a printed wrapper: *The Qualls are the Balls.* "We give one of these to each of the drivers. It's good for three miles an hour."

Their slogan is less facetious than perhaps even The Classics realize. Jerry Grant is running Indy for the ninth time, and it never gets any easier, he tells me. I remember when we were racing together in the United States Road Racing Championship series in 1965, and Jerry had just run at Indy for the first time. "It's not really much different from road racing," he told me, "just more specialized, and all the turns go to the left." But he doesn't see it that way anymore. He's large for a racing driver, six-three and over two hundred pounds. It's ninety-three degrees, with matching humidity. The perspiration beads up on his forehead as he leans against the tool bench, sipping a Fresca. "It's gotten so fast and so technically intricate here." His dark brown eyes fix on mine with a kind of intensity that seems at odds with the casual attitude of his body. They never seem to blink. "You remember when we were racing, how if the car wasn't handling quite right, you could drive it a different way, throw it into the corner a little differently, and make up for the way the chassis was? Well, you can't do that here anymore. This race isn't really much different from any other race I run, but qualifying here is the greatest pressure I'm put under all year. Everything depends on those four laps, so much money and prestige and sponsorship. You just drive it the only way you can and hope everything's working for you, the car, the tires, the track, the air, cause if it isn't, there isn't much you can do about it."

In 1972, Grant qualified on the pole for the California 500 and was the first USAC driver to run an official qualification lap at over 200 mph, but today everything *isn't* working for him, and he qualifies fourteenth. Johnny Rutherford, who holds the one-lap record at Indianapolis and won the pole position in 1973, makes the definitive statement on those four crucial laps after qualifying a disappointing seven mph off the pace: "Some days you eat the bear and some days the bear eats you."

It's a fairly reliable axiom that the best drivers will be offered the best cars, and rookies, unless they're already established superstars, consider themselves fortunate to have any kind of a ride for Indy. Usually they have to struggle with fairly antique and uncompetitive equipment. Billy Scott, the rookie for whom the driver's test at 170 mph had been "a cakewalk," finds that trying to push the same car just twelve mph a lap faster to make the race is a nightmare. And inferior equipment isn't his only handicap. The intimidation of Indianapolis itself, the most important and tradition-bound race in the world, takes time and many laps of practice to overcome. "It's the biggest race in the world," Scott says. He leans close to be sure I can hear him over the din of the bar. "I saw those huge grandstands full of people watching me, and it suddenly hit me where I was. A couple of times it happened during practice. I'd start down the front straight and hear myself thinking, *Gee, I'm at Indy, I'm really at Indy.* Then I'd catch myself and say, *Cut that shit out and drive.* Finally I took an 869-foot spin coming out of turn three and ended up on the grass inside turn four. The car was okay, and so was I, but that really got my attention, like a dog shittin' a loggin' chain."

Scott fails to make competitive speed on two qualifying attempts and is waved off by his crew. The car owner decides to try another driver and puts Graham McRae, an Indy veteran, in the car. But McRae's times are no better than Scott's. "I was pushing that car as fast as it was ever gonna go on this track," Scott explains, "but the old man wouldn't believe it." On his last attempt, Scott overcooks it coming out of turn four. The rear end comes loose, and he makes a spectacular spin down the front straight, shedding fiberglass and suspension parts like a dog shaking water. "Too bad he didn't stuff it beyond fixin,'" another driver quips. "Now some other poor son of a bitch'll have to struggle with it next year."

I TELL BILLY SCOTT about my friend Dave MacDonald, who was killed eleven years ago, coming out of turn four in an unstable car; tell him how Jimmy Clark has followed MacDonald in practice; and told him he should refuse to drive it in the race. "But I couldn't do that." Scott seems shocked by the suggestion. "I mean, if I stepped out of a ride, I'd never get another one. I'd be all washed up."

"THE THRILL ISN'T there anymore." Andy Granatelli, who with his legendary Novis and his turbine car that died four laps short of winning the 1967 race has been responsible for more innovation and spectator interest than any other man in the Speedway's sixty-year history, looks tired and almost on the verge of tears as he talks about his twenty-nine-year lover's quarrel with Indianapolis. "Driving down here each year, I used to get so excited I'd start edging down on the accelerator, going faster and faster, till by the time I got to Lafayette I was driving flat out."

"But there's been too much tragedy," he explains. "That and USAC's continual legislation against innovation. It all comes down to the rules." He gets up and goes to the refrigerator for a can of diet pop. He's lost fifty pounds and waddles less conspicuously than he used to in those STP commercials. "Want one?" I accept. He pops the top, hands the can to me, and sits back down at the end of the couch. "If they went to stock blocks, stock oil, stock gasoline, and street available tires, you'd have a better race, and you'd have something about the cars the spectators could identify with."

"What about the changes they've made," I ask, "like wing restrictions and fuel limitations?"

"That's a start." He pauses for a swig of diet pop. "But they didn't go far enough. Look . . . " He moves up on the edge of the couch and makes an expansive sweep with his hands." You've got a governing board made up of twenty-one car owners, drivers, and mechanics, all legislating their own interests. I mean, you ever see a committee of twenty-one that ever got anything done? No. What racing needs is a czar. Limit the fuel to two hundred gallons. You'd slow the cars down to one-seventy, and you'd have a better race. The spectators wouldn't know the difference. They can't tell if a car's going two hundred or one-fifty. You ever notice during qualifying, how they never cheer for the fastest cars till after they hear the time announced? They can't even see the drivers anymore, can't see their style or the way they drive, can't even see the numbers from the pits anymore."

"They killed my driver and my mechanic." There's a kind of forlorn intensity in his expression which, though he doesn't say it, pleads *Don't you understand?* Two years ago, the last year Granatelli entered the 500, Swede Savage, driving one of his cars, was leading the race after fifty-seven laps when he lost it coming out of turn four, crashed brutally into the inside retaining wall, and suffered burns from which he was to die a month later. A Speedway crash truck, rushing the wrong way up the pit lane, struck one of Granatelli's crewmen from behind and killed him instantly. Those in the pits, already horrified by the explosion and almost total disintegration of Savage's car, saw the mechanic's body tossed like a rag doll sixty feet in the air.

"Swede had just come out of the pits." Granatelli pauses and draws his hand across his forehead. "He'd taken on eighty gallons of fuel, and it was a completely different handling car than he'd been driving a lap earlier."

To understand why Savage lost control in that particular corner, it's necessary to speculate on what he must have been thinking just before it happened.

Bobby Unser, who had previously been Savage's teammate, had insulted him in print, had told the media that Savage couldn't drive, that he wouldn't even include him on a list of the hundred top drivers. Jerry Grant, who, like Unser, had been driving a white Olsonite Eagle, explained it to me: "The track was oily, really slippery in the groove, and Swedie was running high, making time by staying above the groove where the track was dry. I think what happened was that he saw a white car in his mirrors, and thought Unser was closing on him. I guess he didn't realize it was me and that Bobby was a lap down at that point. Anyway, he must have been thinking about what Bobby had said about him, 'cause he dove down into the groove to close the door on me. The car was heavy with full fuel tanks, and he was just going too fast to hold traction when he came down into the oil slick. It just must have been brain fade. For a second there his mind must have been somewhere else."

The race was stopped for an hour and fifteen minutes after the crash, restarted, and then called because of rain after 332 miles. Granatelli's other car, driven by Gordon Johncock, was declared the winner, but it was a sad victory for Andy.

The diet pop can is empty now, and he sets it on the table at the end of the couch. "Last year when we were coming in over the airport, my wife looked down from the plane and saw the Speedway. 'The thrill is gone, Andy'–that's what she said." He looks down at the floor and taps his chest. "It just isn't here anymore."

DAN GURNEY IS balancing on a small bicycle in the Jorgensen Steel garage in Gasoline Alley. I'm leaning against a workbench, and he seems to have me pinned in the corner with the flashing wheels of his unruly mount. He pulls up into an occasional wheelie, and I notice, with some relief, that the frame brace bar is thickly padded. "We can't forget we're in show business." His blue All-American Eagle rests unattended in the adjacent stall, race-ready and immaculate. "We're competing for the entertainment dollar with football, baseball, hockey, whatever's going on at the same time, and those other things are more solidly entrenched and better organized than we are. I think that's the most important thing about this sport to keep in mind, even more important than the rules."

Like Andy Granatelli, Gurney feels the rules, as they now stand, are stifling championship car racing. "I'd like to see us get more in line with the rest of the world, go with the Grand Prix formula and get a full international sanction so we could attract foreign drivers again." I recall Granatelli's complaint that Indy has become too homogeneous, that there are basically only two kinds of cars here anymore, the McLarens and Gurney's Eagles; and no more Jim Clarks, Graham Hills or Alberto Ascaris. "If we had foreign drivers here again," Gurney continues, "they'd have to build a third tier on the grandstands." He also wants to eliminate rules that favor turbochargers. "Turbocharged engines cut down the noise and the diversity of sounds, and frankly, that's a big part of the spectator appeal."

I remind him that the Indianapolis 500 is already far and away the largest spectator event in the world.

"I know that," he smiles earnestly, "but that doesn't mean it couldn't be bigger." A man from ABC interrupts to tell Gurney they'd like to film an interview for *Wide World of Sports*. Dan politely explains that he's busy right now, and that he'll get to it as soon as he's free. I feel slightly impertinent, holding up ABC, like the flea with an erection who floats down the river, hollering for the drawbridge to be raised, but Gurney takes one thing at a time. While they are talking I notice three Indiana State troopers with nightsticks, Sam Browne belts, and mirror-finished sunglasses in the bright alley beyond the garage door. I don't like to reinforce stereotypes, but they look polished, impersonal, and just plain mean, like licensed bullies. Their presence is an integral part of the atmosphere of this race, as is that of the rioters, sadists, muggers, streakers, fornicators, motorcycle gangs, Frisbee players, and drunks who occupy the infield like thirty armed tribes. The faint odor of tear gas is almost as common on race day as beer, popcorn, and hot rubber. The man from ABC will wait outside with his crew.

"Where was I?" Dan smiles in apology for the interruption. "Okay, another thing about turbochargers is that they make the race so technologically intricate that it works against younger, less experienced drivers, so that you've got the same crop of forty-year-olds out there leading the race every year. We don't have a farm system like they do for Formula 1 racing, so there isn't a big crop of young fast drivers coming up all the time, pushing the older guys the way it is in Europe."

Dan's wife, Evi, walks into the garage and talks to Pete Biro, Gurney's P.R. man. The attention of the pit gawkers shifts from Dan and the car to a truly beautiful woman.

"What makes this race unique is tradition and the ripples that it causes all around the world. But what I don't like about it, and I guess it's a part of the tradition, is the amount of time we have to spend here. It's like a whole month in a police state." I smile and notice the troopers are talking to Bobby Unser, who last week was made a special sheriff's deputy, had a police radio installed in his car, and, thirty minutes later, drove across town at unrecorded speeds to be the first on the scene to arrest three teenagers suspected of smoking marijuana behind an all-night market. "Maybe it's necessary for it to be that way in order to put this race on the way it is," Gurney says as he scratches his head and smiles wryly, "but we're all anxious to get back to the United States when it's over."

IT'S THE MORNING of carburetion tests, three days before the race and the last opportunity any of the drivers will have to practice. I'm walking along Sixteenth Street toward the main gate to pick up my race-day credentials. I'm on a hard-packed dirt path just outside the chain-link fence that defines the official boundaries of the Speedway. Beyond the fence is a grass slope, a service vehicle road, then a rise, crested by the concrete retaining wall of the short chute between turns one and two. Above the wall is a catch fence woven of heavy steel cables, but the wall itself is low enough so that I can catch a glimpse of the wing, the windshield, and the driver's helmet as he drifts to the wall, setting up for turn two.

It's a hot morning. There aren't many spectators at the track today, and the traffic on Sixteenth Street is relatively light. There's a deceptively relaxed atmosphere as this day begins. Qualifying is over, and the tension seems to have subsided. I hear the Doppler effect of an engine, wound tight and rising down the front straight. It's getting louder, then seems to fade momentarily behind the grandstands on turn one. Suddenly it rises again, then, *zap,* one startling reverberation off the wall, one strobelike flash of sunlight off orange and white, and it's past, powering into turn two, the pitch rising and fading down the back straight. My stomach tightens. The sheer speed has given me a light punch in the solar plexus and a prickly sensation all over my skin, and I realize how much of that sense of speed is lost on television, where telephoto lenses and elevated camera angles convey the impression of a relaxed, almost slow-motion kind of game.

Television has come a long way in transcribing sports action on a field, court, or track to a circumscribed image composed of dots and spaces on a screen, capable of a multitude of points of view, *but* again, only one at a time. After several years of experimentation, they've learned to photograph tennis matches so that you can actually see both the players and the ball. The same can be said of football. With slow-motion instant replays you can have a more detailed, though still particularized, look at every bone-jarring nuance in your living room, bedroom, or bar than any ticket-buying, pennant-waving, crowd-braving fan in the stadium. But they haven't quite pulled it off with motor racing. They've got it down to covering every turn, accident, and pit stop, interviewing drivers and crews and explaining the particular challenges and characteristics of each track. But the one thing they haven't yet been able to adequately capture is speed.

Anyone who has gotten out and gone to a race after watching them on television is astounded at how fast the cars zoom past. Maybe part of it's being there with the ear-splitting engine noise, the smell of rubber, oil, and asphalt, but when you get out from behind the telephoto lens and see how long those straights really are and how little time it takes a racing car to cover the seemingly immense distance from turn four to turn one, it causes a certain physical sensation in the scalp and at the base of the spine that television viewers never know. "My God, they're going fast." It's no longer the sort of leisurely motorized game you've watched between commercials. You feel the ground shudder under your feet, and it feels a little threatening.

But maybe the camera is better than the naked eye at projecting the driver's experience of speed. Of course there are vibrations, sounds, and G force sensations that the driver alone can experience, but when a man lives long enough at 200 mph, 200 mph becomes the norm, and he slows it down. Through his eyes, as long as he remains in control, things don't happen with the frightening rapidity with which we perceive them. For him, the track isn't a chaotic blur, but a calmly perceived series of sensations now, now, now, and now. He fixes on nothing and is therefore not startled by the brevity of his relationship with any object in the field of his experience. It's a kind of Zen by default in which survival depends upon nonattachment and single-mindedness, a gestalt from which no element can be removed and examined.

MOST OF THE drivers would like to get on with it. The field is set, but tradition dictates the weeklong waiting game between the end of qualifying and race day. Today's carburetion test is the only chance they'll have to get back on the track until they line up for the parade lap preceding the race. Today they are given three hours to get in a little more practice, make a last-minute check of carburetion and tires, experience how the car will handle on race day with a full fuel load, and one hour to practice pit stops.

Twenty years ago a forty-five second pit stop to refuel and change tires would have been considered highly efficient, but today it would be a disaster, costing the driver almost a lap and probably putting him out of contention. The Gatorade McLaren team pulls Johnny Rutherford's car back up the pit lane, then pushes it in to simulate a pit stop. Each member of the crew is waiting in his assigned position, tires, jacks, impact wrenches, refueling hoses ready. For Rutherford it means practice in stopping exactly on his marks. During the race he'll be coming down the pit lane at almost 100 mph and must sight his crew and bring the car to a stop precisely at the spot where each crew member can do his job without having to change position. Tyler Alexander, the crew chief, stands in the pit lane to mark the point where the nose of the car should come to rest. Rutherford stops exactly on the mark, and five men go to work. The refueling and vent nozzles are inserted, impact wrenches twist off the right-hand hub nuts. A jack instantly lifts the right side of the car, two wheels are removed and replaced with another set, the jack is removed, and the tires come back to the pavement. The impact wrenches blast again, the refueling nozzles are removed, the front-tire man jumps out of the way, whipping his airhose clear of the car. I duck to avoid a mechanic as he hurtles over the wall. Only five men are allowed in the pit during a stop, while a sixth man offers Rutherford a cup of water at the end of a rod extended from behind the pit wall. Rutherford never takes his eyes off Alexander. Three crew members fall in behind the car, Alexander waves him off, and the car is pushed back into the pit lane. Teddy Mayer clicks his digital stopwatch: 12.5 seconds from the instant the car stopped until the wheels are rolling again.

NORMALLY, MOST OF the pit stops will be for fuel only. The crew will check the right-side tires and be prepared to change them if necessary. In Jerry Grant's pit, they've made five practice stops with tire changes and simulated refueling, the same procedure again and again until it's become mechanical routine. A sixth time, Grant coasts to a stop, but now he pulls a surprise and points to the left front tire, a frantic series of stabs with his index finger. The front man scurries around to the other side of the car and undoes the nut while the jack man moves to jack up the left side. When the tire man has changed the tire and secured the nut, he scrambles back to the right side of the car and gives Grant the all-clear signal. When the practice stop is completed, Grant motions the front-tire man over to confer with him. They've handled the unexpected tire change flawlessly and without hesitation, but Grant figures it has taken the tire changer an extra second or two to get back to the right front corner of the car to give his all-clear signal. The tire man kneels by the cockpit while Grant tells him to give the signal from the left side of the car in case they have to change the left-front tire.

Adrenaline will be running freely when the actual pit stops are made, and the tension can be felt in this last bit of practice before race day. The driver will be sitting with the car in gear, the engine running and the clutch in, and it's crucial that he has only one crewman to look to for his signals, that there are no misunderstandings. I remember seeing films of Parnelli Jones rolling on the pavement in invisible alcohol flames after a botched pit stop. Thinking he'd been given the all clear, he'd pulled away from his pit with the fuel hose still connected, rupturing the tank, eliminating himself from the race, sustaining some painful burns, and causing a potentially dangerous situation in the entire pit and front straight grandstand area.

I look up and down the row of refueling tanks mounted on scaffolds above the pit wall and realize that on race day I'd rather be anywhere else on the track. One 240-gallon tank of highly combustible methanol fuel for each of the thirty-three cars, and it would take only one careless act, one car out of control in the pit lane, to cause a chain reaction that could endanger hundreds of lives. "I'm surprised something like that's never happened," one driver confides. "I feel a whole lot safer out on the track than I do during a pit stop. It's not just the time lost from the race; I'm really anxious to get away from all that fuel and confusion."

TRADITION DOMINATES EVERY aspect of Indianapolis, and not only in a ceremonial sense. There is a pervading attitude among those in authority that there is a *right* way of doing things, and that way has acquired its mantle of rectitude by virtue of the fact that "It *is* the way we do it." Actually, it may be the only way they are able to run this race, dealing with a group of men as egocentric and opinionated as racing drivers. "I don't know" is a statement seldom heard. Whichever aspect of race procedure is in question, each of them will not only have an answer, he will have *the* answer, and a dictator behind the badge of a Chief Steward is required.

REFUELING TANKS AND the penalty for jacking to get the last bit of fuel from them is the first order of business at the driver's and crew chief's meeting following pit practice. It's a Turkish bath. The main concourse below the tower is packed with rows of folding chairs and sealed off to the public as well as to ventilation by Speedway guards. Spectators press their faces against the glass doors, blocking the reflections of the afternoon sunlight with their cupped hands. From inside the meeting room, they look like visitors to an aquarium. Tom Binford, the Chief Steward, calls the meeting to order. His situation is similar to that of the president of the United States at a news conference, both man on the spot and the ultimate authority.

With each car limited to 280 gallons for the race, fuel and its handling become a controversial issue. Even if a car could mechanically withstand being driven flat out for the entire five hundred miles, with a consumption rate of between 1.2 and 1.4 miles per gallon, it would eliminate itself by running out of fuel in the process. Most of the teams, particularly those of the front-runners, will be depending on a certain amount of the race being run under yellow-light conditions in order to be able to stretch their allotted fuel over the distance. Binford settles the refueling controversy as soon as the meeting has been called to order. Refueling tanks may be mounted at an incline of eleven degrees. Pit stewards will check the angle of incline, and any tanks exceeding this angle or any tanks jacked during the race will be cause for disqualification. This will be the most definite ruling made during the entire meeting. Almost all other aspects of race procedure seem to be open to a certain variance of interpretation, and Binford generally chooses to let the penalties for infractions remain vague.

An argument over the use of pacer lights for regulating speed in a yellow-light situation occupies almost half the meeting time. A. J. Foyt, Bobby Unser, and Mario Andretti argue that while the pacer lights were a good idea, they just don't seem to work. They would prefer the use of the pace car to control speed in an emergency situation even though it would allow the field to close its distance on the leaders.

"The pacer lights stay," Binford states flatly.

"Well, hell," Foyt is on his feet, "those lights screwed up the other day during practice. They got sequenced at over two hundred miles an hour, and I had to scurry the hell outta myself try'n to keep up with 'em." Everyone but Binford laughs.

Grant King, a car builder and crew chief, argues that since most of the drivers would prefer the pace car, why not reinstate it and forget the light system.

Binford says, "Because the regulations call for the pacer lights."

King replies, "But none of these rules are irrevocable."

Binford fires back, "I know that, but the Speedway management prefers the lights." End of controversy.

Bobby Unser is up again, contending that since name drivers like "me and Al and A. J. and Mario are better known and get watched closer than these other guys, we get unfairly penalized for yellow light infractions."

"I guess that's the price of fame." Binford seems unmoved.

Someone raises the question of onboard fuel capacity, covertly referring to the controversy stemming from George Bignotti's insinuations that Foyt had carried an extra five-gallon fuel tank somewhere in his car during the California 500. Binford appears to have been expecting this one and states that they have already made plans to inspect the fuel capacity of the first ten finishers.

Grant King wants to know what the penalty will be for having too many men over the wall during a pit stop. Binford takes a deep breath and wipes his forehead. "Any crew with more than five men over the wall will be penalized accordingly."

"Well I want to know exactly what that penalty's going to be," King insists, "because if it's only gonna be a fifty-dollar fine, I'm gong to have fifteen men over that wall."

Binford assures him that it will be more than a fifty-dollar fine. He wipes his forehead again.

Jerry Grant sips his Fresca. James Garner whispers to Al Unser and Mario Andretti, and all three smile knowingly.

Foyt stands up again, his arms bulging from his short-sleeved sport shirt. He looks impatient and impressive. He always looks impatient and impressive, on or off the track. Several nights ago, I watched him make his entrance in the Speedway Motel dining room. He seated his wife and walked over to another table to talk with four men, aware that every eye was on him. It was almost as if a tiger had wandered into the room, and while nobody wanted to make a scene about it, nobody wanted to lose track of where he was. Foyt now asks Binford whether or not Goodyear technicians will be allowed over the wall to check tires during pit stops.

Binford replies, "No, not if they make the total more than five."

"Well hell, you talk about safety, those Goodyear people are a hell of a lot better judges of whether a tire needs changing than any of these mechanics."

Binford concedes the point. Tire technicians will be allowed. But that doesn't sit well with Billy Vukovich. "But what if I don't have any Goodyear men in my pit? Then it isn't fair."

"You start runnin' out there in front"—Foyt twists the knife—"and you'll have so many of 'em you'll be wantin' to trade 'em off." A wave of laughter spreads through the meeting and then dies away uncomfortably. Salt Walther asks what the penalty will be for improving your position prior to crossing the starting line. I can see the black glove of his left hand, the full use of which he lost in a crash at the start of the 1973 race, a crash initiated by a charging car that bumped him into the outside retaining wall. It's an important question, and a pointed one coming from Walther. Binford states that anyone flagrantly charging before the starting line will be penalized one lap. He goes on to urge everyone not to really start racing until they've come out of turn two and started down the back straight.

"Look," he pleads, "for most of us, our livelihoods and our careers are centered around this one race, and it'd be stupid and pointless to spoil it by getting overanxious at the start of it."

The meeting adjourns with Binford asking several of the name drivers to stay for a briefing of the rookies. At speeds well over 200 mph, the "old boy-new boy" system is a vital part of the Indy tradition. There's a big show coming up in three days, the biggest one in sports, and it has to be made absolutely clear to the rookies how they are expected to play their parts.

IT'S THE EVENING before the race, and Speedway, Indiana, has become a refugee camp. Every field and vacant lot within miles is packed with trailers, tents, motor homes, sweating bodies, piles of empty beer cans, and backyard barbecues. Refugee camps are better organized. These are the Mongol hordes, the Huns awaiting race day to storm the gates of Rome. Campfires glow. I'm certain I can hear the throbbing of tribal drums, unintelligible chanting. Police sirens are as commonplace as the random explosions of cherry bombs. A prison bus with heavily wire-meshed windows speeds past in a clusteral escort of flashing lights. There will be a total eclipse of the moon tonight, and it seems to hype the lunacy. Except for a few nervous mechanics and staff personnel, the Speedway is empty and quiet. From a helicopter it would look like a black oval, a void in a galaxy of fire and chaos.

The motel room I'm sharing with Bob Jones faces Sixteenth Street and is less than one hundred feet from an entrance to the track. It's a convenient bivouac, but only a self-hypnotist could sleep here. During the evening several gaggles of girls from tent city have wandered in to use our bathroom. Invariably their introductory line is, "I know it's a terrible imposition, but this is an emergency."

This one sits down and has a cigarette while her companion uses the plumbing. I offer her a drink, and Jones interrogates her. She's from Indianapolis and claims she's twenty-one, though sixteen seems more likely. When she laughs, she snorts through her sinuses and she laughs at almost everything she says. "You guys got any spare change?" She laughs at this too.

"No, none that's spare."

"You're selfish."

Jones asks her if she left a dime in the bathroom. "Oh, that," she says. "But I left something else." She finds this funny too. Jones and I are infected by her laughter and laugh ourselves because there's nothing to laugh at.

"What do you think about the race?" It's a rhetorical question.

"What race?" she snorts again and we all laugh.

I nod over my shoulder in the direction of the Speedway. She covers her lips with her cupped hand and snorts a mouthful of vodka and tonic through her fingers. "I don't even know who's racing."

I ask her why she's here, and she says it's for the crowd in the camp across the street. "It's the most exciting thing that happens all year. Ya live in Indianapolis, this is like Christmas, it's what ya wait for." I was reminded of all the middle-aged, middle-class women I'd seen cruising the bar at the Holiday Inn, doctors' lawyers' and salesmen's wives, race groupies for whom the race means only a chance to meet a stranger, a mechanic, a tire buster, or a P.R. man, maybe from far-off exotic California. There were also 150,000 fans who would fill the infield, most of whom, by midafternoon, would have forgotten why they'd come there in the first place.

Now the other girl has finished in the bathroom. "Ya know, we don't have to go," the snort queen offers. "I mean we could stay here."

"You could, but you can't." I hear the crackle of radios from the police cruisers along the street and encourage them to go back to tent city.

ALTHOUGH THE GATES won't open until 5:00 A.M., the traffic starts stacking up shortly after midnight. I close the door, turn out the lights, and lie awake with the sirens, honking horns, and motorcycle engines, and the anticipation of the race. I wonder how well the drivers are sleeping, or if they are.

I realize I must have finally fallen asleep, because I'm awakened at 6:30 by an immense pounding on the door. I swing my feet to the floor and sit for a minute trying to remember where I am and to determine whether or not I'd been dreaming. I open the door on the long shadow of early morning light. The traffic is still solid and the police radios are still crackling unintelligible messages. I've almost forgotten why I opened the door when someone grabs my right hand. "Hi, I'm Dayton Spengler. It's a beautiful day, and it's time for you boys to get up and go to work." A puffy, almost featureless, florid face, little pig eyes squinting out from under the visor of a white yachting cap. "You boys do a good job now."

"Thank you." I turn and close the door. Jones is still snoring. *Maybe it's a special wake-up service the motel has for the race day,* I thought. I'd promised Heinz Kluetmeier that I'd cover turn two with one of his motor-drive Nikons, so it did make sense. I did have a job to do. I look at the camera on top of the dresser and feel a momentary apprehension that I've already missed something important. I have barely settled back onto the sheets when the pounding resumes.

"Hi!" My hand is being pumped again. "You remember me. I'm Dayton Spengler."

"Sure." It's true, I do remember him.

"Say, this lady's kinda sick and I wonder if she could use your room to lie down a little while." I peer around the doorjamb in the direction he indicates, to a blonde lady with a beehive hairdo who seems bored and impatient. She is pretending to be interested in the traffic on Sixteenth Street and refuses to acknowledge either Dayton or me.

"Well, gee." I stumble for a moment, trying to figure out what I'll do while she is using my room and how I'll explain it to Jones. After all, Jones doesn't even know Dayton Spengler. Then Jones himself helps me out.

"No." I look over my shoulder and see the whites of his eyes glowing through the dark cave of the room. They don't look the least bit sympathetic toward Dayton's cause.

"No," I say

"Well, that's okay." My hand is being pumped again. "You boys have a good day."

I close the door and look at Jones. He is laughing. "That's Indy," he says. "There's your story."

AT NINE O'CLOCK, two hours before race time, I head over to the track. I've been given a pass to shoot photographs from the balcony of the Penske suite overlooking turn two. It's a precarious, though very pleasant, setup. Drinks, snacks, and air conditioning will be available a few steps away, and the view of the short chute, turn two, and the back straight is excellent, though I'll be sitting less than twenty feet from the edge of the track at the point where the cars begin to exit the turn. I'd felt a little exposed there, watching qualifying, feeling the vibration and heat from the passing cars and gauging the strength of the cables reinforcing the wire fence that was all that separated me from the track. I remind myself now that it is only steel cables that hold up the Golden Gate Bridge, and that if they do fail, anything that happens will happen so fast that I won't have time to torment myself trying to escape.

On the telephone this morning my nine-year-old son asked me to get the autograph of the winner. "It's not likely I'll be able to get close to him after the race," I told him. "Why don't you just pick a driver whose autograph you'd like and I'll get that." There was a long silence at the other end of the line while he searched for a name, then a tentative "Is Bobby Unser there?" I pull a small photograph from the Jorgensen Eagle press kit, slip it between the pages of a program to keep it from getting bent, and set off for the pits with a pre-race mission.

A few steps from the door of my room I can feel the juices begin to ooze from my skin and I expect to deliquesce like a maple-sugar doll. In the pedestrian tunnel that crosses under the track I fall in with a half-dozen slightly flaccid, halter-topped high school girls. They have already begun to pink a bit on the back shoulders and somehow smell like school lunch boxes, the redolence of overripe bananas. I am now part of the great event, a drone filing into the hive, *the people, yes*, and so goddamn many of them, hippies, rednecks, straights, and greasers. We are passed by a seemingly endless line of Buick convertibles carrying celebrities and race queens. I don't recognize any of the celebrities, though we scatter before them like peasants before the coaches of the king. At least a dozen bands are playing, and the atmosphere is already so bizarre that I half expect to see a guillotine in the next parting of the crowd. I'm concentrating on my own pace, trying to maintain some identity, trying not to fall in step with the martial music of whichever band is dominating the moment. But the crowd is moving in time, and I must move with it or be trampled. The Golden Girl of the Purdue Band is attracting all the photographers, who a moment before had been three-deep around A. J. Foyt as he checked over his safety harness and every detail in the cockpit of his Gilmore Coyote. Most of the drivers are staying in their garages, avoiding the crowds and the heat as long as they can. The pit lane looks like Fifth Avenue on Easter Sunday, two ill-defined columns of aimless strollers with pit badges in lieu of bonnets, there to see and to be seen.

The pit crowd is noticeably better groomed than those in the infield, crews in bright-colored uniforms; photographers in bush jackets under tiers of Nikons; and car owners, sponsors, and officials in seersucker suits. I feel a little underdressed in my Levi's and short-sleeved cotton shirt. I decide it's time to head across the infield toward the suites. I cut through Gasoline Alley and stop by Gurney's garage to get Bobby Unser's autograph. There doesn't seem to be a great deal of tension in the garage. It's an hour until race time and Unser is still dressed in blue cotton trousers and a short-sleeved shirt. He gladly signs my photograph and seems relaxed, as if there were nothing special he had to do. Then it occurs to me that there isn't anything special he has to do. If you are a professional racing driver, driving races is what you do, and he's done it almost every week for the last twenty-six years. Indianapolis may be the biggest race around, but still, a race is a race. I thank him for the autograph and remember not to wish him good luck. There are so many uncontrollable variables in racing that drivers tend to be superstitious, and being wished good luck is one curse they'd rather do without. I pass Jerry Grant's garage and think of stopping to wish him good luck without saying it, but the doors are closed and I figure he'd rather be alone. I remember that when I was driving I never really had anything to say to anyone before a race. Any conversation that occurred was like that at a Christian Science funeral, about anything but the business at hand.

A few Frisbees are being tossed on the infield golf course, a few couples are making love in the sand traps, and the sweet aroma of marijuana hangs in the breezeless air.

At the Penske suite, the chairman of the bank whose travelers' checks co-sponsor the Penske McLaren driven by Tom Sneva extends himself to make me feel welcome, points out the bar and buffet, tells me not to hesitate to ask for whatever I need. He even suggests that I might be able to bribe the maintenance man to show me how to get up on the roof. "Anything we can do for you, anything at all, just sing out and it'll be done." A hearty clap on the shoulder. His graciousness seems quite genuine, though I am beginning to realize that my motor-driven Nikon and *Sports Illustrated* nametag represent some fairly heavy credentials. I stake out a seat on the corner of the balcony where no one will be moving between my lens and the track, fix myself a tonic water, and check my focus and exposure. There are no rednecks or hippies here in the suites, a madras and La Coste crowd, collegians of the fifties with a few crow's-feet and gray hairs, not surprisingly, the kind of people one would associate with Roger Penske, precise and successful.

The pre-race ceremonies have begun, the celebrities have been driven around the track, Peter DePaolo, winner of the 1925 500, has taken a lap in the Miller that won the race in 1930, the Speedway has been presented with a plaque designating it as a national historic landmark, and the final lines of the invocation drift across the infield, ". . . with a hand over the heart, a prayer in the soul, and brains in the head." Now everything seems to accelerate, including four hundred thousand pulse rates. Jim Nabors mouths every word of "Back Home Again in Indiana," a thousand helium-filled balloons are released, and Tony Hulman takes the microphone. "Gentlemen, start your *in*juns." The parade and pace laps come off without incident. Some of the drivers wave or salute as they pass the suites of their sponsors. I am reminded of knights dipping their lances to the ladies whose favors they wore. The ritual hasn't changed, only become more commercial. I know the drivers are very calm now. For them the pre-race tension is over and they are locked into that impenetrable concentration that comes the moment they are strapped into the car. As they approach the starting line, everyone becomes very quiet, probably the one moment when not one of the nearly half-million people in this arena has anything to say. The engine noise accelerates, a series of bombs explode in the air, and a great cheer goes up from the crowd. The announcer's voice booms, "And the fifty-ninth Indianapolis 500-Mile Race is under way, the greatest spectacle in racing."

After the start and the excitement of the initial laps, the race, for most of the spectators, diminishes to a monotonous stream of almost indistinguishable cars and anonymous drivers flowing by at over 200 mph. I don't mean that it isn't still exciting. The noise itself is enough to keep the adrenaline pumped up, but you have to rely on the track announcer to understand what's happening. It's very much the way it was all those years I listened to it on the radio, but with a lot of special effects thrown in. I'm aware that Johncock, who had jumped into a commanding lead at the start, has dropped out. It's a five-hundred-mile race. Running away with the early laps may please the crowd and momentarily put a driver in the limelight, but the chances are he'll be all but forgotten when the checkered flag falls. Foyt and Rutherford are swapping the lead now, though I'm seldom certain who has it at any given moment. As the cars scream out of turn two it all seems effortless, though they're fighting the limit of adhesion. They pass so close it almost seems I could touch them. In twos and threes, the engines surge down the back straight like aircraft engines out of sync.

There's a yellow light and most of the cars head for the pits. For a full ten seconds no cars pass, and the silence is startling. I'm keeping my camera ready, watching what's coming out of turn two and trying to answer the questions of the distractingly pretty woman who has taken the seat next to me. Our conversation is disjointed, broken sentences sequenced in the brief intervals between passing cars. Occasionally a whiff of her perfume mingles with and subsumes the perspiration and burning rubber. She's a young Grace Kelly type from somewhere in Pennsylvania. It's difficult to hear, let alone remember, details in these circumstances. She seems unaffected by the heat, which at the moment is causing large drops of sweat to trickle over my ribs.

They tickle, and I know if I touch them they'll show through my shirt. I want to appear to be as cool as she is. I lean closer for her next question, but not too close. At the same time I'm reminding myself to keep my lens and my attention on turn two.

Several times I stand up to watch some passing action down the back straight. Tom Sneva is running a highly respectable fifth and is still very much in contention. He pulls to the inside to lap several slower cars and the precision of his judgment keeps me standing. It seems he won't have time to get past them and back into the groove to set up for turn three, and I realize that at that point he's traveling at about 220 mph. He's deep, almost too deep, but in the last few feet, he cuts back to the outside, clear of the traffic and right in the groove. Then I remember how it always looks more impressive from the outside than it does from the driver's seat. Once at Mosport, during practice for the Canadian Grand Prix, I walked over to watch at turn one while my car was being worked on. I was frightened and astounded at how ragged and perilous it seemed, the cars skidding and vibrating through the reverse camber downhill turn. *Jesus, that's scary,* I thought. *How can they do it?* Then a half hour later I went and qualified on the pole for the G. T. Race. I didn't know how to do it. I just did it.

More laps, more questions, more fragmented answers: "They're limited to"–two cars scream through the turn, nose to tail, and I wait for the noise to fade–"280 gallons, which means that"–another car passes and I can feel the heat from its exhaust–"at the mileage they're getting that they"–this time we're interrupted by the track announcer calling attention to Wally Dallenbach, who started in twenty-first position and is now moving up toward the lead at an alarming rate–"they couldn't finish the race if they didn't do at least"–another car–"a few laps under the yellow."

I've been watching Dallenbach. His engine sounds stronger, higher pitched and wound tighter than the other cars, and another strange thing is that though he's gobbling up the field, his line through the corners isn't following the groove. He's running through the middle of turn two each time he passes, not drifting wide and using the whole track the way other cars do when they're turning hot laps. Each time he passes, it seems he's operating on a separate principle of physics, as if the laws governing centrifugal force have been suspended for him. Later I would hear rumbling that he had a small tank of nitrous oxide (laughing gas) that was being injected directly into the cylinders, giving him an extra 150 horsepower with no increase in boost, and that his unorthodox line was to compensate for the extra sensitivity under his right foot. It occurred to me that if that were true, it might be possible that the nitrous oxide was being injected directly into Dallenbach and that his extra speed was the result of an altered consciousness. Whatever the facts, Dallenbach was laughing on the sixtieth lap when he passed Foyt and went on to open up a twenty-two-second lead.

ONE HUNDRED AND twenty-six laps and almost two hours of racing. Senses are beginning to numb and the stream of cars is beginning to have a hypnotic effect on the afternoon. I have a mild headache, my throat's getting sore, and fortunately, or unfortunately, Grace Kelly is asking fewer questions. The tension begins to dissolve into monotony. I'm less attentive with my lens and have pretty well determined that I won't have to shoot any action on this turn today. Somebody taps me on the shoulder and as I turn to my right. I hear a scream from the crowd, followed by a loud, dull thud. I turn back to my left and there, not forty feet away, and twenty feet in the air, just about eye level, is the top of Tom Sneva's helmet. Flames have engulfed the rear half of his car and it's cartwheeling horizontally along the wire-retaining fence. I have a stop-action image, looking at the car as if from above as it hurtles toward me, but not on film. I've forgotten about my camera. For an instant I am certain I'm witnessing a man's death and that it will also be my own. Things have gone too smoothly, the atmosphere has been deceptively benign, and it now seems this track has demanded another catastrophe. I leap over the now vacant chair to my right, and as I turn toward the suite, I see the reflection of the flames in the sliding glass doors and feel the heat sweep across my back. The instant of danger has passed and I turn back toward the track just in time to see the disembodied engine tumble by in a ball of flame. Debris fills the air like a flight of sand grouse. The Nikon takes over, zipping off exposures, one last somersault before the car comes to rest, right side up and on fire. It really doesn't resemble a car anymore, just a burning tub of metal, not thirty feet away, a driver's helmet protruding from the flames. The original fire had been from burning oil, but now the methanol has ignited and can be seen only as intense heat waves blurring the edges of the wreckage.

The fire marshall is herding everyone off the balconies and into the suite. He sees my camera and press badge and lets me stay, though I've finished the roll and have to change film. At this point, I'm certain Sneva is dead. It's the most brutal, spectacular, and horrifying crash I've ever seen, and I've seen at least a dozen that were fatal. The scene in the suite couldn't be more macabre or more comic. All these people know Sneva in some capacity. Several of them are sponsors of his car, and he's crashed and apparently been annihilated right in their laps. Sneva's wife has gone into hysterics and has been hustled out to the balcony overlooking the golf course on the far side of the building. Grace Kelly, who had been fixing a drink at the time, has fallen backward into a tray of chocolate brownies. The chairman of the bank, in nervous relief, tells me how delighted he is that I've been able to get some good pictures. Though I'm sure it isn't his intention, it sounds as if, in his role as gracious host, he has arranged the crash for my photographic convenience. Everyone looks sick to their stomach, and I am changing film.

"Did you get it?" I look up into the wide eyes of a young executive type.

"Yeah, I think so."

"Did you get Mrs. Sneva?"

"What?" I'm certain I've misunderstood.

"Did you get pictures of Mrs. Sneva?"

I choke on my own saliva and shake my head. "I didn't hear that. No."

"Good for you," he says earnestly, "good for you."

The fire marshall lets me back out on the balcony to photograph the work of the fire crew. There are clouds of chemical vapors, flashing lights, scattered detritus, and crash crews diverting traffic to the grass verge inside the track. Then I see something that, for a moment, I am certain is an illusion. Sneva moves. His helmet is wiggling back and forth and he's put his arms down on the fuselage. He's trying to push himself up and out of the cockpit, but he appears to be stuck. Another driver has abandoned his car and is trying to help the emergency crew get Sneva out of the wreckage. The struggle goes on for several minutes, till they finally free him, dragging him up and out by his armpits. Not only is he alive, but he walks, with help, to the waiting ambulance, lies down on the stretcher, and is taken to the infield hospital. Still, I'm not confident he'll recover. I remember how two years ago Swede Savage rode into the infield hospital sitting up, but died of his injuries a month later.

The emergency crew finishes clearing the debris, and I sit down to try and sort out what has happened. It is at that moment that I realize that two weeks ago to the hour, I had been sitting on this balcony interviewing Tom Sneva, the day after he had qualified. He told me he had been a junior high school principal in Lamont, Washington, and had raced as a hobby until the racing began to be more profitable and more time-consuming than teaching. He was enthusiastic, boyish, and articulate, and appeared to regard Roger Penske with almost the same reverence that a University of Alabama quarterback might hold for Bear Bryant. "We'd like to be racing more than just the Championship Trail," he tells me, "but Roger's got a lot invested in this series, and he doesn't want to take any chances." He reminded me how the previous year Penske had lost his driver in midseason when Gary Bettenhausen was seriously injured in a minor dirt-track race in Syracuse. I asked him about his relationship with the established superstars, like Foyt and Unser. "That's a funny thing," he said. There was surprise in his voice, as if he were only discovering the irony as he told me about it. "I guess they just thought of us as another kid who wanted to be a racing driver. Anyway, they barely paid any attention to us, hardly said hello, until we began to become a threat to them." I asked him why he referred to himself in the plural, and he said it was a habit. "It's a team effort. If we win I don't want to take all the credit, and if we lose I don't want all the blame." I'm sure this *organization man* attitude is largely the result of driving for a no-nonsense, quasi-military business organization like Penske's, but there also seems to be a certain element of the affectionate plurality with which a show jumper will refer to himself and his horse as one being. "Anyway," Sneva continued, "when we started showing them something, that indifference seemed to change; not that they got friendly or anything, but they knew we were there."

I had first become aware of Sneva while watching a television broadcast of the Phoenix 150 several years ago. I remembered having been quite impressed watching this then unknown driver pass Foyt to take the lead. As we sat there that overcast afternoon, he told me the story. "Foyt was having a little momentary problem with his car. He bobbled, and I shot by him like he was standing still. It was no big deal. He was having trouble for a second, and I took advantage of it and got by. But they played it up big on television, as if I'd really pulled something off. Anyway, Foyt wasn't upset about it after the race but later, when people, friends of his who'd watched it on TV, razzed him about it, 'Boy, that Sneva kid really blew you off, didn't he?' he began to get pissed. Then one day he walked up to me in the garage–I mean it was just like something out of the movies–and told me that I'd gotten away with it once, but that if I tried anything like it again, he could bump me right out of the park. It was unbelievable."

The ABC slow-motion replays show Sneva passing Eldon Rasmussen and running just ahead of Foyt in the short chute between turns one and two. Sneva's right rear tire touches Rasmussen's left front, and Sneva finds himself upside down and airborne, heading for the outside wall at almost two hundred miles an hour. Sneva's car slams into the wall tail first, the wing, engine, and rear wheels separating, in a protracted dance with the flames and scattering fragments of metal and fiberglass; the remains of the car cartwheel three times along the wall, then somersault three times down the asphalt to come to rest, on fire, in the middle of the track. It's the kind of accident usually associated with dirt tracks at less than half these speeds.

Three weeks later, Sneva is recovering from his burns and practicing to qualify for the 500 at Pocono when I talk to him on the telephone.

"It was like a dream," he tells me. "We watched the TV replays and it looked like it was all happening to somebody else. We passed Rasmussen in the first turn and thought we were by him in turn two. We glanced in the mirrors and he wasn't there; he was right beside us and we saw that the wheels were going to touch. From there on it was as if we were dreaming, as if we were lying in bed dreaming we were flying through the air upside down. After we first made contact with the wall, we don't remember anything till we woke up in the track hospital and wondered how the car was." I ask him how it's going at Pocono and he tells me that the first day out he was pretty cautious. "The second day we started running hard through the corners, but I noticed that we still weren't trying to prove anything in traffic. It takes a little while," he concludes. "It makes you realize you really could get hurt doing this kind of thing."

After Sneva's crash, the 500 begins an anticlimactic slide toward a rain-shortened conclusion. Dallenbach, who has maintained his lead, drops out thirty-six laps later, claiming his air intakes have gotten clogged with litter from the wreckage, causing him to burn a piston. Some drivers have other theories about what caused the burned piston, but it is a sad end to what had been one of the most spectacular, come-from-behind drives in the history of the race.

The sky darkens radically, the wind begins to whip up hot dog wrappers and dust devils in the infield, and within minutes the 500 has been transformed into a hydroplane race. The checkered and red flags appear simultaneously and cars spume rooster tails, trying to make the start-finish line. There are multiple and relatively harmless spins and crashes, cars sliding, looping lazily down the straights, up the pit lane, and through the corners. It is Bobby Unser's good fortune to be leading when the sky splits open, and in a delicate ballet with his now tractionless tires, he creeps toward the start-finish line. There are twenty-six more laps that will never be run and there will be seemingly endless theories and arguments by and for Rutherford and Foyt that had the race run its full course, they would have certainly won. It is the luck of the draw. It's made heroes and corpses without discretion.

Back in my motel room, I fix myself a drink and watch the rain pour down on the policemen channeling the postrace traffic on Sixteenth Street. I notice that the hair on the back of my arms has been singed; it balls and crumbles off like melted plastic. This whole month in Indianapolis seems like an abruptly ended dream. Two weeks from now, most of these drivers will be racing at Milwaukee, and it won't much matter who won today. The race has been important only because 400,000 paying spectators and millions more by their radios and TV sets have, by agreement, made it so. But now it is all over and another "agreement" is in force. The following day's sports section will carry the news that the Golden State Warriors have beaten the Washington Bullets for the National Basketball Association championship, and the cover of *Sports Illustrated* will carry a picture of Billy Martin, "Baseball's Fiery Genius." I have an autographed picture of the winner for my son, and I'm beginning to get drunk.

The next morning there's a photograph of Sneva's crash on the front page of the *Indianapolis Star*, and I recognize my own figure, fleeing ignominiously from the flames. On my way to the airport I drive past the Speedway, and all I can see is litter, two feet deep, in every tunnel, passageway, and concourse, more than six million pounds of it. I stop for a red light and notice one more thing: the corpse of a huge tomcat lying next to the chain-link fence. Someone has considerately propped its head up on a crushed beer can and crossed its paws in repose. There's my story, I think. After twenty-five years of listening and dreaming, I've seen my first Indianapolis 500, and this is the one picture that will stick. Another great event chronicled in trash, another discarded container.

1976

I'M FOLLOWING RICK MUTHER'S ancient, borrowed Barracuda down a winding Indiana country road toward the complex where he has taken an apartment for the month of May. Suddenly I realize we've fallen into a high-speed parade with a four-wheel-drive van leading Rick and another pickup truck joined in behind me. We're in a road race on a fairly tight course, each vehicle in turn driving on the apex of each bend in the road, dropping one front tire into the gravel, then sliding wide to the outside shoulder. It seems like old times. I first met Muther more than a decade ago when he was racing sports cars in California. In fact, he was one of the first non–Formula 1 road racers to break into the crew-cut, left-turn-only fraternity of Indy drivers. He has told me about a letter he received from then USAC president Henry Banks in 1968 suggesting he shave his mustache if he wanted to run at the Speedway. Muther complied. He shaved his mustache, but let his hair grow into the frizzy mane that has since become his trademark. Times are changing, and even tradition-bound Indianapolis has had to make some concessions. If he is persistent, and has the necessary degree of skill, even a California hippie can't be kept out of the club.

I'm delighted with my pickup truck, which takes the corners smooth and flat. We're playing a game of mechanical horse, each trying in turn to duplicate the line of Mike Mosley, who I will discover is driving the van in the lead. Now we are winding through a maze of identical modern mansarded apartment buildings. Mosley slides his van to a stop in an empty carport, and Muther, I, and Mark Stainbrook, Rick's mechanic, park alongside. Muther introduces me to Mosley, and we go up to the apartment to have a few beers and watch the rebroadcast of the second day's qualifying on television. Mosley is all smiles, like a kid who's just made a date with the homecoming queen. He's turned in the fastest time of the day, and third-fastest overall, edging out Bobby Unser's time by seven-hundredths of a second. He's a small, fairly delicate-looking man with steel-rimmed glasses and a sensitive, boyish grin, hardly fitting the mythical stereotype of the brawny, two-fisted Indy driver.

Muther and Mosley form perhaps the nucleus of the unofficial club of freaks among the drivers, mostly a new boys' club, which they identify as the "good guys," as opposed to the straights, or "bad guys," the old-school Indy drivers like Foyt, the Unsers, and Andretti, who have come to be regarded here as "the establishment." Mosley, in beating out Unser's qualifying time, has scored a big one for the "good guys," though he'd be the last person to laud it as such.

"You beat Bobby Unser's speed by eight-eight hundredths of a mile an hour," says the track announcer, soliciting a victorious comment.

"Yup. That's pretty close," Mosley says, being characteristically modest and noncommittal.

"What's the secret? Where'd you get the extra speed?"

"I can't tell you," Mosley replies, his voice on the edge of jubilation. "That's why it's a secret."

The apartment, which Muther is sharing with Mark Stainbrook, is spacious and fairly empty, a place to keep their clothes for the month of May, furnished only with black lights that give it a subdued, psychedelic atmosphere, and enormous pillows to lean back against while sitting on the floor. It's about as California as you can get on a modest budget in Indiana. Muther, Mosley, Mark, and I are sitting crosslegged in a semicircle around the television set, waiting out *Hee Haw* for the taped report on the day's qualifying. Janet Guthrie has dominated the news for the past week, and though it seems like a tired question by now, I ask Rick if he thinks that, if she is able to qualify, she will have the physical strength to drive the entire five hundred miles.

"I don't know," he says, turning to gaze out the window at the last light of an overcast evening. "It's a crush for sure. I get pretty wrung out by it, but you do get a second wind in this race." Mosley nods in agreement. "After the first two hundred miles," Muther continues, "you think it's impossible, especially if it's hot. But then, all of a sudden, you feel like you're starting fresh again and it seems almost easy."

We talk about the tension and the charged atmosphere of race day. A promo blurb for my article in the current *Playboy* describes Indy as the closest thing America has to rollerball. Muther comments on the description. "That's it all right. It's like three hundred thousand crazies drawn mysteriously to the same spot in the middle of America at the same time every year."

"Rollercar," Mosley interjects, "that's what we called it after we saw that movie." Mosley suffered two bad crashes at the Speedway in consecutive years, in 1971 and '72. He retired after winning last year's Milwaukee 200, but found that the quiet life he had sought back in California was too quiet, that his bank account was suffering from lack of income, and that all his friends were gone to the races. Most of the drivers agree that he is a consistent charger who would be just about unbeatable in a really first-rate car.

I tell my story of standing on the inside of turn three with two motor-drive Nikons at the first false start of the 1973 race. I'm describing the unearthly sensation of watching, hearing, and feeling those thirty-three cars go by, with only a few feet of grass between me and them.

"I'll bet it would be," says Mosley. "I took a friend over to watch from the suites on turn two, and it's real scary there. It feels like you're gonna catch someone in your lap."

"I know," I nod in agreement, flashing on Sneva's airborne car hurling toward me in flames.

"It's hard to believe how fast those cars come off that turn," he continues, "and some of them seem really bent outta shape. It looks a lot easier and solider for me looking from the inside out than it does from the outside in."

We have another round of beer and Muther and I reminisce a bit with some road-racing stories from the early sixties. "Did you ever want to drive here?" Mosley asks.

"Yeah, I did," I reply. "Sure, from as far back as I can remember. But coming here seemed quite a jump. It was always something almost mythical to me, so much different from any other race."

"It's different all right," Mosley laughs, and he and Muther exchange knowing grins.

"I was a pretty good driver at the kind of racing I did," I go on with my explanation. "I mean, I won my fair share, but I never really knew if I was good enough to make it here."

"I guess you still don't know, do you?" Mosley smiles.

"No," I agree, "I guess that's something I'll never know."

Mosley grins at Muther and then at me. He has tried it, and is better than just good enough. It's the grin of a man who knows.

Buck Owens and Roy Clark finish their last duet and it's time for the films of the day's qualifying. We're watching Foyt's rather disappointing run, which put him in the middle of the second row–disappointing to A. J., that is. His car is loose, oversteering, the rear end coming out too easily on the corners. His first lap is a respectable 187 mph. His second falls to 186, his third to 184. On his final lap, his right rear tire kisses the wall coming out of turn four, an error that would have caused most drivers to lose it and probably write off their car as well, but when you see that kind of smoke from the tire and the car bobbles, only to straighten out, you know it's got to be A. J. Foyt. And you know that when he pulls off his helmet he's going to be wearing his mad mask.

"That was a pretty good run," says track announcer Del Clark, trying to keep an upbeat tone for the almost 150,000 race fans who expected A. J. to take the pole for the third year in a row.

"It's a disgrace to me, my crew, and my car," Foyt snaps back.

"Well, what went wrong?" Clark asks, recovering from the momentary shock of A. J.'s bluntness, only to be blasted again.

"The damn thing wasn't handlin.' If you'd had your eyes open you coulda seen it for yourself."

"Did you hear that?" Mosley gasps, rolling backward with laughter. Both he and Muther are again amazed at the plain talk from Super Tex. It was all down on tape and no P.R. man had had a chance to launder it for public consumption. By now, however, that short fuse and lack of tact have become part of the Foyt legend.

It occurs to me that Muther and Mosley seem to get more fun out of racing; not that they don't take it seriously, but they seem to take themselves less seriously than the Unsers and the Foyts. They don't have a tough guy, almost legendary race-driver image to maintain. Though Muther is forty and Mosley twenty-nine, they project the impression of a couple of kids who are happy to be doing something they realize only a handful of people in the world are capable of doing, and happy to have been good enough and fortunate enough to have gotten away with it so far. As I sit here in front of the television set in this dimly lit room, I feel like I'm sitting with a couple of young World War I aces, ordinary men, except for what they are able to do with a race car, who are dedicated to taking life moment by moment.

John Martin is qualifying now, and though the television cameras and the subdued recorded sound make it seem almost leisurely, Muther is pointing out to me how Martin is diving down on the corners early, dropping a tire over the white line and pushing the car wide coming out, stretching the capabilities of his car to get the absolute maximum from it. "Martin's getting pretty damn good," Muther comments. Mosley nods in agreement. This is Martin's sixth year at the Speedway, and it frequently takes that long for a driver to begin to realize his full potential here. Several days ago, I heard Billy Vukovich say that for his first five years running here he felt completely lost, and that it was only after thousands and thousands of times around the two and a half miles of asphalt that he began to feel at home and to really get control of what he was doing.

Now Dick Simon is out, trying to qualify what Mosley and Muther consider to be an inferior-handling car. "That thing just isn't going through the turns," Muther shakes his head. Still, Simon is turning in laps in the 182 range.

"It's a banzai run," Mark exclaims, meaning an attempt made mostly on courage, a do-or-die effort to make an ill-handling car go around the track faster than it's really capable of going. Simon completes his fourth lap, and though we know we're watching him on videotape, we're relieved when it's over, and so is Dick Simon, relieved and delighted to have put his car in the middle of the sixth row, securely in the race.

I ask Rick and Mike what they do on race day mornings, what time they get up and head for the track. "Oh I don't like to get up too early," Muther says. "About nine, I guess."

"And you can still make it through the traffic?" I'm a little surprised. I have a nagging apprehension that I'm going to get caught up in a traffic sweep that will carry me irreversibly to Terre Haute and funnel me down a dead-end, one-way street with a cop car sitting at the open end.

"Sure," Mosley chimes in, "the crush is pretty well over by ten o'clock."

"Don't you ever worry about not making it in time for the race?"

"I'll drive down sidewalks, over fields, or anything I have to do to get there race day," Mosley says, and I get the impression that those kinds of maneuvers might help to alleviate the tension of the hours before the race. "It's sure a rush to see all those people, though," he goes on. "It's like the whole world has turned out to judge your performance. Those grandstands just vibrate."

I tell them about being with a girl who was wearing a chartreuse Day-Glo blouse in the pits, and how when we walked past Johnny Rutherford, he stopped and said, "Ah, you're the girl in the first turn," which was where she had been watching practice and taking pictures that morning.

"Yeah, there's a spot there where it seems fairly slow," Muther nods.

"He probably spotted her on his warm-up laps," Mosley suggests. "I do that a lot. You're going slow and everybody's looking you over, but really, I'm down there peeking out of that cockpit, watching all those people, picking out faces in the crowd. Boy, it's a rush."

In 1953, Thomas W. Binford was an Indianapolis businessman who manufactured and distributed lubricants for heavy earth-moving equipment. He had no particular interest in auto racing, apart, that is, from the interest more or less imposed on anyone who lives in Indianapolis, but he was persuaded by several friends to chip in with them and rent a race car. They entered the car in the 1953 race. It practiced, but blew its engine the day before qualifying started, and, lacking a spare, they towed it back to the garage and called it quits. Two years later, when the AAA, which had run the 500 since its inception, pulled out of racing in reaction to the horrible crash at Le Mans that killed more than ninety spectators, a group of Indianapolis businessmen organized the United States Auto Club, to take over the 500 and to become the sanctioning body for championship racing. As a capable young executive, Binford was asked to serve on its board, and was, at the age of thirty-two, elected president. Although he still did not feel really close to racing, he took it on as a civic responsibility and served until 1969.

"I don't know how I got to be chief steward of this race," he says, pausing to light his pipe. "I think I have Ray Marquette of the *Indianapolis Star* to thank for that. When Harlen Fengler resigned,

Marquette ran a headline that read, "Binford to be Chief Steward?" That was the first I knew about it, though I guess he'd checked it out with the Speedway management and they'd already made the decision." Not that Binford really needed the additional responsibility to fill up his already full spare time. He was chief executive officer of the largest bank in Indiana, president of DePauw University, and organizer and part owner of the newly formed Indiana Pacers basketball team.

Fengler had resigned after the 1973 race amid a great deal of controversy about his competence and his sometimes dogmatic and autocratic methods. "I don't think all the charges made against Harlen were justified, but he'd become defensive and had gotten a lot of bad press. Anyway, when I took over I had to create a discipline, overcome a nice-guy image I'd had." He lights his pipe again, watching the flame through his dark-lensed, tortoise-shell sunglasses. He's a compact, well-built man, who, now in his mid-fifties, radiates competence and an almost total absence of self-importance. We are sitting in a rather bare concrete room under the grandstands along the main straightaway which serves as his working office at the Speedway. The furnishings consist of one ancient steel desk and two metal chairs of the same vintage. We can hear the muted sounds of racers diving into turn one, trying to get up speed for the upcoming first day of qualifying.

"I had never been a race official before, and suddenly here I was, chief steward. Well, I was pretty nervous that first year. I mean, racing is a hobby for no one. It's not like officiating a football game or a basketball game. You can never be frivolous about it. There are lives on the line. There's that presence of death that makes it different, intensifies everything, but also there's a spirit of adventure about it that's getting hard to find in our everyday life. Anyway, that first year was tough for me, and there was that decision about Johnny Rutherford that made me unpopular with Rutherford and his crew and probably some of his fans as well."

I didn't attend the 1974 race, so I ask him to explain that decision to me.

"Well, the rules state that in order to be assured a chance to make a qualifying run on the first day, and thus to have a chance at the pole, a car must be continuously in line in the position its owners have drawn in the qualifying order. Well, Rutherford's crew removed his car to the garage for half an hour to do some work on it, and I ruled that they must thereby forfeit their place in line. It was a tough decision to make and it cost Rutherford his chance to run for the pole, but I figured if I stuck to the rules with a Rutherford or a Foyt, I wouldn't have any trouble enforcing them with a Salt Walther or a Boom-Boom Cannon. Well, as you can imagine, Rutherford was furious about it. Fortunately, he won the race that year, and he couldn't continue to be mad at anyone. But for me it was just a matter of the rules."

I ask him if he doesn't think some of the rules governing the race are a little outdated.

"The rules don't have anything to do with right or wrong," Binford laughs. He's about to explain when he gets a call over his walkie-talkie, which keeps him constantly available for consultation. He answers a few questions concerning a driver's credentials, and relights his pipe. Shim Malone, the assistant chief steward, brings in a form for Binford to sign, officially certifying that Billy Scott has successfully completed his refresher test. "A pretty consistent job," Binford says, looking over the lap times.

"He looked pretty good," Malone agrees.

"As I was saying," Binford continues, "the rules don't have much to do with reason. They don't even have to make sense. They're just the agreements under which we run this race. Some of them, I'm sure, are pretty outmoded, but they're tradition, and tradition is the glue that holds this race together. Tradition itself answers a lot of questions, but it's a two-edged sword. I can't see for the life of me, for example, why we start this race with three cars abreast. Every other race is started with two cars abreast. It makes imminent good sense, but I can't get anyone to listen to me when I suggest changing it. There are a lot of things like that."

I begin to feel the pressures that must be crowding in on his time. I tell him that I'm aware he has many people making demands on him, and I don't want to monopolize his afternoon, but he puts me at ease. "They can reach me if they need me." He smiles, holding up his walkie-talkie.

"You were talking about tradition," I say, leading him back to his narrative.

"Everything gets magnified here." He rests his elbows on the desk and leans toward me for emphasis. "It's the richest race in the world, the most dangerous, and most of the famous drivers spend an entire month here every year. In fact, we've got so much time here that every little thing gets chewed over and we've got to be careful they don't get magnified out of proportion. We've got journalists, as you know, who have to spend a month here too, and if there isn't some kind of controversy, they almost have to create one to keep the interest up."

"Has your own interest in racing increased since you've become chief steward?" It's hard for me to imagine how someone could have taken on this demanding and rather thankless job—which requires him to deal with some very egocentric racing drivers, crew chiefs, car owners, and lesser officials, some of whom have held their jobs since the days when the race was run with riding mechanics aboard most of the cars—if he didn't have an almost consuming passion for the sport. Yet before I've finished the question, I realize that those difficulties and complexities, that intricate network of egos and mindless tradition are the very elements that would make this job attractive to a man like Tom Binford.

"Oh, yes. I've had to become interested in it. The intensity of my involvement here almost demands it." He pauses to light his pipe again. "There are a lot of races I enjoy watching more, but this is always *the* race. Nurburgring is impressive and they get 220,000 spectators there, but they're all spread out. Here, you can't help but feel intimidated on race day. I look at all those people and realize that nobody could control them; nobody could run this race. You almost get the feeling that if all the officials went away, the race would run itself."

I clear my throat and reposition myself on the straight-backed chair. I don't know why I should feel uncomfortable asking him about Janet Guthrie; I suppose it's because she's gotten so much attention and so much publicity that any question about her has already begun to sound like a cliché.

"I think it's great we've got a woman trying to make this race. I think it's probably overdue, and I'm glad it's someone who's really qualified and sincere about her effort, rather than someone just trying to make a point, to just break down barriers."

"Some of the other drivers don't seem to be thrilled about her being here," I say, recalling conversations in Gasoline Alley and some graffiti, "Janet Guthrie, Nookie of the Year," on the wall of the men's room behind the pits.

Binford leans back in his chair and scratches his head. "Obviously, she's getting some breaks here because she's a woman, but everybody gets breaks, one way or another. I think those drivers who complain the most about her being here are the ones who feel most threatened by her presence, drivers who've gotten some breaks here because of who they were. They've all proven themselves." He holds up his hands. "Don't get me wrong, but you know that Billy Vukovich or Gary Bettenhausen wouldn't have gotten their first rides here as easily as they did if their names had been Binford or Gerber." His pipe has gone out again, and he gives up on it and lights a cigarette.

"I think it's too bad she doesn't have a better car and that there has to be so much pressure on her. It's tough enough being a rookie here, without all the attention from the media."

"The last two races here, since you've taken over as chief steward, have been remarkably safe." I'm trying to soften what has to sound like a pretty blunt question, but he's not going to wait for me to ask it.

"I like to think I've done everything I could to make them safe, made improvements in the track and spectator areas, the pacer light system, tried to foster a discipline among the drivers, but I realize that just plain luck has had a lot to do with it. Sooner or later, that record will get tarnished. I'm horrified when there's an accident, just like anybody else, but I've got a job, something I have to do. I can't justify racing. You either like it or you don't. It's just the way it is."

TONY HULMAN IS having problems with his Cadillac Seville. Each time he puts it in gear, it stalls. He doesn't seem to be flustered by it. He sits erectly behind the wheel and starts it again. "I don't know what the problem is," he says in a very quiet voice, turning to glance over his shoulder at me. "You all right back there? I'm sorry about the mess." The front passenger seat and half the back are piled high with books, pictures, luggage, and a breathing machine he uses to alleviate his emphysema. He has cleared a space for me by piling some of this paraphernalia to the left. I'm holding a marble penholder on my lap. It bears a plaque recognizing his thirty years as head man at the Speedway. Finally, he tricks the balky fuel system and gets the car moving. We drive away from the Speedway office behind the pits and head for the new office building and museum just inside the southeast turn. I notice how every official, gate guard, and traffic controller, most of whom seem to be old men, recognizes this black Cadillac and seems to nod and wave respectfully as it passes. It's as if Hulman were *El Patron* in this separate empire within the Speedway gates.

We stop at the infield hospital so that he can have the doctor check over his breathing machine. He shows me around and points out with pride that this hospital could, in a pinch, serve the emergency needs of a city of 350,000 people, which, in effect, on race day, it does. He pauses to interview a young doctor, new to the Speedway. The intern has just graduated from the University of Iowa, and Mr. Hulman shakes his hand and warmly welcomes him to Indiana. The intern seems as grateful for the recognition as if he'd just been officially certified by the Indiana State Medical Board, and I can understand his reaction. This mild-mannered, handsome, still almost athletic-looking man of seventy-five is the voice I've heard on the radio every Memorial Day I can remember, exhorting the "Gentlemen" to start their engines. I don't know how it was for my contemporaries in New York or California or Iowa, but in one small town in Michigan the sound of those words represented the most intensely exciting moment of the year.

Tony Hulman is just settling into his office in the new Museum Building. It's a very large room with a long conference table. He hasn't yet organized his pictures, books, and the plethora of service award plaques piled on the long credenza behind his desk. I take a seat in one of the leather-upholstered chairs in front of his desk, and after scanning a few pieces of mail, he comes from behind the desk and takes the chair to my right. It's a democratic gesture, removing the formal expanse of rosewood between us.

I ask him when he first became interested in auto racing, and he tells me that he was never particularly interested in it. "Golf was my sport," he says, nodding toward the nine fairways in the infield of the Speedway, "golf and deep-sea fishing. I used to see this race sometimes, because it was a local event, but mostly I would listen to it on the radio while I was playing golf." He went to Yale and then came back to Terre Haute to work for the family wholesale merchandise company. "I sold and promoted our Clabber Girl Baking Powder from 1928 till after the war, when the ready mixes came in." He smiles. "They sort of took the juice out of the baking powder business. And I did a lot of deep-sea fishing, too; that was really my sport back then. I was captain of the U.S. Tuna Team until 1952."

"What about the Speedway?" I ask, trying to tie it in with baking powder and tuna fishing.

"Well, the Speedway got pretty run-down during the war, and Eddie Rickenbacker decided to dispose of it. Wilbur Shaw had been looking around and thought about getting a number of companies interested, but"—he pauses to light a cigarette and looks at the ceiling as he continues—"he decided he didn't want eight or ten bosses. I wasn't a rabid race fan at that time, but I thought maybe it'd be worth taking a chance on. So I bought the track and put Wilbur Shaw in as president, and he ran it till 1954 when he had that plane crash coming back from Detroit." He puts his left hand in the pocket of his suit coat and looks at the ceiling again as he takes a long drag on his cigarette. He takes a moment to sort out his memories, then seems to hit on the one he's been looking for. "We had a hard time getting the track ready for the 1946 race. The grandstands were run-down. We put up what now seem small grandstands, and I wondered how we'd ever fill 'em. Wilbur was afraid of fire; the grandstands were wooden then, you know. So we used to wet them down with a fire hose every night, and we were always afraid they might collapse.

"We wondered if anyone would come, but we found that people had lined up the night before, and some of them couldn't get in before the race was over. I must have gotten a thousand letters about that. But we just couldn't handle the traffic." He seems to be enjoying the reminiscence. "I always remember"—he puts his hand on my arm for emphasis—"there was an article in the San Francisco newspaper about how lucky Captain Rickenbacker had been to find a couple of Hoosiers," he draws out the "ooo" sound and laughs to himself as he does, "to take that white elephant off his hands."

I've often wondered about the term "Hoosier," and I ask him if he knows its origin.

"I don't know where it comes from," he says with a slightly bewildered smile. "I've always been one, but I've never been able to find out what it means." He clears his throat and continues his story. "Everybody said, Why would anybody want to watch a car go one hundred miles an hour when boys were flying airplanes at five hundred or six hundred miles an hour? Well, race day came, and I got caught up in traffic, clear over on the other side of town, and almost missed the race. I had no idea where all those people were going. It didn't occur to me that they could all be going to the track. Anyway, Wilbur and I had to get out and run, down sidewalks, through fields, and barely got here, all soaked with perspiration."

I tell him that all that must seem like ancient history now, and he nods and looks out the window at a car flashing through the southeast turn. "I think about everything's changed here except the track. The old roadsters got pretty unsteady on those bricks. Jack Brabham talked to me about it in 1962 when he came here with the first rear-engined car, and so we thought we'd pave it and make it safer. But we didn't want to change the slope or the configuration. We wanted that to remain as a constant. We've seen the development of the automobile around this track, you know, and the speeds here have always sort of been a yardstick." He leans toward me, smiles, and touches my arm again. "If somebody had told Pete DePaolo back in 1925 when he won the race at about one hundred miles an hour that there'd be cars going one hundred and eighty to two hundred miles an hour here, he'd have told 'em to go look for a psychiatrist."

It's getting late, and I thank him for taking the time to talk to me.

"Oh, thank you," he says, "I'm delighted that you want to come down here and write about all this." He insists on giving me a ride back to the pits.

As we're walking toward his car, we are stopped by an old man in a Speedway Safety Patrol uniform. "Have you heard where we'll be working this year, Mr. Hulman?"

Tony is taken by surprise and at a loss for an answer. "Oh, um, I don't know." He's struggling to be gracious. "Have you asked Clarence?" (He's referring to Clarence Cagle, the superintendent of grounds.)

"He hasn't made up his mind yet." The old man sighs, and it occurs to me that this "old man" is probably at least ten years younger than Tony Hulman.

"Well, good to see you," Tony says, taking the man's hand.

"Thank you, Tony," the man says reverently, making a small bow. He opens the car door for Tony and waves again as we drive away.

JANET GUTHRIE IS walking down the concrete alley that separates the tower grandstands from the garage area. It's a rare moment when she finds herself alone. She's been the biggest news at the Speedway this year and has generated at least a twenty-five percent increase in pre-race publicity, not because she's the hottest rookie in recent memory, or because she's one of the half-dozen drivers who actually might win this race, but simply because she's a woman.

Four years ago, women weren't even allowed in the pits or in the garage area. It was quite a shock to the traditionalists when the restrictions were lifted in 1973, permitting wives and girlfriends of the drivers and even female journalists to walk on this ground that had, theretofore, been sanctified exclusively for male soles. Yet equal opportunity laws had to come, even to Indianapolis, and this year, for the first time, you might find a driver or a mechanic flirting with one of the gate guards. And most of them would probably even admit that they find these young women in hard hats and well-fitting Levi's a definite improvement over the old-timers, some of whom have been manning their posts for so many years that they seem to have become part of the facility.

But a woman in a driver's suit—I mean, a woman actually out there in a racing car on the same track with the A. J. Foyts and Bobby Unsers—that's something that the yardbirds, those denizens with grooves in their elbows from leaning against the infield fences, can't quite bring themselves to accept. There are all the other drivers, and then there's Janet. When she goes out on the track, they all crowd the fences to get a glimpse of her blue McLaren flashing by, and try to convince themselves that there's actually a woman driving that car, a woman just like their mothers or their wives or their sisters. But she's not like their sisters or their wives or their "sainted mothers," no more than they are like A. J. Foyt or Johnny Rutherford. This woman happens to be a racing driver with thirteen years of experience, and, in her own mind at least, she's come here like any other rookie to try and qualify for the biggest auto race in the world.

It's tough enough being an ordinary rookie at Indianapolis. It's a scary track, sometimes even for drivers who've driven the 500 a dozen times or more; there are so many tricks to learn, so many quirks about its four totally individual turns that can keep a new driver from getting up to speed or can put him into the wall. And a rookie is under constant scrutiny. He has to prove himself to the veteran drivers and to the army of technical observers who are watching him every moment, trying to pick out flaws or inconsistencies in his driving, any imperfection that might indicate that he isn't quite good enough to be allowed a chance to try and qualify. But for Janet Guthrie, that's only half the pressure with which she has to contend. She's big news, and if I want to find her at any moment, all I have to do is look for the paparazzi, that cloud of photographers, reporters, and TV crews that hound her constantly. It's news every time she puts on her driving suit or goes to the ladies' room. She's being photographed every moment she's at the Speedway, and I'm certain that if a photographer could catch her picking her nose, it'd make the front page of the sports section.

Though some of them may resent her being here, most of the drivers, crews, officials, and spectators are at least polite to her. Oh, there are a few catcalls and whistles when her name is spoken over the public address system, and privately some of the drivers grumble about her getting a ride "just because she's a woman." But most of them will admit that if she had a better car, she'd stand a pretty good chance of getting it in the race, and when the airlines lost her luggage, Billy Vukovich loaned her his driving suit so she could practice and get ready to take her rookie test. And she feels she's been treated fairly. She just wishes the press would leave her alone so she could concentrate on her driving.

On this particular morning, however, as she is walking to the Speedway pressroom to meet me for yet another interview, she is stopped by two slightly beer-crazed twenty-year-olds. "Hey Janet," one of them calls, "you gonna qualify?"

"I hope so," she replies, smiling, perhaps a little nervously.

"Well we don't," the other boy calls back to her. "We hope you crash and burn where we can see you."

She is obviously a little shaken by the encounter. Race drivers do sometimes crash and burn, but they don't talk much or speculate about it, and they'd like to think that that's not the reason all those people come here to watch them.

"That's really the only bad treatment I've experienced since I've been here," she tells me. She has a disarmingly sweet smile and a definite feminine air about her, not at all the butch sort of toughness I'd preconceived about any woman who would try to compete in this most difficult and dangerous of all sporting events.

There is no doubt in her own mind that she will be able to drive the entire five hundred miles if she should be able to qualify. "I've proven that lots of times in twelve- and twenty-four-hour races." I can tell she's a little tired of having her strength brought into question. I tell her that some of the other drivers have complained of sore necks and shoulders from the time they've spent practicing. "Well, they must be out of shape then," she replies, "because I feel just fine."

Paula Murphy, the world-record-holder among female drag racers, has been in town and has made some comments in the local papers that while she thinks women can compete in drag races and road races, she feels they have no place on the super speedways, that they simply aren't strong enough. At the mention of Paula Murphy's name, Janet hisses. I laugh. "I read that," she explains, "and she came by to tell me she really didn't mean all that, and to wish me well, sort of in spite of my being a woman, but what does she know? She's a drag racer. They only have to drive for six or eight seconds."

"The rookie test was no problem," she goes on. "I was confident I could do that. I'd pretty well established that at Trenton. But when we try getting up to qualifying speeds, that's when it'll get tough."

"Have you had any flashes about what you're doing?" I ask. "I mean, have you had any trouble bringing yourself to realize that you're really driving at Indianapolis?"

"I've been so busy." She takes a deep breath, blows it out, and blinks her eyes several times rapidly, as if she were, just this moment, trying to sort it all out. "I haven't had much time to think about it being Indianapolis. Only, at a few odd moments, I've looked up and seen that Gasoline Alley sign." She seems to relax a bit, and I get the feeling that, for the first time, she's not regarding me as an adversary.

"I first came here in February when it was all deserted and the trees were bare, and there was nobody here but some birds," she explains. "I remember watching two doves soaring up and perching on the top of the grandstands. It was so quiet, it was almost spooky. I tried to imagine the leaves coming out and the stands filling up with people. I've been warned about the effect it can have on you, seeing all those people and realizing they're looking at you."

"What about the wall?" I ask. I know that some highly skilled road racers, like Chris Amon, haven't been able to cope with it whistling by at two hundred miles an hour, a few inches from their right ears, and most drivers say they never really get used to it.

"It's definitely a concern." Janet flattens her palm out above the table, and her eyes open wide. "I've encountered walls before, at Daytona and at Trenton, but they were never going by quite this fast. I haven't really been up to it yet; till I work up to qualifying speeds, I guess I won't really know till then. But my biggest concern has been in the pits." She laughs.

"In the pits?" I ask, wondering what she could be talking about.

"Yeah, to keep from running over all those photographers."

It's the Happy Hour, that period between five o'clock and the six o'clock closing on practice days when the track is usually reserved for veteran drivers. The Happy Hour is another sometime practice that has become one of those unwritten rules Tom Binford talked about. Late in the afternoon the wind usually dies down, the air is a bit cooler, and the turbocharged engines can operate at peak efficiency. It's the time the hot shoes usually choose to wring it out and turn in some fast pre-qualifying times that might psyche their competitors. There's no rule that says that rookies can't be running then, but if the track is fast and crowded, the officials will usually pull them in. And that's what's happens to Janet Guthrie on this particular Friday afternoon, the last day before the first weekend of time trials. All week she's been plagued with mechanical difficulties, and now, just as she's ready to complete the final phase of her rookie test, twenty laps at any speed over 165, A. J. Foyt, Gordon Johncock, and Tom Sneva come screaming down the front straight, pushing their lap speeds to the upper 180s, and Shim Malone decides it's no time for rookies to be learning their way around.

Jerry Sneva, Tom Sneva's younger brother, is hanging around Gasoline Alley, looking for a ride. "It'll be easier finding one next week," he says, "after the first weekend of time trials. There'll be cars that haven't gotten up to speed by then, and owners will be gettin' in a panic, lookin' for any change that might help 'em make the race."

"That's kind of a tough way to try and make it, isn't it?" I ask him. "I mean, with a car that some other driver hasn't been able to do anything with."

"Sure it is." He raises his eyebrows in a comic gesture and stiffens up momentarily, like a toy soldier. "But," he adds, "if you can make it go, people pay a lot more attention." He makes a gesture with his hands as if he were holding a steering wheel, sawing it back and forth. "On the other hand"–he pauses to bite his lower lip–"if you go slower, that's not so good, 'cause they notice that too. You've just got to put your foot in it," he says, making the steering gesture again, wiggling his hips as he does. "That's what it's all about."

I WONDER IF Indianapolis is anything like this in, say, February or July. I tend to think of it, apart from May, as a fairly conservative Midwestern city, distinguished by its two gigantic war memorials and a plethora of banks and financial institutions (Wall Street on the Wabash), and as the birthplace of a writer named Vonnegut, a name still seen on several hardware stores. But this evening, as I'm driving from the Speedway toward downtown to meet some friends for dinner at St. Elmo's Steakhouse, it seems more like Los Angeles or maybe even Tralfamador.

I've seen a lot of weirdness here, but most of it in and around the Speedway. There are the Thursday night amateur topless go-go contests at Mother Tucker's, which more often than not become bottomless as well, local ladies of the night gyrating in every imaginable posture in a desperate effort to outgross the competition for the loudest applause and a cash prize. Those are things I've more or less sought out. But on this particular evening I don't even have to look for it. It comes to me as if my air-conditioned car were a sealed space capsule traveling through some sort of an X-rated amusement park.

I've just crossed the Wabash and am passing a used-car lot when I notice someone standing on top of a car. As I get closer, I can see that the person is wearing a bikini and red terry-cloth booties, and that she's dancing on the car roof to attract patrons to *The Aloha Club Topless Dancers*. It's kind of like some hamburger stands, where they have a clown out front to beckon customers in off the street, except this silent barker has a special trick that I rather egocentrically assume is intended just for me.

As I'm just a few yards short of the Aloha, she turns away from me, pulls down her bikini bottom and flashes two melon-shaped globes at me, so dazzlingly white that for several seconds I see spots before my eyes as if I've just been shot, point-blank with a flash gun. I turn down Merridan, still blinking and trying to refocus my vision, and then pass a parking lot in which I notice two men circling one another. Again, the timing is perfect. Just as I'm in position to see them clearly, one man punches the other in the jaw. The strikee falls backward, his head bouncing off the pavement like a semideflated basketball. The striker then begins to kick him in the ribs, but my view becomes obscured by a parked car. A third man is standing by with his hands in his pockets, more as if he were watching a crap game than a street brawl. I'm surprised that I'm not disturbed or startled by these passing vignettes. I tell myself that they probably have nothing to do with the race, but after a couple of weeks here in the month of May, they just seem like part of the big show, and I wouldn't be surprised to learn that the two men in the parking lot were fighting over the usable horse-power of the Drake Offy as against that of a Cosworth Ford.

BILLY SCOTT IS back this year with a better car, one that might actually make the race. I'm talking with him in the pits between practice runs when Larry McCoy, a second-year Indy driver, stops and asks him what kind of times he's getting.

"Mid 170s," Scott says, shrugging his shoulders.

"Same as everybody else." McCoy nods his head and stands with his hands on his hips, looking over Scott's car.

"Yep."

"You holding your breath yet?" McCoy grins.

"Not yet." Scott looks at McCoy as if to say, *Are you crazy?* "It's too early for me to be holding my breath. I don't have a backup car."

"Well, we're getting 180s," McCoy says, matter-of-factly.

"You holdin' *your* breath yet?" Scott glances at him sideways, so as not to seem too interested in his response.

"I had sore lungs last night, literally," McCoy says, and they laugh away the tension between them.

Another driver is hanging around the pits, wearing his driving suit long after his car has been towed back to the garage, and Scott looks at him disdainfully. "He probably wears it when he goes out at night, to make sure everybody knows he's a driver."

"He's a rookie," I say. "He's excited."

Billy wrinkles up his face in an exaggerated smile and then lets it go slack. "Big deal," he says.

IN THE LAST few minutes of practice before the qualifying begins, I hear over the P.A. system that Billy has been involved in an accident. Then I hear him being praised for his evasive action in missing Spike Gehlhausen, another rookie who hit the wall in turn one, shedding three wheels across the track in front of him. Scott dove to the inside to avoid the wheels and spun on the grass inside the short chute. I find him in the pits near the tower, where he's just been interviewed by the track announcer.

"Boy, it was really neat," he tells me as we walk back toward the garage, "just like in the movies, stuff flyin' off that car, comin' around me and past me, and I'm goin' right through it. The only bad part of it is, though"—he makes a face as if he'd just smelled something—"we probably flattened out our tires, and it's the only set we've got scrubbed in to qualify on."

Gordon Johncock stops Billy to tell him that with all the delays in getting qualifying started, he'll probably have time to scrub in new tires before his number comes up. It's a magnanimous gesture from a veteran toward a rookie. "I didn't mean to spin," Scott explains to Johncock, "but as soon as I hit the grass, it was *adios.*"

One of Bignotti's crewmen hollers at him as we pass, "Ya change your drivin' suit yet Billy?"

"Naw, nothin' like that," he replies. His manner is that of a kid who has just pulled off a new trick on his dirt bike. His tires are dirty and flat-spotted badly, but he can't move his car out of line without losing his chance to qualify. Fortunately, the track closes before his number comes up, so he'll have time to scrub in a new set in the practice period tomorrow.

His best time so far has been 177 mph. The next afternoon, in a qualifying attempt, he turns three laps consistently at 178 and change, but Jim Wright, his crew chief, waves off the attempt as he feels it might not be good enough to make the race. When he pulls in, Scott complains that he doesn't like the way the car's handling, that it's getting loose in the turns. His crew changes the angle of the wing, and adjusts the crossweight. A Goodyear technical adviser checks the temperatures and measures the circumference of the tires, and his crew puts an extra one-eighth inch of bump rubber on the right-rear shock to alleviate the pushing coming out of the turns, but the track closes before he has another chance to qualify. "Well, it gives us another week to see what kind of speed we can get up to," he says. "I'd rather worry about that than about somebody else bumping us if we had taken that 178."

During the five days before the second weekend of time trials, he manages to get his speed up to the high 179s, still not fast enough to be sure about qualifying. But just before noon on Friday, he has what will turn out to be a bit of racing luck; he blows the last engine he has and is forced to call his sponsor, Warner Hodgdon in San Bernardino, to ask if he can buy a new one.

"Are there any available?" Hodgdon asks.

"Vels-Parnelli's got one for fifteen thousand," Billy says, a little tentatively.

"Buy it," Hodgdon says.

Scott takes the new engine out to warm it up in practice Saturday morning. "The first time I stood on it, I knew it was the best engine we'd ever had," he says, "but we didn't get a chance to turn any hot laps to see what kind of times we could get with it." About five o'clock in the afternoon, he gets his chance to try it out when he takes the green flag from Pat Vidan at the start of his qualifying run. "On the first lap I knew I was going fast, but I had no idea we were turning a 184.6. I wasn't even holding my breath. We waited till late in the afternoon when there was nobody waitin' in line so we didn't have to wait around and think about it. We couldn't decide whether we ought to refuel and scuff up the tires.

"I went out and ran one lap. When I came in, Jim just said, 'You turned a 181.8. Get in line.' We checked the fuel and found we had just enough to qualify with if we didn't take more than one warm-up lap. We got in line. They checked the wing height, inserted the pop-off valve, cleared the track, and I took off. I mean, I was really pumped up and ready to go. I was pushin' it, but it seemed almost easy. I mean, I didn't even have to hold my breath." I thought about how different it must seem when everything is working for a driver, different from the banzai run of Dick Simon, who must have been holding his breath the whole four laps. "We finally had it dialed in, and I knew we were going to make the show." He pauses a minute to catch his breath and to let his story catch up with him. "Jim didn't signal me any speed. He just gave me a plus sign to let me know I was going fast enough. If he'd of signaled me a 184.6, I'd probably have been so startled I'd have dropped down to a 150 on the next lap."

As it was, he dropped only to a 183, and maintained an average of 183.383, making him the fastest rookie in the field, edging out Vern Schuppan by 1.5 seconds for the ten-mile run. "Hey, I got fifteen hundred and a trophy," he tells me. He's a kid who has gotten what he always wanted for Christmas. "Of course, the money won't last long," he shrugs, "but that trophy'll be nice to have." He puts his hand on my shoulder. "There aren't many people who have a trophy from Indy."

I drive him back to the apartment he's taken with his crew. We stop at a twenty-four-hour grocery, and he buys a bottle of Pepsi and a box of animal crackers. He opens the box of crackers and begins munching them as we get back in my truck. "Sunday's my day." He stretches with excitement. "I don't want to sleep too late. Sometimes I wake up at two in the morning, and I've had a nightmare that I've missed the race. I want to be there for all the parades and pageantry."

"It sounds like you're excited," I laugh.

"Is a frog waterproof?" He rocks forward in the cab of the truck, then rolls back, crosses his legs, and uncrosses them again, as if he doesn't know what to do with himself to pass the time until race day.

IN 1971, RICK MUTHER was following David Hobbs out of turn four when Hobbs suddenly lost power. Muther swerved to the left to miss Hobbs, hit the inside wall twice, and careened back across the track into the outside wall. As Muther's car collapsed around him Hobbs, who had fallen behind the carnage, hit him broadside, tilting him up on two wheels and sending him skidding sideways down the front straight like a Joey Chitwood stunt driver. "I was lucky that time," Muther smiles and rolls his eyes toward the sky. "We were running aluminum wheels instead of magnesium; otherwise they'd of caught fire for sure." As it was, he came out of it with a broken sternum and dashed hopes.

This year his luck has been less spectacular but nevertheless bad. No thrill ride for the spectators on the main straight; in fact, no ride at all. His car owner burned up two engines, testing in California, and arrived at the Speedway a week late. "I don't know, señor," Muther says, shaking his head. He lets all the air out so that his shoulders almost seem to collapse on his navel. "He used bearings people stopped using four or five years ago. I guess he got a good deal on 'em, I don't know. We didn't get a good crankshaft till the night before the last day of qualifying. I drove out to the airport to pick it up and Mark and I stayed up all night to get it in, but we didn't have time to run a block leak test. We started it up the next morning, and there was water in the cylinders. The block was cracked, and there isn't much you can do about that."

It's the following Thursday now, three days before the race, and Rick is getting ready to leave for the airport to catch his plane back to

California. "You've just gotta come here prepared," he tells me, "A month seems like a long time, but you gotta be ready to race when you get here." In his flowered Hawaiian shirt he slumps on a toolbox and looks at the immaculate but nonfunctional blue and yellow Eagle that won't get past the pit gates again this year. "When I started out in this game I was going to be rich and famous, señor. Now I've got to go back home and start all over again, tryin' to scratch up a sponsor. Well, at least I've still got my arms and legs, and no bad burns." He sighs. "At least I'm still pretty."

"I wish you were going to stick around for the race," I tell him.

"I can't." He shakes his head and slides on his mirror-finished sunglasses, as if they'll filter out all the reminders of his disappointment. "This place makes me sad if I'm not in the show. It's just too intense to watch from behind the fence. I'll be on the beach Sunday, señor." He smiles. "Maybe I'll listen to it on the radio. Maybe I'll be ridin' a wave."

Later that afternoon, I'm sitting with Mike Mosley on the wall that separates the pits from the track, watching the final moments of pit-stop practice. It's a pleasant sunny afternoon, the grandstands across the track are empty, and there's a deceptively low-key atmosphere. The ABC TV crew is filming some practice pit stops for their delayed broadcast of the race, and the buses that take museum visitors around the Speedway are running again for the first time since the track opened three weeks ago. One stops behind us while the driver explains what's going on in the pits, and we turn and wave at the faces behind glass—like mechanical figures in a Disneyland Raceworld. We are talking about the drivers' meeting, which is due to start in a few minutes. I tell Mike about having snuck into the meeting last year and ask him if he feels the drivers really do heed Tom Binford's exhortation about the start, not to begin racing till they come out of the second turn.

"I don't know," he says, glancing over the Tower Terrace stands, "It's pretty wild out there the first few laps. When they're over you kind of settle down, and it's all right."

"Does being three abreast add to it?" I ask.

"Yeah, here it does, 'cause it's so narrow. There's no room if anybody makes a mistake. I don't like it much, to tell you the truth." He laughs. "In fact, I don't like it at all. They clean the track, but there's still a lot of sand and you can't see very well. You have to wear three or four face shields to rip off as they get dirty, and each one of them distorts things a little more. I just hope everyone keeps it together and doesn't try to win it on the first lap."

The sound of the impact wrenches fades, and the last car is wheeled from the pit lane. A few crews are still working on their refueling tanks. A lady with a really outstanding décolletage walks past, and we are both silent in a moment of admiration.

That evening, we are back in Mark Stainbrook's apartment in Claremont, where I first met Mosley. We are all feeling Rick Muther's conspicuous absence and listening to a new Charlie Daniels Band record, *Saddle Tramp*. Mike breaks our rather melancholy trance by lamenting that he can't have music in his racing car.

"If you could work it out," I suggest, "you'd have to program your tapes pretty carefully. I mean, you'd have to predetermine what kind of a race you were going to drive: seven minutes of hard rock for charging at the start, then fifteen minutes of easy travelin' music for pacing yourself, a little Orange Blossom Special for puttin' the hammer down again, a soft guitar interlude for runnin' under the yellow, and then eighteen seconds of frantic harpsichord music for a pit stop."

Mosley laughs. "It'd be like having music for the movie."

"If we really got civilized, you'd have air conditioning, automatic transmissions, and cruise control."

"Next you'll want TV." Mosley's chuckle is a soft Woody Woodpecker laugh, with no hard edges.

"Maybe even remote cameras, so you can watch the race you're driving from any one of a dozen points of view, from the first turn, from the Goodyear blimp, maybe even from inside the car."

We end up with thirty-three drivers driving the race in a penny arcade with a preprogrammed track and traffic pattern on a continuous roll, over which they guide their miniature cars. "Or we'll have slots in the track," Mosley caps it off, "and we'll just be passengers in the cars while somebody back in the tower is pushing the buttons."

Clifford Haverson, who works as a mechanic for Dan Gurney's

team, brings up the latest antics of A. J. Foyt, who was fined twenty-five dollars for refusing to wear his Nomex underwear, got mad about that, and skipped the drivers' meeting, winning himself another hundred-dollar fine. "It's just a popcorn meeting," Foyt said, "just a lot of bull we've heard before. I've been arguing with them all month, and I don't want to argue anymore."

"Why don't you ever do anything like that?" Clifford asks, "You're just always Mike Mosley, nice-guy race driver."

Mosley smiles.

"I can see the headlines when you win it: Unidentified Driver Wins 500."

Mosley laughs again, and it's infectious.

"I could hover over the track in a helicopter," Clifford mimes, "and pull you out of the car as you take the checkered flag. Then we could go somewhere and watch the search for you on television."

"That'd be great." Mosley seems delighted, as much by the idea of the monumental prank as by the idea of winning, and the smile behind his steel-rimmed aviator's glasses is almost more than his face can contain.

"Hey, Mike, you're gonna win."

"Go get 'em!"

"Hey Bobby!"

I've never seen a 500 Festival Parade through downtown Indianapolis. I still haven't, but I'm watching something better: the faces of the people who are watching the parade, four hundred thousand of them, the organizers claim. Whatever their number, the spectators are a great parade themselves. Mike Mosley has asked me to ride with him in his pace car, one of thirty-three identically painted Buicks, one for each of the drivers. Each car has a sunroof so that the race drivers can sit on the roofs and wave to the crowd. I'm in the backseat of the car, peering through the windows at all the people who are looking at Mike and at Bobby Unser and Boom-Boom Cannon, who are riding atop the cars

on either side of us. I feel as if I am a rare fish in an aquarium, looking back at the multitudes streaming past my tank.

Following the formal drivers' meeting, the drivers, their families,
and guests have ridden from the Speedway to the parade-marshaling
area by the Indianapolis National Guard Armory in two police-escorted
buses. Spirits on our bus are pretty high, the race drivers egging the bus
driver on as he speeds in his cocoon of sirens, weaving intricately
through the halted traffic. There's a surge of power and importance, the
whole city stopped and waiting for us. "Of course," Johnny Rutherford
says. "Without us they wouldn't have a show."

"I'm not so sure," I suggest. "I'll bet if they stopped running the
race next year, almost all those people would come anyway. It's a ritual as much as a race. They'd fill up those grandstands and the infield
and make something happen."

"Maybe you're right." Rutherford smiles. "It'd probably go on for
another three or four years anyway."

Dick Simon is wearing his hairpiece for the first time this month
and whooping out rebel yells as people along Sixteenth Street stand
and wave at the busloads of celebrities.

Drinks are being served at the Armory before the parade, and as
we go in to get a Coke, Mike and I pass Bob Hope and Tony Hulman
coming out to take their places at the head of the parade. We walk
through the corridors of the armory, past the ominous rows of barred,
cell-like doors, to the reception room. It's crowded with familiar faces:
those of the drivers, of course, and TV and movie stars, some of them
familiar only from commercials. Barry Goldwater is shaking Mario
Andretti's hand. Martin Milner wishes Mike good luck. Through the
crowd I can see Phyllis Diller, Claude Akin, and General Jimmy
Doolittle.

Outside on the street, the bomb goes off to signal the start of the
parade, and we hurry back to our cars. The streets are packed with people, standing, sitting on stools and lawn chairs, on balconies and
bleachers, filling every visible window of every building, even on
rooftops, and as we pass a six-story parking ramp, I notice that standing room has been sold along the outside edge of each ramp so that it

looks like a huge multilayer human sandwich. I notice an isolated niche high up on the war memorial, and there's a man standing in it, waving to the drivers below. It's a Roman mob scene worthy of Cecil B. De Mille.

As we move down the street, I forecast a pattern of those spectators who will root for Bobby Unser; seconds later, with amazing accuracy, my projection is borne out. "Hey Bobby!" I see their lips moving, banging together twice, "Baa-Bee!" *"The Indianapolis 500 festivities will be heard round the world on the world's largest radio network,"* I hear the parade announcer say.

Near the end of the two-mile parade route, we pass a motor home in a parking lot. It faces the street and there's a loudspeaker on the roof. Behind the windshield, a woman is holding a microphone. She's blushing. I can see even through the tinted windshield that her rather porcine features are flushed with a wide-eyed, manic smile. She's thrilled, having the volume of the speaker at her command, but she doesn't know what to do with it. "Halooo." Her voice takes on the quality of a siren, and her excitement is hyped by the sound of her own voice. "Wooo, Wahooo." Now she's bouncing up and down on the driver's seat; her blond curls dangling like flaccid springs. The microphone has control of her, and she's not about to go into orbit. "Halooo. WoooWeee." As the sound of her screaming fades behind us, I imagine her being dragged off to a rest home, driven totally insane by the sight of Bobby Unser and the self-perpetuating narcissism of the sound of her own voice.

BACK AT THE Speedway, people are lined up for a quarter mile to get into the museum and to take a bus ride around the track. The sky is overcast, but nobody wants to talk about the possibility of rain for tomorrow. In Indianapolis, that just isn't done. The race has been halted by rain two of the past three years, and nobody can bear the thought that it might happen again–or worse, that it might be delayed until or have to be restarted on Monday.

The difficult thing about trying to talk with a driver before the start of a race, especially this race, is that there's nothing to say. I'm standing on the track with Mike Mosley. We are leaning against the pit wall, facing the fourth row of cars, the row in which he will start from the middle position. The bands have passed, and the celebrities, and now there are only drivers, crews, officials, and photographers on the track, about a thousand of them nervously milling around to kill the fifteen minutes before Tony Hulman will tell them to start their engines. Everyone seems a little zapped by all the pageantry and perhaps simply by the presence of another estimated 399,999 people. It's hard to realize that in a few minutes this piece of asphalt on which we're standing will be crowded with cars traveling 220 miles an hour. Perhaps foolishly, in an attempt to focus this moment, I make a stab at conversation. "Well, when it gets to this point," I say, "it must seem just like a race."

"Yeah," Mosley nods philosophically, "it looks like it's going to happen, so there's no point in worrying about it."

A man with a tape recorder comes out of the crowd, thrusts a microphone in front of Mike's mouth, and makes my lame attempt at communication seem almost profound. "Mike, what's your race plan? Can you talk about it?"

I imagine Mike saying, "Yeah, if I can just keep from throwing up all over your microphone." At this point the tension is so high I can feel it resonating through my legs and up my back. I'm as nervous as I've ever been before driving a race, and here I'm only a spectator. But Mike keeps it together and deals with this inane question as straightforwardly as he would have if it had been asked two weeks earlier: "We're just gonna try and get through the first few laps and then drive as hard a race as we can."

"You've got a pretty good car this year, don't you?"

"Well, we'd like to have a little more power. I just hope it can run all day."

"What would it mean to you to win this one, Mike?" *Jesus*, I'm thinking, *this guy doesn't quit.*

"It'd be . . ." Mike tries to find an intelligent answer to this obvious question, then shrugs his shoulders. "It'd be great."

Now it's time for the drivers to get in their cars. I shake Mike's hand. "I'll see you . . ."

"Wherever." He smiles.

I run to the front of the starting field. An overly ardent singer with a group of hyperactive dancing children who all look like they've stepped out of a toothpaste commercial is melodramatizing the national anthem to the point of sedition. I wince at each high vibrato, hoping he'll swallow his uvula and spare my ears. I'm trying to get a photograph of Tony Hulman as he speaks *those immortal words,* but he's lost in a forest of microphones. Jim Nabors again drawls through "Back Home Again in Indiana," and a barrage of red, then white, then blue balloons is released against the now darkly threatening sky. Tony Hulman speaks, the starters grind, engines begin revving, and I'm sprinting to take up my camera position on the inside of the first turn.

I'm thinking about Billy Scott in his first Indy start as the field passes on the parade lap. When I talked with him earlier in the morning, he was thrilled by the pageantry, as if it were all in celebration of his having made the race. He seemed excited rather than nervous, more as if he were going to ride in a parade than be caught up in the sweep of 24,000 HP. Mosley is late getting started and hurries past to catch up with his place in the formation. The field passes again, faster this time, the cars snaking violently to heat up their tires, and the track announcer's voice follows them around. *Down the back straight . . . taking their positions through turn three . . . looking good in the north chute . . . into turn four now, the pace car dropping down, pulling into the pit lane, Johnny Rutherford now in control, bringing them toward the start, in good formation, keeping their interval,* AND THEY'VE GOT THE GREEN. The low roar of the engines glissades to a scream, the air is saturated with the vapor of methanol fumes, and I can feel the vibrations in the grass beneath my feet and against the exposed skin of my arms. *And the sixtieth running of the Indianapolis Five Hundred is under way, the greatest spectacle in racing.* The cars disappear into the short chute and a dozen bombs explode in the air in rapid succession. I'm startled and wince, momentarily mistaking them as reports from a horrendous crash. I hear an enormous cheer from the hordes in the snake pit behind me and from the grandstands across the track, so many voices that I can hear them resonate over the scream of the cars. I've completely lost myself. The excitement blurs my vision and all I see is a chain of bright colors.

There are a few moments of silence, and I can hear a cricket somewhere in the grass between me and the track. I can hear the roar building again as the cars zoom back down the front straight, and I imagine what the drivers are seeing, the wings and tires ahead of them, blurred by vibrations and by the dust and smoke, dodging and darting, testing for an opening to pass. The first cars blast past me and the roar becomes a scream again, raw from their exhausts. This time I get control of myself and begin sorting them out, Rutherford in the lead, followed by Johncock, Sneva, and Foyt. On the third lap, Foyt is on Rutherford's tail. On the fourth lap, just in front of me, Foyt passes Rutherford. But there are no gaps. The whole field is close. Rutherford and Foyt will dice like this, swapping the lead between pit stops, throughout the next 250 miles. I see Mosley trying to pass in the short chute, but he seems to lack the power to get by the car ahead of him. He goes high on the outside, then is forced to drop back to set up for the second turn.

Thirty-five laps have gone by, and the field is running under the yellow. There's a moment of silence; the first turn is empty. Then the spectators in the stands across the track rise in a wave as the green light comes on. They can see what's coming down the main straight. Ten cars pass, nose to tail. There's another brief moment of silence in their wake, and I can hear ten thousand excited conversations like ten thousand fragments of falling glass, as they settle back in their seats. Then their voices are blanketed by another wave of four cars.

At ninety-one laps, Mike Mosley coasts in, out of fuel. His crew runs down the pit lane to meet him and pushes him to his pit. I'm standing in the pressroom, watching the race on a TV monitor; it's the one way I can see what's happening all around the track.

I FEEL THE wall behind me vibrate as the cars dive into the first turn. At 101 laps, the rain starts falling and the race is stopped. Rain is getting to be part of the Indy tradition; it has stopped the race three of the last four years. This time it passes, and a parade of pace cars and crash trucks and an absurd-looking jet-powered blower circles the track to dry it out for the restart. The race cars pull into the pits and a curiously relaxed half-time atmosphere prevails. There's nothing to do now but wait.

I find Billy Scott sitting on the pit wall by his car. I sit next to him and ask how he dropped so suddenly from sixteenth to twenty-third.

"I had a loose wheel," he says. "I went into turn one, and it wouldn't turn. I went way up in the gray. I looked at my left wheel, and it was turning, but the right one was just going *oooha, oooha, oooha.*"

"And then you went *oooha, oooha, oooha,*" I suggest.

"Yeah," he laughs, "at least I was sure something wasn't right."

"Either that or you forgot something important about this track."

"Yeah, really." He laughs again.

"Well, have a great second half," I tell him as I get up to go.

"Thanks, coach," he says. "We gotta drive this one harder. That wheel mighta cost me Rookie of the Year."

I stop by Foyt's pit and hear him explaining to a group of news-men how Johnny Rutherford had picked up twenty seconds on him under the yellow.

"Did he do anything you wouldn't have done?" one of them asks.

A. J. hesitates a moment, then smiles weakly. "No, I guess not really," he says and turns back toward his crew.

At 3:00 the track is judged dry enough for a restart, and the cars are lined up single file in the pit lane. While the drivers get strapped in, I hurry back out to my spot inside the first turn. At 3:10 it starts rain-ing again. The crews cover the cars and drivers with tarps and sheets of plastic, and everyone who can runs for cover. At 3:20 the race is called in one of the most anticlimactic finishes in its sixty-year history. Johnny Rutherford is declared the winner of the Indianapolis 255, beat-ing out Foyt by 3.7 seconds, and is the first driver in the history of the race to walk, rather than drive, to victory lane. Foyt is furious and distraught, foiled again by the weather. For the past nine years he's been trying to become the first man to win the 500 four times. In his frustration, he threatens to file a protest, but eventually realizes it would be futile. There's no recourse against the rain.

The party is suddenly over, and everything is confusion. The multitudes in the infield have run for their cars or broken out sheets of transparent plastic to cover themselves and their drowned picnics. They will sit and steam for hours as the greatest spectacle in traffic congestion tries to sort itself out. I'm in no hurry to join the crush, and will let it ease up before I drive back to my motel.

I stop by Mike Mosley's garage and have a beer. The car sits outside under a tarp, and a party is going on in the one-stall garage. Running out of fuel had dropped Mike back to sixteenth place. He has his driving suit half off, folded down around his waist, but has given up the idea of changing in this crowd. It's raining harder now, really pouring. Everyone, except perhaps Rutherford, would have liked to have seen the race restarted and run to its conclusion, but they are, nevertheless, relieved that it's over.

Clifford Haverson has joined the party. He tells Mike that Vern Schuppan, Dan Gurney's Australian rookie driver, said to Gurney during a pit stop, "I think I'm getting the hang of this. This is fun," then went back out and improved his speed markedly.

"Boy, he's really a nice guy," Clifford says earnestly.

"Yeah, he is." Mosley nods in agreement.

"Really easygoing and . . ." Clifford looks at Mike and they break into laughter, complete the thought simultaneously, "dumb."

"Yeah." Mosley is still laughing. "Anybody who thinks that's fun out there is dumb. It's just scary, that's what it is." I'm delighted with his frankness, and we all laugh again with relief.

I stop by Billy Scott's garage to say good-bye. Everyone is crowded in around his beautiful red, white, and blue car. They all seem happy, especially Billy's mother. His loose wheel cost him seven places and the Rookie of the Year Award he'd been working toward all month. "But that's racing," he says, shrugging his shoulders. He knows he's run well and has the experience of one Indy behind him. "I hope I see ya before next year," he says as we shake hands. "Give me a call when you get to California."

Epilogue

Our revels are now ended. These our actors
As I foretold you, were all spirits and
Are melted into air, into thin air . . .

How COULD I be so naive? The race had seemed to fade so insignificantly in the downpour that it had taken on a dreamlike quality. It was almost as if it had been a rather pointless fantasy we had constructed in the rain, there in Mike Mosley's garage. No one could take issue with the weather. It played out its pattern, as totally indifferent to the greatest spectacle in racing, to this mid-American celebration of the rites of spring, as if it had drowned out a pastoral tryst or a sandlot baseball game. And because the race had been so arbitrarily terminated, did I assume that the multitude had likewise been dissolved? What did I think was going to happen to those 400,000 people?

In past years, the postrace traffic has been merely a stream to be crossed on my ten-minute walk back to the Speedway Motel. But this year I am staying at a Ramada Inn, a short three miles away. I have killed an hour and a half following the race and figure that, by now, it will be a moderate, if perhaps mildly circuitous, drive back to a hot shower and some dry clothes. I know I'll have to follow the traffic pattern east on Sixteenth Street until I can catch a left to Thirty-Eighth, turn left again and cruise to the door of my room. I pull out of the garage area parking lot, get into the flow through the tunnel and out of the Speedway with no delays. *All I'll need is a little patience,* I tell myself. I flick on the radio. "I know it may seem like they're sending you to nowhere," the voice oozes, "but the police really have your best interests in mind. So follow their instructions and they'll direct you as quickly and safely as possible to your destination." The traffic is six lanes one way, like water running out of a bathtub, 400,000 half-drowned lives funneling out into America.

A mile or so down Sixteenth Street, I catch a left through a residential area. This street takes me to Lafayette, which my map tells me will intersect with Thirty-Eighth, and it does. It's been twenty minutes, and I'm cruising down Thirty-Eighth Street, three blocks from my motel. The traffic's heavy, but I'm home free. But wait! Two cars ahead of me, a police car is pulling across all three lanes of traffic. He's stopping us, making us U-turn and go back the other way. Now I am lost, on a freeway to No-Name Creek. I take the first exit, head north, and begin an hour-and-a-half search for a safe route to the Indies. It's pouring again now. I find a freeway that will take me right to my motel, but there's no southbound entrance ramp, anywhere. I turn back and search, circumnavigating accidents, circling defensively to find a weak spot in the outboard flow. Finally I see a police car parked on the shoulder. I pull up behind him, get out into the deluge, and knock on his window. "I need help." My voice is on the edge of cracking.

"It's easy," he says. "Just take a left here, go two miles to the light, turn right, and you'll be on Thirty-Eighth, real close to where you're going."

"Thank you sir." I feel an impulse to kiss him.

Now I'm coming up on the light. I make the right turn on Thirty-Eighth Street and I'm right back at the same roadblock where all my problems began. I'm being directed to U-turn and start all over again. *The Ramada Inn? You can't get there from here.* I work my way to the right, pull onto the drive of an abandoned gas station, switch off my engine, and tell myself, between measured breaths, that the world isn't really a conspiracy against me. It just seems that way. I wait half an hour, but there's no letup in the flow of hapless drivers being sent back out into Hoosier oblivion. A great day at the races. This is the real carnival ride, a Sartrian *No Exit.* Just me and my pickup truck, doomed to wander endlessly until . . . Oh, cut it out. I'm losing my mind. I'll walk up to that cop who caused all my confusion and ask his advice, a return to the source.

"I don't know anything," he tells me, sighing heavily, "I live six miles outside of Cincinnati and I don't know anything about this town. I go through this once a year and I can't stand it. I've been out here in the rain for hours, I've been yelled at, threatened. I just want to go home. I want a dry uniform and a cup of coffee. You can do anything you want, 'cause this street's open right now." He gets into his car, backs it off the street, turns and heads for the nearest McDonald's. I watch his red lights disappear and spend a moment regretting I couldn't have been more comfort to him. But my odyssey isn't over. I will circle for another three-quarters of an hour, trying to make a left turn, and will eventually, during a break in the oncoming traffic, make a banzai run the wrong way down a divided highway and pull into my motel three hours and ninety-seven miles after leaving the Speedway.

As I collect myself in the bar, I construct a scenario of the one truly mythical character of the Indianapolis 500, the Phantom Race Fan, who left the Speedway after the 1949 race and hasn't been home since. No one knows for sure where he is, but at least once each May he is seen passing the Speedway in his decrepit 1948 Ford, his head swiveling involuntarily, his eyes glazed with a vague, directionless longing.

Africa

FOREWORD

*In the summer of 1974 I made my second trip to Africa—I had traveled in Kenya,
Tanzania, and Ethiopia in the winter of 1973—with Robert F. Jones on assignment
for* Sports Illustrated, *to do stories on what was to be "the last great safari." We were
accompanied by my late wife, Virginia; by Bill Winter, a near-legendary professional
hunter; and for most of the trip by our three African game scouts, Lambat, a
Wanderobo, Otiego, a Turkana, and Machyana, a Samburu. Bob Jones was to do
the big-game hunting and I the photography. We would travel the northern reaches
of Kenya to the Somali border and cross the Chalbi Desert to Lake Rudolph.*

The Heart Is One

I REMEMBER HOW everyone crouched down beside the Toyota and plugged their ears when it was my turn to sight in the .458. I adjusted the ear protectors, nestled my elbow into the pad across the hood of the truck, looked through the iron sights, held my breath, let out a little, and began squeezing the trigger. The black dot of the target danced, then settled atop the front sight, and I watched it with a certain kind of detachment until the recoil knocked me back and I saw the entire side of the mountain which rose above our camp as an enormous target I might easily have missed. The noise seemed less startling than when Bill and Bob had fired, I suppose because I'd been concentrating on the target rather than flinching in anticipation. The .458 would be used primarily by Bill Winter as a backup gun for Cape buffalo, and it was unlikely that Bob or I would ever fire it again, but it was as close as either of us would come to shoulder-firing a howitzer, and there was all that boyhood mythology of the power of the elephant gun. At least we could say we'd done it.

I hadn't done much rifle shooting since I'd won my Junior Marksman medal at summer camp several decades earlier, but apparently I hadn't lost my touch. With the .458, as with the .375 and the 7mm before it, I had either hit the bull's eye dead center or broken the ring of it, confirming my suspicion that there really wasn't all that much difficulty involved in sighting in a large animal and turning it into meat. I had a bird hunter's prejudice, having been raised in Michigan on pheasant, duck, and ruffed grouse, and the previous day had shot two yellow-neck Francolins which provided our dinner. Although Michigan is famous for its white-tailed deer, I had never hunted them, mostly because my father had never hunted them. Hunting is a tradition you are either raised with or you view from some distance with amusement and righteous indignation. Consequently, bird hunting seemed to me a noble celebration of autumn, while deer hunting or big-game hunting of any kind was for egotistical greenhorns from Detroit, for meat gatherers either too lazy or incompetent to trudge through swamps and cornfields all day, constantly tuned to the explosion of wings and the almost instinctive snapshot that meant the difference between a game dinner and simple exhaustion, the two outcomes almost equally satisfying.

But here I was, involved in a big-game safari on a plain called Marilal in northern Kenya, though not primarily as a hunter. I had come along to take the photographs for a feature article Bob had been assigned to write for *Sports Illustrated* on "the last great African adventure." Originally we had planned to travel by horse and camel-back from Marilal to Lake Rudolph, then back to a campsite on the Uaso Nyiro River, affectionately referred to as EDB (Elephant Dung Beach). But all the horses and most of the camels we were to have taken had died in the drought the previous spring, so we found ourselves traveling in two more prosaic but far more practical Toyota pickups. Bob was going to do the hunting, and except for some Francolins and sand grouse, I would do all my shooting with a camera. Yet, I had one question, one unconfirmed assertion. I had always maintained to my non-hunting and deer-hunting friends that I could, if necessary, shoot and field dress a large animal, and Bob had persuaded me that the time was right to make good on it. "You'll never really know until you do it," he chided. Wichira, the ancient fire tender, threw on another dry acacia branch, and a few lambent sparks rose into the still, moonless night.

"You poets," he snorted, only half in jest, as he emptied his glass. He stared into the fire a moment then turned his head at the cackle of a hyena. Bill and Virginia, my wife, seemed remote in their silence, basking in the weariness of the day's hunting. The cackling stopped and Bob turned back to me, his face oddly segmented by the light of the fire. "It's not like shooting a piece of paper," he sighed. He had sensed my generalized distaste for the idea of killing purely for sport, to fill up a trophy room, to document a personal history with corpses, and he wasn't going to let me rest in the righteous security of the observer. We would be out for a month and would be living on what we shot, and, in addition to the meat from the trophies Bob would take, we would need an additional impala or warthog for the pot.

Though both Bob and Bill had assured me that I would find it more difficult to zero in on a living animal than on the black circle of a paper target, I was confident of my marksmanship. My only concern was that I might not make a clean kill, that I might wound my prey and have to fire several more times. I had seen an eland wounded and stalked through heavy cover for over an hour before it was finished at close range with a shot to the head, had seen a zebra spinning around a shattered foreleg, and had a nightmare about shooting an impala in the hindquarters, having to pursue it through thorn bushes as it dragged its maimed quarters, shooting again and again to bring it down. I awoke, startled by the shrieks of baboons from the rocks behind our tent. Earlier in the night I had heard the cough of a leopard, and now knew from the cries of the baboons that it had been successful in its hunt. I heard the cackle of another hyena not far from the tent and remembered the day before: watching vultures tearing apart the carcass of a zebra, and finding a human skull on a hillside not a mile from camp, a delicate green butterfly perched in the empty socket of its eye. As the time for my hunt drew closer, my empathy with the animal I would stalk became more intense. I had formed some definite ideas about the ritual into which I was to enter, and I knew that everything would have to be just right before I could begin to squeeze the trigger.

In the morning we looked unsuccessfully for buffalo in the damp, moss-hung forests on the mountain ridge about Marilal, then returned to camp to lunch on the chops of a Thompson's gazelle Bob had shot the previous afternoon. It was the last of our camp meat. Bob had shot a buffalo several days before, about thirty miles from camp at a place in the mountains called Tinga, but we had given most of the meat to the Samburu, who lived in that region, saving only the tongue and tail for ourselves. In addition to Bob, Bill, Virginia, and myself, there were thirteen men—trackers, skinners, and camp keepers—who would need to be fed that evening. "Well, it's up to you, *Bwana*," Bill said, leaning on his elbows over coffee and cheese. "A bit of meat for the pot. I hope your eyes are clear, because we're depending on you for our supper." I felt an elemental kind of exhilaration at the idea of all these people depending on me to put meat on the table. I was familiar with the process, of course, but only indirectly, having been paid for writing articles or books and having taken that money to the supermarket and exchanged it for meat, sanitarily cut and packaged. I had, of course, provided pheasants and grouse, but they were ritual meals, taken only as sacraments in place of the pork chops, ready in the refrigerator in case I'd been lazy or unsuccessful. Now, I, the deer-slayer, would set out, after our midday nap, to provide for seventeen mouths that would be salivating by the time the sun went down. Of course I would have expert help in locating our dinner. All that would be required of me would be a steady aim and a smooth squeeze on the trigger, or so I thought. In the heat of the equatorial sun on the tent flap, I tried to read Rimbaud, but my gaze kept drifting from *A Season in Hell* to the plain below. I could hear chanting from a Samburu *manyata* down the valley, and a noon bird singing like a rusty swing.

Lambat was the sullen one, a Dorobo tracker who smiled only while holding his battery-powered cassette recorder to his ear for the sounds of the Rolling Stones or the chants and songs of his village. As in all our previous ventures from camp, I would ride standing behind the cab of the truck with Lambat and the two other trackers—Machyana and Otiego—only this time, instead of my cameras, I would use the .375 Winchester Model 70 which lay in the canvas tarp at our feet. As we rolled down the hillside from camp, I resumed my Swahili lesson with

Lambat, Otiego, and Machyana, pointing at objects and repeating their Swahili names. "You *piga.*" Otiego laughed and pointed at me.

"*Piga*?" I looked perplexed and shook my head. "*Piga*?" His manner didn't seem insulting. Then I remembered, "*Piga*, kill," I said.

Otiego smiled, slapped his palms together in a glancing blow, and then raised his arms and cocked his head as if holding a rifle. "*Piga*, kill," he said, laughing and nodding deeply. "*Pahali a Mungu*," he said, this time pointing at the sky, which had turned a gunmetal gray and formed an anvil-like cloud that resembled a storm crossing a wheat field, as Thomas Hart Benton might have seen it.

"Place of God," I said, remembering the Swahili way of saying sky. "*Pahali a Mungu.*"

"*Dume.*" Lambat shouted. *Dume* means male or herd bull, and I was about to pantomime horns spiraling above my head when I realized that the Swahili lesson was over. Lambat was tapping on the windshield with a stick to get Bill's attention and pointing ahead and to our right. The Toyota jerked to a halt. I jumped to the ground, and before I had even spotted the *dume*, Lambat had racked a shell into the chamber of the .375 and handed it to me. "*Piga, piga.*" He whispered hoarsely, pointing at what I could see was a large male impala standing broadside to us, not more than forty yards down the slope of the hill.

"He's a beauty," Bill said, looking up from his binoculars as I knelt and steadied the crosshairs just behind the *dume*'s shoulder. I hadn't had a chance to look at him before I saw him through the scope, and he was beautiful. He was upwind of us, but I don't know why he hadn't seen us. He simply stood there like a target cut-out, as if he were watching something in the thorn trees below, the sky gone almost black behind him. "Lambaste him, *Bwana*," Bill whispered. It was a perfect target. Too perfect. I watched him through the scope for a moment, then relaxed my aim and stood up. The *dume* spotted me, sank slightly on his haunches, turned in the air, and was gone. It had been too perfect, too easy, no stalking, no sense of a hunt. There, not five minutes out of camp, was the best impala Bill had seen in years, almost begging to be shot. But it wasn't what I had in mind for my one big-game kill. There would have been no ritual. Bill looked at me, the corners of his eyes creased in a question. "Too easy," I said, "I just couldn't do it."

I FELT THE rifle jerked out of my hands. Lambat was scowling. "You go back to America," he said. "You take pictures." He climbed back into the truck, unloaded the rifle, and stood staring at the storm cloud ahead of us. It had grown noticeably cooler. Bill spoke to Lambat in Swahili, "He doesn't want to shoot something beautiful like an impala. He wants to shoot something ugly like a warthog." Bill tried to explain, tried to soothe him. But Lambat had no ideas about hunting, no Western sense of sportsmanship. For him, you killed what you could, the easiest way possible. Our next meal had been presented to us, and I had arrogantly refused it for all of us. Lambat spoke slowly and solemnly to Bill, then turned his back to us and hunkered down in the corner of the truck bed.

"What?" I asked. I felt in some indefinable way ashamed and at the same time amused by the cultural gap, at this portrayal of two men seeing one thing with such disparate eyes. Bill put his hand on my shoulder and smiled as he spoke. "He says, beautiful or ugly, the heart is one."

We got soaked on the way back to camp and dined on bread, cheese, and cauliflower brought along from Bill's garden, and we talked about other things; about the deserts we would cross on our drive to Lake Rudolph, about the abundance of Cape buffalo we would find at EDB, and about the human skull we had hidden in a cave above camp. The rain beat down on the canvas above our heads, and Bob asked me if I would dare to climb up to the cave that night to retrieve the skull. It wasn't much different from ghost-story dares around campfires I remembered from childhood, except that here there were leopards, lions, and snakes, real dangers in the night as well as those we might imagine, and we speculated about which would cause us the most apprehension on the climb we well knew we would never make that night. I wanted to explain to Bob and Bill that I hadn't refused the shot because I thought the impala was too beautiful. Though that might have had something to do with it, my sense of the aesthetic had been put to shame by Lambat's simple recognition of the truth. But it really had been too easy. Though that excuse was at least as silly as my discrimination against warthogs, I was stuck with the idea that a hunt without effort wasn't really a hunt. This would be a one-time experience for me, and I had to at least make it memorable.

During the course of the safari, it had become a nightly custom to make up limericks about the events of the day. Many of Bill's clients were French, German, or Italian, and so to spend a whole month with people who spoke, more or less, his native tongue was a rare treat for him. After we had finished our meatless dinner, Bill poured some brandy and proposed, not a toast, but rather the first couplet of a limerick:

> *There was a young poet named Dan*
> *Who would shoot an impala for the pan*

Now Bob Chimed in:

> *But when it came time to do it*
> *He chose to eschew it,*

There was a moment of silence while everyone but me searched for a final rhyme. Our limericks were always without mercy. Finally it was Virginia who delivered the coup de grace:

> *And we all sighed, 'How hungry I am!'*

We laughed, but it was true. Here we were in Eden, surrounded by more meat on the hoof than the King Ranch could lay claim to, yet going without because of what now seemed my perverted sense of sportsmanship. I decided not to explain. My excuse didn't even make sense to me anymore. In the morning I would hunt again, and I wouldn't think about it. I would take my shot however it came.

An hour from camp, I spotted three young Grant's gazelles 150 yards beyond a dry riverbed. Bill stopped the truck. I grabbed the .375, crept down the slope, crossed the dry stream, and rested my elbow against the bank of the other side. "Remember," Bill had cautioned me, "don't hold your aim too long. Let those crosshairs settle behind the shoulder and lambaste him." The sense of detachment I had felt the day before was gone. My heart was pounding as if I were the prey rather than the hunter. I was determined to shoot, and I wanted to hit him clean. Though there were three *dume*s to choose from, it was a far more difficult shot than the one I had had the previous afternoon. Slightly uphill, they stood in a clearing of thorn trees, their tails flicking nervously, their heads raised, alert to something in the scrub to their right. I wiped the perspiration from my eyes and took aim, then remembered that I had forgotten to rack a shell into the chamber. I was glad the sulking Lambat had stayed in the truck. I worked the bolt and settled back into position, but the steady hand of my target shooting had deserted me. The crosshairs bounced crazily. I picked the gazelle on the right, but either he wouldn't stand still or the frame wouldn't stand still. It bobbed like a boat on a choppy sea. The crosshairs swung across his shoulder, then back over his flank. I took another deep breath. I knew I had to take this shot. The crosshairs came back toward his shoulder and I pulled the trigger. I saw a puff of dust where the bullet hit in front of him. The gazelles started but didn't move. They seemed confused about the direction of the shot. I worked the bolt and fired again, another cloud of dust, but when my eye settled back to the scope, the clearing was empty. We searched the ground where they had been standing, for any blood spoor, but I knew there wouldn't be any. I could have sworn I had seen Lambat smile as he'd come from the truck. Maybe it'd been a smirk. "I'm getting hungry, *Bwana*," Bill said. "Maybe we should check those sights." We found a clearing and set up a small cardboard case as a target. Since both shots had been an almost equal distance short, Bill thought it might be an adjustment in the scope. I nodded in agreement. The scope might have been off a little, but not as far off as the confidence of the hunter.

Bill took two shots, and to my relief, they both kicked up little puffs of red clay dust in front of the box. My pride was at least partially restored, if only by a technicality. Bill talked me through several shots and sight adjustments, this time telling me to take my time, to let the crosshairs settle on the center of the box, to gradually tighten my grip around the stock and not to anticipate the recoil. "Spot on!" Bill lowered his binoculars. My fifth shot was square in the center of the box. "Now I wonder if you can do that for our supper," he mused. "Well?" Bob asked rhetorically, raising one eyebrow. He absorbed his laughter and climbed back into the cab.

An hour later we spotted two young impala at a distance of about 250 yards, standing near a grove of acacia trees. I lay on my belly in the red dust and adjusted the sling while Bill studied the impala through his glasses. The one on the right had a better head. "You sure you don't want a trophy, *Bwana?*" Bill asked, still watching them.

"No, just meat." I assured him.

"Then take the one on the left. It's a pretty good distance, so aim a little high."

It seemed easy now. The young *dume* was just a target, at least for the moment. He lowered his head to graze as I watched him through the scope, then raised it. Now he turned away at a slightly oblique angle, and I couldn't see his shoulder. "Remember where his heart is *Bwana*," Bill whispered, "right behind those ribs." The crosshairs were steady now, just ahead of his flank. "The safety," I thought. I'd almost forgotten the safety. I flicked it off and had barely begun to squeeze on the grip when I felt the recoil in my shoulder and against my cheek. I held my aim and looked again, but the scope was empty. There were only the acacia trees and the sunlight on their leaves, but I knew he was dead before Bill confirmed it. We paced off 240 yards and found him shot through the heart. "*Nakwisha*," Bill said in Swahili, "finished."

We hoisted him on a low branch of one of the acacia trees, and I made my first tentative cut down the center of his chest and along his belly. I had a strange feeling, putting my hand around his still-warm heart and severing the last tissue around it with my knife. Strange to feel the weight of it, as if it could have been my own. There was a hiss as I punctured the membrane around his intestines, and I had a sense of this life carried on by those of us who would eat him, whether we were men, lions, or jackals. Lambat was smiling now, actually smiling. He grasped my still bloody hand and shook it. I was welcome again. The heart is one.

Distant Thunder

IN THE PREDAWN darkness, the odor of blood was overwhelming. The truck rocked violently several times as it rolled down the hillside from our camp at Nibor Kedju, and my shoulders bumped first against Machyana and then Otiego. Behind us Lambat nestled into a tarp against the cold. Did they bathe in blood, I wondered? It was the first time we'd all been confined together with canvas stretched over the braces above the truck bed like a Conestoga wagon, and I was feeling mildly nauseated. It wasn't like the odor of cow dung that permeates everything in the vicinity of a Samburu *manyata*. I'd gotten used to that. No, this was dried and congealed blood. I couldn't see it, couldn't see anything in the darkness of this enclosure moving onto the still-dark plain, and I hadn't been aware that blood could have such a devastating smell. I'd tasted it, a slightly metallic, salty flavor, on the occasions of five broken noses and numerous dental extractions, but this . . . this was like a blood cologne. I imagined a deep maroon coating, cracked and blackening over the black skin of their forearms, a residue from skinning. Was it to protect them from spirits, the cold, or insects, or had there simply been no water to spare for washing it off?

It was a choice between nausea and the cold, and since I was apparently the only one bothered by the smell, the canvas would remain closed to keep out the wind.

We were headed into the Karisia Hills, southeast of Marilal in northern Kenya, to a place called Tinga, in search of Cape buffalo. Against the glare of the headlights off the track before us, I could see the silhouettes of Bob, Bill Winter, and Virginia through the rear window of the cab. There was a heater in there, and it would smell only of smoke or of Bob's breath, stale from too many cigarettes. That halitosis would seem almost sweet to me now.

By the time I'd made my peace with the blood smell, it was past dawn and the chill had lifted enough to raise the side flaps. The sky was gray and the land was rolling red clay covered with dry scrub. We were climbing gradually. The engine whined in second gear, and the land made me think of Wyoming. Ahead and just before the final climb into the hills, there were wire fences and a cluster of three wooden shacks with corrugated roofs. Bogo Boots stood in an alley between the shacks. I didn't know his name, but Bogo Boots fit. He was wearing a wool army jacket, a blanket around his waist, and combat boots which appeared huge and bulbous at the ends of his thin, bare legs. He stood with his hands on his hips, as if he'd been expecting us, and Bill brought the truck to a stop in front of him. He walked around the truck to Bill's window; several other tribesmen appeared, and there was some excited conversation in Swahili. I recognized the word *simba,* uttered repeatedly, with gestures and pointing toward the hills to the south. They told of a man from their village who had been sleeping out on the plain with a sick cow and had been dragged off by a lion during the night. Later we learned that the cow had died and the man had spent the night feeding on it, till the lion came and dragged him away from his feast. Near dawn, the lion had released the man, relatively unharmed, and he had returned to the village and cursed his companions for not responding to his cries for rescue. Bogo Boots explained that they had all been asleep and hadn't heard him, but the man who had almost been a meal himself refused to be mollified. He stood apart from the rest, shaking his fist and babbling at the hills as if pleading with the lion to come back and carry off his heartless brothers. Bogo Boots picked up his spear, climbed into the back with Lambat, and we left the village and the lion-crazed beefeater below.

On a high plateau we found a handsome eight-year-old herdsman with unusually bright eyes. His name was Peringin and he was Machyana's brother.

"*Wapi bogo?*" Bill asked him where the buffalo were, and Peringin replied with a sweeping gesture of his arm. "Honest to Christ, isn't that always the way?" Bill turned to us, laughing. "He says, 'Oh *Bwana*, you should have been here last week. The hills were black with *bogo*.'"

While we were discussing which way we should go, Peringin was joined by his friend Leyteyan. Together they pleaded with Bill, *Bwana Winja* as they called him, to let them come with us. They hadn't been on a hunt before, but they weren't really children as we think of eight-year-olds in the so-called civilized world. These two had spent as much as a week at a time on their own, with responsibility for the welfare of a herd of cattle in this wild, high country.

"All right," Bill gave in. They could come along on the condition that they stayed with the truck wherever we went. A Cape buffalo is as unpredictable as a shark, and when pursued will just as likely turn and charge as flee for cover.

A few miles further on we stopped for a breakfast of coffee and chocolate bars, while Lambat, Otiego, Machyana, and Bogo Boots scouted the area and surveyed the surrounding hills for any black shapes that moved against the background of yellow grass. It was mid-morning now. The canvas on the sides of the truck had been rolled up, and in the light I had discovered that the blood smell that had nauseated me earlier came not from Lambat, Otiego, and Machyana, but from the ribs of an eland they'd brought for their lunch, stashed under the bench on which we'd been sitting.

I'd just poured my second cup of coffee when we heard a rumble, first like distant thunder, then more like an earth tremor.

"*Bogo.*" Bill jumped to his feet. We saw Lambat motioning us down the slope of the hill. Virginia stayed with Peringin and Leyteyan while Bob, Bill, and I grabbed rifles and followed Lambat. My pulse rate had already picked up. Any creature that could make the ground shake like that deserved at least 120 heartbeats per minute. Lambat motioned us to keep low, and we crept with him toward a small thicket. In the cover of the bushes, we stood up slowly, and there were buffalo everywhere. There must have been fifty of them, now grazing quite peacefully, not thirty feet down the slope from us, trees to the right and below them. Now we were all nervous. The wind blew up the hillside, carrying their scent to us, and we spoke in the faintest whispers, searching the herd for a large bull. Then something moved in the trees to the right. It was Machyana throwing stones, trying to get the tightly grouped herd to circulate so that we could spot the bull. What if they stampeded? It was the question I was in the process of asking myself when we heard another rock falling through the branches, and the earth let go with another tremor. But this time it was a full-blown quake. I wasn't even aware of it beginning, but suddenly we were huddled together in the bushes, and buffalo were charging past on either side of us. The ground shook, the air was filled with dust, hooves clattered against stones, and they were past us. "Come on!" Bill yelled, and we ran after him, following the stampede down the side of the hill. I was choking, all but blinded by the dust, guided only by the slope falling away beneath my feet, when it hit me, a solid punch in the ribs and I went down on my shoulder against the side of the hill. The young springbuck struggled to its feet and continued its flight, apparently as startled by our collision as I had been. I watched until he crested the hill, then looked down through the dust at Bob and Bill, still running. But it was futile. The herd ran on into the forest of thorn trees and disappeared in the valley below.

ON A GREEN ridge I lay in the thick grass, leaned back against the trunk of an acacia, and washed down my eland sandwich with a few swallows from Bill's canteen. It was as if I were sitting on a hilltop in northern England, looking over the rolling, forested landscape in the foreground, at the entire state of Utah beyond. I'd spent perhaps a dozen summers in the American West, in the "Big Sky Country" of Wyoming and Montana, but the sky had never seemed as vast as this, nor had the land beneath it. In a grove behind us, Lambat, Otiego, Machyana, and Bogo Boots were roasting the eland ribs over an open fire, and I was feeling drowsy, basking in the realization that the stinking bloody ribs would no longer be with us, and making one of those "by God" pacts with myself that if Bob shot a buffalo, he, not I, could stew in its blood smell on the ride back to camp. Bill and Bob were discussing the lack of imagination in the writings of the earlier African explorers, agreeing that the land they traveled was so harsh and so vast that if they had been given to introspection, to musing rather than to a single-minded devotion to survival, they never would have lived long enough to report their discoveries. I had seen the harshness of the land in the lives of its people, the impersonal cruelty of nature, more evident here than in the Michigan woods but really no more cruel; seen men and animals riddled with infection, made blind by the infestation of flies; been moved by the contrasts of pain, death, and beauty; and it had made me feel vulnerable, helpless, and at the same time more vitally aware and alive. I must have been listening to their conversation as I dozed off. Maybe I had been musing on Machyana's stories of his youth in these hills, of fleeing from the Suk and Turkana raiders from the north, and I was back with the blood smell again, back in the stifling darkness of the truck. But this time it was human blood, and in my dream it was Bob not bothered by the blood or the cold, because it was his blood as well as the buffalo's, the heads and haunches of each jostling together on the long drive back to Maralal.

It was midafternoon when Bill woke me, and a light rain was falling. I seldom sleep in the daytime, and when I do I have a hard time shaking it off. I couldn't shake off the visions of my dream, either, and before I checked myself and considered how absurd it would sound to those who hadn't been dreaming, I considered suggesting we call off the hunt. If a poet has a place in a land like this or on a flight to the moon, he'd better have a pragmatist along to keep him on course.

Leyteyan and Peringin were told to stay with the truck until they heard shots, and we set off in the now-steady drizzle, hiking the ridges above a sea of thorn trees. Machyana and Bogo Boots had gone off to scout the other side of the plateau. During my unsettling nap we had been joined by an ancient *Mzee* with deep-set wrinkles and white stubble on his chin. The *Mzee* (Swahili for "revered elder"), whom Bill had nicknamed "Bogo Face," was related to Leyteyan–his grandfather, we assumed. Later I was to learn he was Leteyan's father, and since the Samburu don't keep track of years, we speculated that he could have been anywhere between fifty and one hundred years old.

It was a silent march in the rain, and except for the occasionally recurrent images from my dream, I might have forgotten why we were there. We must have been walking for over an hour when Lambat appeared ahead of us, waving his arms and pointing toward the next ridge. He'd spotted a large solitary bull, napping in a clearing about two hundred yards below. We followed him to the ridge, then crept down the slope to a small thorn tree where we could see the bull below us. The forest of thorn trees surrounded him on three sides and he lay in the tall brown grass, occasionally lifting his huge head to sniff the air. The rain had stopped now and there was no wind. Bill watched him through the binoculars, then passed them to Bob. He was a big one, not a spectacular spread to the horns, but clearly more impressive than any bovine creature I had seen before. Bob, Bill, and Lambat would sneak down the ridge to the left and get into a position to shoot from the trees at the edge of the clearing while Otiego, Virginia, the old *Mzee*, and I waited by the thorn tree. We were in plain sight of the bull and would have to remain absolutely still until Bob got off his shot. We watched them until they disappeared below the curve of the hill, then watched the buffalo in silence. He looked so peaceful at this distance, an old bull enjoying the lazy afternoon. I could imagine butterflies fluttering around his head in some Disneyesque fantasy. I was still drowsy, still on the edge of a dream. The old *Mzee* cautiously opened his pouch and pulled out a handful of shiny green leaves. He broke a few off from the bunch and handed them to me. I looked at him, not understanding, and he took the leaves from my hand and put them in my mouth. He gave some to Otiego, and they both began to chew them. He spoke in a low voice to Otiego, and Otiego spoke to me. "If you have a watch to keep," he said, holding a leaf to his lips, "you will never go to sleep." The leaves had a green and bitter taste. They made my mouth feel slightly numb, but soon my drowsiness was gone. Later, I learned that the plant, which grew only in the high country, was called *mira, murungi* locally, and *khat* by the Arabs, and was related to the coca plant of the Andes from which cocaine was extracted.

We sat in silence for forty minutes, watching the bull, cramped but not daring to move. We heard a faint shriek overhead and saw a goshawk swoop low with a small starling in his talons. I raised the binoculars and watched the starling, still flapping its wings, trailing feathers as the goshawk disappeared with it beyond the next ridge. More silence.

It seemed an absurdly long wait. There couldn't have been more than an hour of daylight left when the *bogo* got to its feet. It seemed to sense something. It turned and sniffed toward the trees below us, then lowered its head and began to charge. It couldn't have been more than twenty feet from the trees when we heard the shots, first the sharp crack of Bob's .375, followed immediately by the deeper roar of Bill's .458. Before the shots had faded, the bull was into the trees, and my nightmare was becoming a reality. Trees were thrashing and clattering together, a few of the smaller ones going down in clouds of dust and leaves as if a small twister had touched down and was tearing a path through the forest. Now it was well past where Bob, Bill, and Lambat would have been, and we sat, horrified, looking down at the storm, listening for human voices, wondering where their paths might have crossed, and then it all stopped. The trees swayed more gently, then stilled. The dust drifted skyward and dissolved in the air like a ghost. But whose? Otiego looked at me, and I looked at Virginia. The old *Mzee* stared impassively down at the trees. And then, as if a signal had been given, we were all scrambling down the slope, heels skidding over sand and rocks, which broke loose and raced us to the bottom.

We stopped at the edge of the trees and looked up. Bob was standing on an outcropping above and to our left, Lambat and Bill coming up behind him.

"We thought you were dead." I got the words out between gasps for breath.

"Very kind of you," Bill said, being British, "but I think old Bob here nailed 'im cold." We heard another clattering sound, and a bull broke from cover, charged across the clearing, and disappeared into the trees on the other side. I looked back up at Bill for an explanation.

"That must be another one." He shrugged his shoulders. Now we could see that there had been a ravine separating them from the bull, and the holocaust we had witnessed had been the bull charging and falling down the densely forested slope, taking trees with him, as we had brought rocks and sand with us in our panic.

We made our way slowly down the path the *bogo* had cleared for us, a river of loose sand and uprooted saplings, through brush and thorn trees, down the steep slope, and found him, dead, at the edge of a precipice. One horn, hooked into the earth, was all that had kept him from going over, but he was still perilously close to the edge. The old *Mzee* mumbled a few words of Swahili and shook his head. "Too bad," he said, "if we try to butcher him we will all go over the edge."

"We can tie him with a rope," Bill said.

But the *Mzee* shook his head again. "No rope will hold a bull that big."

"But we have magic," Bill said.

"What magic?"

"It's called nylon."

When the rope was laced four times between the buffalo's haunches and the base of a tree he had spared in his crash toward the valley, the *Mzee* sat on his flank, patted him tenderly beside the tail, squeezed the last dung from his anus, and smiled. "White man's magic is very strong." He laughed and twanged the taut strands with his fingers. "When I was young, we would hunt *bogo* with spears. But it was very hard, and the rifle is much better. We will eat well tonight."

Machyana and Bogo Boots had come at the sound of the shots, and soon Leyteyan and Peringin joined us. Lambat and Otiego began to butcher the bull while Bob, Virginia, and I carried the rifles and gear back up the steep slope to the clearing. We were exhausted and relieved. We sat on rocks in the tall grass, broke open a flask of Jack Daniels, and compared perspectives on what had happened. We watched as pieces of the bull were brought up the grade, Lambat bent low under the head and cape, Leyteyan and Peringin carrying a leg. We left the old *Mzee* below, where he would spend the night feeding on the carcass, which was too heavy and cumbersome to be brought up the perilous slope. Leyteyan and Peringin were fighting over the bone marrow in the leg they had laid claim to, as American children would fight over candy, and it was well after dark before we started the long trip back to camp. We kept the head, tail, and tongue, dropped two haunches at the *manyata* of Machyana's brother and one with Bogo Boots at the village where he had joined us that morning. The man who had been dragged off by the lion was quiet now. No one holds grudges when there's fresh meat to be shared.

On the drive back to Nibor Kedju I enjoyed the warmth of the cab and shivered in comfort, thinking of Bob, riding in back, very much alive in the blood smell and the cold of the high plains night.

Thanksgiving on the
Fourth of July

FOURTH-OF-JULY heat, but not as I am used to it. This is hotter, windless, unearthly, with no trace of the Midwestern humidity that wilts picnics and in which a cold drink will slip from your hand in its own sweat. This is the heat of another planet, closer to the sun, and those distant mountains, if they actually exist, were constructed solely for ambush. Far ahead, just approaching the next ridge, I can see the dust train of the other truck and guide on it. The road is barely visible, the ground rock strewn and baked, impervious to tracks. This is the Kaisut Desert, so the map says. The name is exotic enough to conjure visions of a caravan but the landscape is more like the moon, and I curse it with each jolt of the Toyota. My head aches from the heat and vibration, and I know that Lake Rudolph will be even hotter, the earth a black bed of hardened lava. I glance across the cab at Virginia. She is dozing off, and I'm irritated that she isn't staying awake to suffer with me. I glance in the mirror and see Lambat, the Wanderobo gun bearer, impassive, rocking easily with the motion of the truck. If he feels any irritation I'm sure it's over my driving, feeling he should be driving instead. At several stops I had asked him to join us in the cab, but he had refused, preferring to sulk in the shadeless box behind us.

Now the other truck has dropped from sight, leaving its dust cloud in the motionless air above the ridge like a smoke signal on which to navigate. I have purposely kept a mile back so that we won't have to breathe their dust, though I can feel a fine layer on my skin, and the windshield is coated. If we don't appear within a reasonable time, Bill, who is driving the lead truck, will stop and wait until he spots us. We are carrying the gasoline and he, my friend Bob Jones, Otiego, the Turkana, who is Bill's other regular gun bearer, and Red Blanket are carrying the water. Red Blanket is a Samburu, we think, though he doesn't wear the traditional beaded ornamentation or braided long hair of the tribe, but rather a modified Afro, the first I have seen here, and a simple red blanket wrapped around his waist. He appeared while we were hunting plains game in Maralal, simply joined us and assisted in the tracking and skinning, and with the maintenance of the camp.

We are traveling through the country of the Rendili, a tribe similar in culture to the Samburu, but more remote and with a separate language, and Red Blanket asked to come along. He claimed that, unlike the rest of us, he could speak Rendili. That is his ticket, and he will soon be called upon to validate it.

We are going to Lake Rudolph, ostensibly to fish for Nile perch, and I have brought my fly rod along to see if I can take a tilapia on a streamer, which, as far as I know, has never been done. But the deeper reason is just to be there, to see and to suffer in the least hospitable spot on Earth, where rainfall is more rare than snow in north Florida.

I wonder about Red Blanket. I suppose that leopards, though always in proximity, are seldom seen even by Samburu. Early that morning when I had spotted a cheetah with two cubs near the road and had jumped from the truck to pursue them through the scrub with my camera, Red Blanket began hollering frantically, "No, no, *Bwana, chui* (Swahili for leopard), *chui naguisha, chui.*" I looked back at Bill and he waved me on, indicating it was perfectly safe. Then, a hundred yards further in the brush, I came into an open spot where the cheetah and her cubs had stopped and stood looking at me. I stood for a moment, so stunned by their beauty and apparent lack of fear that I forgot to use my camera. They were clearly cheetahs, high-haunched, rangy, and traveling this plain in daylight as no leopard would likely be. They stood sideways to me for several seconds, then turned and trotted into the brush as if they had stopped a moment simply to show me they weren't afraid. My hands rose dumbly to where my camera hung from its strap, then just as dumbly raised it and took a photograph of the vacant space in which they had stood. When I got back to the trucks Bill was waving his arms, arguing with Red Blanket, incredulous that he could have mistaken the cheetah for a leopard. But Red Blanket refused to be convinced, even by the fact that I had returned alive, which would have been unlikely if it had been a leopard. Finally Bill simply threw up his hands and told Red Blanket to get back in the truck. "Old Red Blanket says you are a very lucky fool," he said, turning to wink at me. "Or maybe a ghost," Bob added. And the way Red Blanket was staring at me, I was inclined to favor Bob's interpretation.

Beyond the ridge, we drop down into a low country of dry washes, thorn trees, and lifeless acacias. Several times I have to stop and drop the Toyota into low to climb what appear to have been, in some more pluvial era, the steep banks of a river. The engine sputters, stalls, then catches again, grinds almost to the top of the bank and dies. I hold us with the brake, ease the transmission out of gear and let us roll gently back down into the wash. I turn the starter several times in vain until Lambat, who knows we have run out of fuel and knows also that he had forgotten to fill the tank that morning, jumps out and draws his finger across his throat, signaling me to stop. He is angry with himself, angry with me, and angry with Bill, whom he knows will be angry with him. But now there's nothing to do but wait until they discover that we are no longer following them and return to rescue us.

What we gain in the ease of not being jolted over ruts and rocks, we lose in the withering stillness of the air around us. The full weight of the heat comes down, as if the sun were trying to compress us into the sand beneath our feet. Lambat squats on his haunches beside the truck, accepting more readily than I that there's nothing to do but breathe what air we can find and wait. We have the gasoline, but in two seventy-gallon drums, and they have the pump. At moments like this you begin to question the concern of your closest friends. I know they will have to return, because they don't have enough gasoline to reach Lake Rudolph without us, and we don't have enough water to survive long without them. In fact, we haven't any. Then I remember why we're traveling in two trucks rather than all together in one. I remember the water in the radiator but decide I'm not that thirsty. I hear the clumsy flapping of wings and notice, not fifty feet from us, in the vestige of an acacia, a dozen or more vultures. I wonder what they could possibly find to feed on in this wasteland. The flies are beginning to bother us. I look at Virginia, still nodding with sleep, waving them away from her face, and the answer becomes obvious.

Soon we heard the whine of the other truck coming back. It seemed to take an absurdly long time to reach us, and I couldn't determine whether it was because sound carried so far in the desert or because any wait would seem too long in this heat. Bill simply shook his head while Lambat got the pump and began transferring gasoline from one of the drums to the tank of our truck. "I swear, *Bwana*," he said, still shaking his head, "there's a cultural gap here I just cannot bridge. Lambat doesn't worry about anything, and I worry about everything. I can't say that he's wrong and I'm right, mind you. His attitude's probably healthier." He sighed deeply. "It's just so bloody different."

An hour later we stopped in a dry riverbed for lunch. We pulled the trucks into the meager shade of trees that appeared to be dead, lining the bank of this now-dead river. We needed the rest and refreshment, but this lunch was also to be a celebration—three Africans, three Americans, and a Brit celebrating the Fourth of July, celebrating independence, which, it occurred to me, was probably the real reason we were here. To live for a month depending on ourselves and independent of what we knew as civilization, but not totally independent. There was a large ice chest in Bill's truck which contained not only ice, beer, and the buffalo tongue from which we would make our lunch, but also, for this occasion, a bottle of champagne. It was totally absurd, seven sweating, dust-coated travelers drinking champagne from plastic cups in one of the most God-forsaken settings on Earth. Bill proposed a toast to our having made it half way to Lake Rudolph, and we had barely finished drinking to it when I heard Bill say, "Oh, oh, we've got company, *Bwana*. Now we'll see if Red Blanket really can speak Rendili."

Walking toward us, down either side of the riverbed, were ten Rendili warriors. As they approached, I could see that they resembled Samburu, with the same leaf-bladed spears, but their hair was short, not braided and colored with red clay, and they wore fewer beads and had a leaner, harder, more austere look about them. I was amazed that they looked as fit as they did, that they could even survive in this seemingly lifeless landscape. Bill had explained that this district was so remote that the Rendili saw few people from beyond it and therefore had little occasion to speak Swahili, that they weren't known to be hostile to intruders, but that they were so primitive, so totally innocent of the twentieth century that they knew nothing of white men's laws against killing and stealing outside the tribe. When he had been a colonial policeman, a decade earlier, Bill had had little difficulty finding lawbreakers, because, in their innocence, they took no precautions to cover their tracks. "Just be calm," Bill said, "as if we were expecting them."

The Rendili approached us from either side, their spears sheathed and pointing toward the sky. The tallest of them spoke. Bill looked at Red Blanket. Red Blanket looked at Bill, a look that was all we needed to tell us that he understood no more Rendili than we did. Then their apparent leader spoke again. "Magi," Swahili for water, and, "tombaco." Red Blanket spoke Swahili to Bill, telling him that these men wanted water and tobacco. "Brilliant," Bill grimaced, "I'd have never guessed." Red Blanket busied himself inspecting a tire while Bill passed a jug of water and parceled out handfuls of tobacco from the nearly empty bag we carried for this kind of occasion. Rather than the Fourth of July, this celebration was beginning to resemble the first Thanksgiving. The Rendili, flanking us on either side of the space between the two trucks, seemed happy, and we were happy that they were happy. The champagne had gotten warm during the tobacco passing, so we put ice in our cups and Bill poured another round for all but Bob, who had taken a bottle of Kenyan beer called "Tusker" from the ice chest. We toasted our guests, but they seemed unmoved by it. They passed the water jug and began chewing the tobacco.

I had eaten half my buffalo-tongue sandwich when I glanced back down the riverbed and saw the scene repeating itself. Rendili, again approaching on either side, but this time there were more, perhaps twenty. They joined their tribesmen and made it known that they, too, wanted water and "tombaco." Bill smiled at me as he spoke, "We've got a problem, *Bwana*," he said, sustaining his smile like a ventriloquist's dummy.

"What's that?" I could already feel my pulse rate tracking Bill's as I glanced at the unsmiling faces beyond his shoulder.

"They want water and tobacco, too."

"Well?" It hadn't come as a surprise

"Well, we don't have any more tobacco," he said, still smiling.

"Oh!" I had a momentary vision of how our bones might look among the tireless trucks and empty cups of our last Fourth of July. Bill raised the empty tobacco sack and showed it to the tall one who had first spoken to us. He turned and spoke to the men next to him, and the unintelligible conversation spread around us, becoming rapid and excited. Lambat, Otiego, and Red Blanket looked as ill-at-ease as I felt. We all kept our eyes on what we were eating, either to pretend the Rendili weren't there or because we were afraid that eye contact might provoke them.

"Take my picture, *Bwana*," Bill said.

"What?" I couldn't believe he could think of commemorating this moment we were all so uncertain of surviving.

"Pretend you're taking my picture so you can look behind me and tell me what you see."

"Okay." I raised my camera to my eye, hoping our guests knew that a camera was not a weapon, and focused beyond Bill's left shoulder. My worst fears were confirmed. In the frame of the eyepiece I could see spears being unsheathed and shaken as if they were beginning some ritual hunting dance.

"They're unsheathing their," I swallowed, "their spears."

"I know," Bill said, giving me his Hollywood smile again. "I peeked."

"What do we do?" I asked, as if he would have a formula for handling this kind of a situation.

"Keep smiling," he said, "pretend you're having a good time, but get Miss Ginny into the cab and lock the doors. The seven-millimeter is under the canvas in the truck to your right. Ease over and get your hand on it, because I have no idea what's going to happen."

I got Virginia locked in and stood leaning against the fender of our Toyota. The distance to where the rifle lay seemed enormous. On Bill's instructions, Bob was edging toward the twelve-gauge, and Bill, his back to me, was speaking quietly to the gun bearers. Most of the Rendili were still grumbling and shaking their spears, but the tall one stood rather calmly, about ten feet from me, in front of the truck. I had a feeling I had this all confused with some movie I'd seen. There I was, on the Fourth of July, in an alien landscape, a glass of champagne in my hand, trying to seem jovial while expecting to be skewered at any moment for the lack of a few handfuls of tobacco. I wondered if there wasn't some way they could be convinced to take an I.O.U. The idea of a shoot-out seemed so final. I swallowed the rest of the champagne as a gesture to cover my nervousness, and the ice cubes rattled against my mustache. The tall one stood watching me, with no trace of either malice or friendship in his expression. Then I did something I can't explain. Maybe it was just out of fear. Maybe it was an attempt at appeasement. I don't know. But there were these ice cubes in the cup in my hand. I picked one out with my fingers and offered it to him. Suddenly all his men were silent, watching him take whatever it was I held in my hand. He held it between his fingers for no more than a second, then screamed, dropped it in the sand and took several steps backward, as if he'd been burned.

Now there was fear and confusion on his face. The voices rose again, and I knew I'd made a mistake. One by one the tribesmen darted to where the ice cube lay melting in the sand. They half snuck up on it, as if it were a firecracker that had failed to explode, touched it, screamed, and jumped back, convinced it was a new kind of fire. The tall one no longer seemed amused. He had composed himself and stood staring at me while I fished another ice cube from the cup and put it in my mouth. His jaw dropped and his eyes grew wide with amazement. His men stopped darting in to touch the ice and stood staring at me, apparently convinced I was eating fire. What had begun in fear now seemed to have become an illusion of power. Here was a man with the courage to suck ice cubes.

I fished another ice cube from the cup and held it up to the tall one's mouth. Now I could see that he was nervous. He was being challenged, and his men gathered around us to see if he would take the fire in his mouth. I could feel my heart pounding as he opened his lips and accepted the ice cube. He stared at me for over a second, two seconds, three. His men waited and watched. No one was breathing anywhere in the world. Then he began to break. With his mouth still closed, a smile emanated from his jaw and spread slowly to his eyes, grew broad, and broke into laughter. His men began to laugh. I looked around and we were all laughing as the tension dissolved into convulsions of nervous relief. The magic of ice had eclipsed the desire for tobacco, and the Rendilis all wanted to try it. We gave each of them an ice cube, which they held in their mouths while they laughed and leaped with excitement. Now it was a real celebration. The spears lay on the ground, and those of us from the twentieth century drank a toast to ice.

I became interested in photographs again. I'm not sure if the Rendili were familiar with cameras, but they seemed happy to pose for us. One of them picked up Bob's bottle of Tusker from the fender of the other truck and took a mouthful of beer while several others watched. His face contorted with an expression that reminded me of my six-year-old daughter the first and last time she tried a raw oyster. He spat the beer on the ground and began shouting, "*umbuya, umbuya*"–bad, bad. He looked at the picture of the elephant on the label and began shouting and gesturing to his friends, pointing to the elephant, and I didn't need Red Blanket to tell me that he was convinced that the crazy *Muzungu* had a taste for elephant piss.

The celebration had just peaked when Bill suggested we pack up and get out before their thoughts returned to tobacco. We left a large container of ice, all we had, happy to sacrifice it. We still had a long drive to Lake Rudolph, though the heat didn't seem nearly so oppressive as the last acacias along the riverbed disappeared behind us.

Along the Uaso Nyiro

SOMEWHERE IN *Seven Pillars of Wisdom*, T. E. Lawrence refers to that most brutal and unforgiving part of the desert, "The Anvil of the Sun." The earth is baked hard and fissured like the skin on the back of my hand, absolutely flat in all directions. There is no point of reference but this two-track groove we are following across the Chalbi Desert, the shortest distance between Lake Rudolph and Rendille Wells. In mirage, shimmering above the horizon, mountains appear, shift, and reappear as if the demonic illusionist of this land were trying to lure us off course with a specious promise of shelter from this heat. For almost half an hour we've been watching the improbable silhouette of a double-decker London bus wavering in the distance ahead. Night winds have obliterated all traces of tire tracks, and it's evident that we're the first vehicle to make this crossing in several days. We regard the London bus with the same jaundiced eyes that see mountains where the map and Bill's familiarity with this country tell us no mountains exist.

Our destination is an actual mountain called Marsabit, but it's still a hundred miles distant, and I wonder if our constant diet of Nile perch has caused a hallucinatory chemical imbalance in our sensory tracts. We've been out for nearly a month, living almost entirely on what we can catch or shoot. Normally I love perch, but three days ago, trolling from a decrepit motor launch on Lake Rudolph, I caught one that weighed 126 pounds, and it's what we've lived on, morning, night, and noon. It wasn't even a memorable fight. The fish gave one good run and then died, but in that heat, I was grateful for his lethargy.

Lake Rudolph is not a place one visits for pleasure. I believe *Mungu* (Swahili for God) designed it to demonstrate to man the kind of beauty he might expect to find on Mercury. Its brackish water is surrounded by miles of craters and volcanic ash in which nothing flourishes but snakes and the Turkana, a tribe of massively built goat herders and fishermen who live as proof that life on any terms is possible. The sun rises and sets at six o'clock every day of the year, the daily temperature is a dependable 120 degrees Fahrenheit, and the only thing that allows for sleep is an eighty mile-per-hour wind that rises at midnight and blows until four every morning. The lake also has the world's largest concentration of crocodiles, which, along with the slimy water, discourage recreational bathing. But on the southeastern shore, at Loingalani, there are springs, an oasis, and a hotel of sorts. A few years ago, the "hotel" was attacked by Shifta raiders who murdered Guy Poole, the innkeeper, and his only guest at the time, a Catholic priest. The Shifta are Muslims from Somalia who believe this northern frontier of Kenya is rightfully theirs. I wonder what a Shifta looks like, and if I would recognize one before he tried to kill me.

The London bus is growing taller, though it's gotten no closer, or so it seems. We are traveling in two Toyota pickups, for reasons of safety as well as supply. Virginia, Bill Winter, and I in the lead truck, Bob Jones, Lambat, Otiego, and Red Blanket, whom Lambat and Otiego call simply "that man," following. If we only had this one truck, I wonder aloud, how would we deal with a breakdown on this seldom-traveled way? "Well, *Bwana*," Bill begins cheerfully. He's had twenty years experience in this country and delights in such hypothetical questions. "That's easy. We'd crawl under the truck to keep out of the sun. We'd drink our water, then we'd drain the radiator and drink that, and then. . . ." He pauses, as if pondering the next step, and I should realize he is baiting me.

"And then?"

"And then we'd die"

"Oh."

"Of course there's always the odd chance someone might happen by to rescue us."

My confidence is inspired, and while I'm ruminating on the apparent simplicity of it, I have a feeling that something dramatic is about to happen. Bill and Virginia are intent on the London bus, and as I turn my gaze back to it, it suddenly transforms into an olive drab Land Rover that rockets out of the mirage like a flaming arrow from a 3-D movie. We pull to a stop and regard it suspiciously for a moment. It's a fairly ordinary Land Rover, but in this waste, anything that moves is a curiosity.

"Major Rodney Elliott," Bill announces, and the man who steps from behind the wheel is almost a caricature of that name. "Check the Empire Builders." Bill grins, referring to the major's baggy shorts, twenty-three inches around the thigh and three inches above the knee, which could serve as a reasonable surrogate for the Union Jack. Four uniformed game scouts pile out of the Land Rover and stand at ease while Rodney and Bill greet each other in a reserved, British sort of way. Any chance meeting in the desert (except with Shifta, of course) is cause for a celebration, and especially among old friends. Bill and Rodney had served together through "The Mau Mau Emergency" in the Colonial Police and in the Game Department. We break out warm Cokes and the Major tells us that he and his men are searching for a young American scientist, an assistant of Richard Leakey's, who, while searching for the origins of mankind, wandered a few hundred feet from his camp to commune with the desert and got lost. According to historical accounts from the time of Teleki, no man has survived in this country unprotected from the sun and from thirst for more than twenty-four hours, but later we are to learn that this American was found, barely alive, after three days. He was young and kept his head, traveling only at night. The last night he crawled less than a hundred feet, and was found by a trail of photographs he was known to have been carrying. He died after several days in a Nairobi hospital.

Rodney and Bill exchange a few hunting stories, the way two salesmen traveling the same territory might compare notes on bars and waitresses, and Rodney tells us of a young friend, out plinking with a .22, who was treed by a rhinoceros. Then, as abruptly as we met, we shake hands, climb back into our trucks, and become dust clouds again.

BY EARLY AFTERNOON, the desert has turned to salt, and it reminds me of an enormous Michigan hayfield after the first light November snowfall. We pass through the oasis at Rendille Wells and see several Borana camel trains. It's difficult for me to realize that this is the real thing and not just a collection of extras for *The Adventures of Haji Baba.*

If Rendille Wells seemed an illusion, however, Marsabit is as incongruous as the Matterhorn at Disneyland, one cone-shaped mountain completely surrounded by some of the bleakest desert country in the world, an extinct volcano, heavily forested with moss-hung cypress. The air is cool, and it's raining as we climb to the perfectly circular crater lake at its summit. I pull on my jacket against the chill, and several times we must stop to wait as elephants cross the road ahead of us.

After a comfortable night in a government game lodge built into the mountainside, we get an early start for our next camp at EDB (Elephant Dung Beach) on the Uaso Nyiro River, where Bill's camp crew is waiting for us. It's another long, hot drive, though this desert, the Kaisut, is broken by arid mountains. I find myself trying to sort out the past few days in terms of sequential time, but there is no time in this country, only the clustered memory of events: fly-fishing for tilapia and tigerfish while balancing on the rocks of the Lake Rudolph shore, where Virginia was almost bitten by a sand viper; Lambat pulling her back and nailing the snake with a rock; the perfect red enormity of the sun setting across the thirteen-mile width of the lake; the flamingos and the crocodiles (called *mambas* in Swahili); the bull elephant who surprised us by the edge of Marsabit's crater lake, forcing us to hide in a cluster of rocks; and, most vividly, the interminably shimmering London bus. Yet on this day's drive, what we notice and what most disturbs us is the emptiness of the land. In this country—which at times reminds me of Arizona—gazelle, impala, ostrich, even giraffe and lion are fairly common sights, and it's unusual to drive for more than ten miles without seeing Samburu or Borana herdsmen with their cattle or a lone *moran* (young warrior) with his throwing spears and *fimbo nyusi* (black stick). Today all are conspicuous by their absence. Bill mentions it first, and as the day wears on we find ourselves looking for some sign that we are still on Earth. This emptiness becomes eerie, and we grow silent. We stop for lunch and speak of nothing but the quietness. I can see the uneasiness in the faces of Lambat, Otiego, and Red Blanket, who know this country well. They keep looking and listening, and never seem to relax. Since this is my first time in this part of Kenya's Northern Frontier country, I probably wouldn't have noticed anything unusual, but Bob, Virginia, and I are now cuing our expectations from the faces of our more experienced companions. Bill does his best to maintain his facade of good cheer, and two hours later we are relieved to find the rest of Bill's men by the river and our camp ready and waiting.

Before we can see the Uaso Nyiro itself we are startled by the continuous stretch of doum palms and the strip of verdure that flourishes several hundred feet deep on either bank. As soon as we are in camp we have an explanation for the bareness of the country we've just come through. Ganya, an old sergeant of Bill's from his game department days, tells us that he's heard reports of three hundred armed Shifta raiders in the region. He's seen a former colleague of Bill's, a district policeman, who has told him that five miners and three road workers have been killed within the last week and that he's had reports that a giraffe has been poached somewhere in the vicinity of our camp.

I wonder why we are staying here if there are Shifta about but I don't voice it, not wanting to be the first to admit the apprehension we're all feeling and figuring Bill knows his business and has our welfare at heart. Besides, it may just be rumors. Maybe Bill is used to stories about the Shifta. I reassure Virginia, who is asking the questions Bob and I have suppressed.

My apprehensions are compounded an hour later, when, having settled into camp, we set off just before dark looking for *bogo* (Cape buffalo) along the river. Not more than fifty yards from our campsite we discover the butchered remains of a giraffe, the skin, entrails, and a few large bones, the still-warm ashes of a campfire, and several fragments of an army shirt soaked in gun oil. "Well, someone has poached a giraffe," Bill sighs. He doesn't seem at all startled, merely philosophical, and I remind myself that this man has been through three wars and countless skirmishes with murderers and cattle thieves. And what he says is true; all we really know is that someone has poached a giraffe. But I can't restrain my question. "What are we going to do?"

Bill shrugs his shoulders as if there are really no alternatives. "Hunt *bogo*," he says, and we head into the thickets along the river. Just at dusk, Bob gets a clear shot at a big bull on the opposite bank and drops him cleanly. At least the buffalo haven't been driven from the river by the reputed Shifta menace, and I can't quite believe that Bill would be so nonchalant if we were in any imminent danger. At dinner, I broach the subject circuitously by asking what one should do if taken prisoner by the Shifta.

"Learn to pray," Bill quips.

"Oh, of course." I'm becoming irritated by his refusal to deal seriously with what I consider to be a serious situation.

"No, I'm quite serious, *Bwana*." He pours coffee for us and tells us of a friend, a district police officer, who, with his men, was ambushed by the Shifta. They killed all his men and took him, as a prisoner, back to Somalia. Now it happened that this policeman was also a student of Middle Eastern religions, and he had the inspiration to bow toward Mecca and to pray to Allah. This behavior apparently convinced the Shifta that he might not be an infidel. At least it confused them sufficiently so that they were wary of killing one who might be a fellow true believer, and they let him go.

"Can you give us a quick course?" I ask.

"Not I," says Bill. "But I can give you a twelve-gauge to sleep with, if it will make you more comfortable."

"Why are we staying here, if the Shifta are threatening us?" Finally

I care less about losing face than about being made into trinkets and sold in some Somalian bazaar.

"It's a big country, *Bwana*. There's always danger of some sort. The Shifta are out there somewhere, but the chances are slim they'll bother us. Besides, we can't do anything about them tonight. Tomorrow we've got to register at the police outpost at Merti, and we'll see what they know."

ON THE DRIVE to Merti I am riding in the back of the truck with Lambat and Otiego. They are giving me another language lesson, pointing at whatever we pass and repeating the Swahili name for it. "*Kume, kushoto.*" Otiego gestures with his right hand, "*Kume,*" then with this left, "*kushoto.*" I imitate his gestures, "*Kume, kushoto, right, left.*"

"*Ndiyo, yes.*" He nods gleefully. He seems delighted to have found a *Muzungu* capable of learning something. He points to a large rock. "*Mwamba, mwamba.*" But the truck is slowing, and before I can respond, it lurches to a stop. We hear Bill and Bob step out of the cab, and stand up to see them walking toward the torn and burned out wreckage of what was once a truck. I jump to the ground to join them. It looks as if the truck has exploded, and I can't imagine what kind of collision could have caused such devastating results on this seldom traveled road. "Mine," Bill says.

"Mine?" I ask. Bob and I look at each other, unsure or unwilling to be sure of what we've heard.

"Mine," Bill repeats. "A favorite weapon of the Shifta." I can see that Bob is startled, and I'm sure he's reading the same reaction in my blank stare. Somehow I had imagined Shifta armed with spears and ancient muzzle-loaders, but now Bill is telling us they plant mines and carry machine guns, automatic rifles, and grenades. I realize I've been harboring images from movies about the Zulu wars and feel a little silly in my assumptions. Modern weapons are available to every other kind of terrorist and guerilla raider. Why wouldn't the Shifta have them? The remainder of the drive to Merti passes in an uneasy and watchful silence, and I notice Bill is driving more slowly now. We pass the wreckage of another truck. Lambat and Otiego only glance at it. Lambat is leaning over the roof of the cab, watching the road, and Otiego seems quite relaxed, scanning the desert as we pass.

At first, Merti looks like a movie set from *Casablanca*. The mission church is a white building with Moorish arches, and we manage a little comic relief from the large red letters spelling *Castlegondolfo*, the name of the pope's summer residence, displayed across its facade. The police barracks are a large rectangular compound of barbed wire, protected by machine guns with trumpetlike flash suppressors on towers at each corner and surrounding several ancient wooden buildings which look like relics of a C.C.C. camp. I can smell something familiar in the air, something strong and sweet that reminds me of America. Marijuana. Otiego notices me sniffing the air and smiles knowingly.

"*Nan na gani?*" I ask rhetorically.

"What *is* that?" Lambat asks, quite clearly in English.

"*Bhangi?*" I use the Swahili word for hemp.

"*Bhangi?*" Lambat stretches his neck in my direction with an incredulous smirk.

"Oh, I've tried it," I admit.

"I smoke *bhangi*," Otiego laughs.

Lambat hunches his shoulders and holds up his thumb and forefinger, indicating one inch. "I smoke *bhangi*, that much once, and it make me crazy." His voice is high, straining for emphasis in the back of his throat.

We enter the police compound to register, and the sergeant who greets us is noncommittal when Bill asks him what he knows of the Shifta. "Oh, Shifta, very bad." He shakes his head and affects a dour expression.

"But what do you know of their presence in this district?" Bill asks again.

"We do not like them." The sergeant wags his head almost a full ninety degrees. "Very bad, Shifta. We do not like them here." It's obvious we aren't going to learn anything from the sergeant, but it's also quite clear we have no disagreement about the Shifta.

The town of Merti resembles an Old West ghost town, several rows of shacks with overhanging front porches. We stop in one, which turns out to be a *duka*, or bar, with a dirt floor and several makeshift shelves constructed of scrap lumber, on which are displayed a dozen or so dusty bottles of Tusker, the Kenyan national beer. Bob buys a carton of cigarettes and we share several bottles of the warm Tusker. A Borana boy has made an ingenious toy car from scrap lumber and several old pieces of wire. It has a twelve-inch wheel base and a steering column about four feet long with a wire steering wheel so that he can walk along behind it and steer the front wheels. Lambat takes over the controls and drives the toy up and down the hard clay street with childlike glee.

It's close to dusk when we start the seventy-mile drive back to camp, and we drive slowly, watching the surface of the road in the headlights and the brilliant stars of unfamiliar constellations. Suddenly Otiego begins banging on the roof of the cab, his signal for Bill to stop the truck. At first I think he's spotted a mine, but he points with his stick, motioning for Bill to pull to the shoulder and to direct the headlights toward a clump of thornbushes. Otiego jumps down and points to a small creature perched wide-eyed in the glare of the lights. "Is that what you people call a bush baby?" he asks.

"No," Bill laughs. "That's what we call an owl."

IT'S WELL PAST dark when we get back to camp, and in the eerie light of the campfire, or what at least this night seems eerie, Ganya tells us that four Shifta, out hunting with their dogs, stumbled into camp, apparently by accident, and exchanged a few shots with the camp crew as they fled. Bill takes the news matter-of-factly, asks if anyone was wounded (no one was), and remarks that at least they now know we're armed. He seems to take satisfaction in that. We have a light supper of buffalo-tail soup and buffalo-tongue sandwiches. Wichira, the ancient fire tender, tells us that most of the buffalo meat has been given to local tribesmen and that the camp crew has feasted on the rest.

Bill retires early, leaving Bob, Virginia, and me to finish our coffee by the campfire. Though we've had a tiring day, no one is eager to go to bed for the sleep we know will be hard in coming. In the daylight in this vast, arid country, we seldom think of the Shifta or of any danger not immediately before us. Hearing buffalo snort in the thicket, as we had the previous evening, or hearing the thunder of their hooves, our attention becomes riveted to what we are doing. The Cape buffalo is, with the possible exception of the crocodile for the unwary, and the Shifta, of course, the most dangerous and unpredictable of African animals. But danger, of any kind, when it's confronting you at the moment, demands concentration, and while it may cause your pulse to accelerate and the adrenaline to flow, that concentration leaves little mind for fear. Our days have been like that, full of intrigue, demanding concentration, and any hazard encountered is dealt with or evaded and not dwelled on. But nights like this make demands only on the imagination, or rather on one's ability to suspend or control it. Everything closes in to the circle of light around the fire, and the unseen world beyond, filled with unfamiliar sounds, is made fuller by an idle mind.

This Shifta threat is a temporary condition for us, a matter of a few days which we'll leave behind and later regard, as I am now in the telling of it, as an adjunct of an adventure. I muse that this must have been the daily experience of settlers on the western plains of America 150 years ago, simply another condition of life, knowing there were hostile Indians about, not letting it disrupt their lives more than the threat of floods, tornados, or corn blight, living daily, and nightly, with the knowledge of their presence. We discuss our situation and agree that the danger is real, but we also agree, at least philosophically, that Bill knows this country as well or better than any other white man and must believe our chances of being attacked are pretty slim. Intellectually we've sorted it out, but our speech is strained and the sound of crocodiles splashing in the river and of lions roaring not forty feet beyond the fire (we confirm this distance by their tracks in the morning) do little to settle our stomachs. Just before we go to our tents, we watch a tiny red scorpion struggling through the white ashes at the edge of the fire.

Virginia and I pull our cots close together. I've taken Bill up on his offer of a loaded twelve-gauge, and it's nestled between us in the space that, when at home in Michigan, would normally be occupied by our Labrador retriever. I know it won't discourage three hundred Shifta, or even three, but the idea of it is more reassuring than having my shoes ready to throw.

We hear the lions again and, oddly enough, it's a comforting sound, like having huge watch dogs prowling outside our tent, knowing any man, even a Shifta, would be foolish to roam there.

IN THE MORNING, on our way to *Maji Moto* (hot springs) to hunt sand grouse, we discover the skeleton of an elephant, apparently killed by poachers, who have stripped it of its tusks and left the rest to the vultures and the hyenas and to rot. Scenes like this were fairly common before Kenya's total ban on the sale or exportation of animal products. In *Serengeti Shall Not Die,* Bernhard Grzimek tells of finding scores of wildebeest and zebra in a single clearing, strangled or strangling in wire garrote traps set by poachers who took only the tails and left more carrion than the scavengers could eat. I walk among the bones of the elephant as if among the ruins of a miniature city, and Bill tells us he's afraid that, except perhaps in a few restricted game parks, the elephant is doomed. Modern medicine has increased the longevity of Kenyans, and the population is expanding dramatically. Consequently, much more land is needed for agriculture, and agriculture and elephants are not compatible. My immediate impulse is to say, "Well then, screw agriculture," but in a week I'll be flying back to the United States, from which it's easy to look back at Kenya as the world's zookeeper. And I know that if faced with the choice of killing elephants or seeing my family starve, my sympathy for elephants would be severely eroded.

At the hot springs there are literally millions of sand grouse. They swarm in each morning like locusts, turning the sky black as they pass. It seems it would be impossible to miss them, but Bob and I find that they are almost impossible to hit, at least the way we begin going about it, blasting at whole flocks in our excitement and confusion. The birds are borne on a stiff morning breeze and pass us from acute angles at nearly sixty miles per hour. Only when we've settled down and begun taking aim—with a considerable lead—on individual birds do we have any success, and still our average is no better than fifty percent. When we have enough for dinner, we collect them and head back to the river. It's our last day before returning to Bill's home at Nanyuki, near Mt. Kenya, and I want to spend the afternoon just relaxing and climbing in the rocks above camp.

In the beauty of the afternoon, looking down on the doum palms and the desert country, Shifta seems only a word, a vague remnant from last night's dream. In three days we'll be in heavy traffic in Nairobi, and four days from now, in New York, which doesn't even seem like part of the same planet. I know that tonight I'll have to battle my imagination again, but I remember nights at home made sleepless by an attack of unexplained noises in the house. We watch the setting sun reflected off the muddy water of the river winding below us, and I feel certain that if I were told I could not go home again, I'd simply shrug and say, "Oh." But the next morning as we finish packing the trucks, I find my appetite rushing ahead to a large serving of fettuccine Alfredo at Lavorini's in Nairobi, to a chocolate milkshake at my local drive-in, to movies, to water in which one can swim without fear of infestation or being eaten, to football on TV. And I don't feel the slightest remorse about abandoning this land to the Shifta, though now that we're packing up to leave it all behind, I find it easy to be cavalier.

But there's one more incident to be recounted, a simple reminder that the idea of security is always an illusion. About ten miles down the two-track by which we'd come into this country, the truck skids to a halt. I'm thrown against the rear of the cab, not injured, but jolted from my smug sense of place. I pull myself up off the floor and see Bill crouching in the road about twenty feet ahead of the truck. I jump down and join him. "They must've heard us coming and been scared off," he muses.

"What?" I haven't quite recovered from my reverie and am still slightly dazed by this interruption.

"This." Bill points to a freshly scooped-out hole in the road, a foot and a half across and maybe a foot deep.

I don't have to be told what it might be for. "Mine?" Bill nods. "If we'd have come along a few minutes later we might not have seen it."

I still wouldn't recognize a Shifta if I saw one, but it's an ignorance I'll be happy to sustain. We get back in the truck and creep, in second gear, all the way back to the main road south.

At Sea

The Dry Tortugas Express

 S AILING IS MORE fun than trailering, though in the realm of trailering, towing a Stiletto isn't bad. You get so much attention, pulling what appears to be a pair of Salt Flats motorcycles or a matched set of Titan missiles. At almost every stop, some perplexed pump jockey would look at those twin twenty-seven-foot hulls, compressed from their normal thirteen-foot-ten-inch beam to an absurdly narrow-looking eight-foot carrying width, and ask, "You guys headed for Cape Canaveral?"

We were, in fact, en route to Key West, where we would assemble our pituitary Hobie Cat and sail it to the Dry Tortugas. When a truck driver in an adjacent lane said, "I bet she's unsinkable," we thought immediately of the *Titanic*. Some encouragements are better left unspoken.

Now, I can't claim that sailing a twenty-seven-foot catamaran (albeit without auxiliary motor or two-way radio) seventy miles west to the Dry Tortugas constitutes a heroic voyage, but there would be moments, finding ourselves at the mercy of the elements, and one evening in particular, nearly becalmed at Rebecca Shoal with lightening to the north and west, darkness coming on, and one of the strongest currents in the Atlantic urging us out to the freighter lanes of the Gulf Stream, when we would tacitly agree that this failing wind could mean an end to all our plans.

Anyone who's taken a small boat well beyond the sight of land, into waters edging the limits for which it was designed, has experienced clearly and viscerally his lack of individual significance on the sea. We didn't do without a two-way radio or auxiliary outboard by design; it just worked out that way. The outboard refused to start, and we couldn't line up a radio. Not wanting to delay our departure, since the boat was lent to us for a limited time, and not wanting to let the fair weather in this October hurricane season get away from us, we left without them. And finally we rationalized that sailing without these backup devices would up the ante a bit, though if I had it to do again, I'd risk losing the weather to ensure that we at least had the radio.

I did, however, have two invaluable backup systems: my sailing mates, Don Kincaid and Dink Bruce. Both native Conchs—Don a highly esteemed treasure diver and underwater photographer and Dink a consummate Jack-of-all-seagoing-trades—they know these waters as well as anyone, and have the reputation, in the Keys, of being the only two perpetually unemployed people who bathe.

Named *Tortugas* by Ponce de Leon in 1513, because of the copious sea turtles he found breeding there, these islands form the outer reef of the Florida Keys. Most people assume that coral becomes sand through the erosion of wind and tides; but the fact is that seventy to eighty percent of the sand in this area was transformed from coral by the digestive systems of parrot fish, who nibble on the reefs. This fine white fish crap, along with bits of coral from the lower Keys, was carried by ocean currents and deposited in the relatively static waters at the far edge of Rebecca Channel. The Tortugas, which today comprise America's least-visited national park, began to emerge.

To anyone who's made the trip in a normal, monohulled sailboat, four days to make the Tortugas, do any exploring there, and return to Key West would seem a preposterously short time. But not many sailors have navigated these waters in a Stiletto. With a basic sail area of 336 square feet, flying main and lapper, and a displacement of only 1,100 pounds, the Stiletto has about the most impressive power-to-weight ratio of any production boat, and has been clocked at speeds of up to thirty-one miles an hour. With her centerboard up, she has a draft of only nine inches, and this combination of shoal draft, allowing her to skim over reefs that could bring disaster to a deep-keel boat, and her great speed, are invaluable attributes in waters as varied and unpredictable as the lower Keys. With this lack of ballast below the waterline, though, we had to be aware that it would be possible to capsize her. In one of our test runs off Christmas Tree Island, sailing close-hauled in winds of almost thirty knots, we lifted the windward hull a good ten feet off the water; the sensation was dramatic enough to convince us to keep the mainsheet uncleated and ready for release in heavy weather.

THE STILETTO'S BUILDERS claim she can be assembled and rigged for sailing in only forty-five minutes, though in our inexperience we managed to have her ready in just under two hours. Our gallery of spectators numbered at least a hundred by the time we were ready to launch in Key West Harbor, and included Hunter S. Thompson and Bill Murray, fellow commodores of the Amazing X Navy, and one aquatic English sheepdog, who retrieved a dropped bowline from the water for me and then chose to play tug-of-war at the crucial moment of casting off. Once the dog's attention had been diverted by a Frisbee, I leapt aboard, and Don dropped her off the wind and made a series of masterful jibes through the crowded moorings that brought our breath up short and had the spectators cheering.

At 10:30 the following morning, with gear and supplies loaded (including a bottle of meat tenderizer to soothe the stings of jellyfish and man-of-war), we are sailing away from the Pier House dock and out the northwest channel with an east-northeast wind at ten to fifteen knots. We pass Mullet and Mule Keys, the harbor current so strong the flotsam appears to be swimming against it. The Coast Guard cutter

Cape York tows in a disabled shrimper. Pelicans and cormorants scatter as we round the outer channel marker and cross the ominous, dark line of the jetty–eight miles out in the first half hour. The moderate chop drops off to easy swells as we take up a westerly course on a broad reach. We gain a few knots, hoisting the drifter, and on Dink's portable radio, hear a Cuban station playing a tribute to Che Guevara that sounds like a marriage of Henry Mancini and Xavier Cugat. Switching to WA1A from Miami, we hear that the secretary of defense is inspecting the Boca Chica Naval Air Station. We see two radar reconnaissance planes heading south in close formation, perhaps among the first in reaction to the Soviet Brigade Crisis. Dink takes the helm, and we snake down the backs of the swells on a sleigh ride. Boca Grande, the westernmost of the regular Keys, fades behind us, and the Marquesas, which form the only true atoll in the Atlantic, come up on the port beam. We're now in the Gulf of Mexico, no land to starboard until the Texas coast.

Occasionally we catch a gust coming off the crest of a wave and shoot over the next four or five almost as if they weren't there. A ballyhoo skims the swells, evading a predator–a kick, a flash of silver, and then the tiny aura of spray as he touches down again, a self-propelled skipping stone.

Our regular compass is out with an oil leak, and Dink tapes a small hand compass to the starboard deck. We spot the Ellis Rock marker and jibe southwest toward the Quicksands. We are sailing wing on wing in a confused sea, the wind coming from one direction, the surge from another. We accelerate rapidly, then wallow almost to a stop at the bows. Dink trolls a spoon from a Cuban reel off the stern. A loggerhead turtle surfaces ahead of us, and when I look back, the Marquesas are gone, no visible point of land, and for the next few hours, the perspective changes. There is only the horizon, and rather than the sense of vulnerability I'd half anticipated, I feel myself for the first time fully settling into the rhythm of the trip.

One of the six-packs we've brought contains beer from six different countries. We drink each bottle communally and sample the world. Don spots the mast of the *Arbutus*, a 187-foot buoy tender belonging to the Treasure Salvors. It is anchored at the site of the *Atocha,* a treasure-laden galleon that foundered on the Quicksands in 1622. Over the centuries these waters have claimed so many ships that salvaging was the primary industry of the early 1800s. After the Wrecker's Court was established in Key West to settle disputes between salvage crews, most wreckers worked out of the Tortugas. There, during storms, they waited for the treacherous waters of the Rebecca Channel to do their work and for the currents to take control of becalmed vessels and run them onto the reefs. The wreckers were so enthusiastic about Rebecca's propensity for disaster that they made a song of it:

> *Den down to Key West we soon will go*
> *When quickly our salvage we shall know*
> *And when you are passing by dis way*
> *On the Florida Reef should you chance to stray*
> *Why we will come to you on the shore*
> *Amongst de rocks where de breakers roar.*

Across the Quicksands, we come about and head west-northwest on direct course for the Tortugas. A three-foot barracuda leaps completely out of the water, turns over, and strikes the handline. Dink pulls him in, but just short of the stern he breaks off our lure. We have a spare hook, but our only bait is a Pepsi can, from which Dink cuts a pear-shaped spoon. He wires it to the hook, and during the course of the afternoon pulls in two respectable Spanish mackerel. We will cut one in strips and marinate it raw in teriyaki and lime juice for our dinner, and grill the other on the hibachi for tomorrow's lunch.

Past Half Moon Shoal we leave United States waters and enter the narrow DMZ that separates them from the contiguous zone of the Dry Tortugas. We are in the dark blue of Rebecca Channel, where the Gulf of Mexico empties into the Atlantic. The swells are noticeably deeper here and the wind fresher. Our speed picks up to eighteen knots, and it feels like we are flying. Four shrimpers idle at Rebecca Shoals, their nets up on the booms, waiting for sunset, in about an hour, when they'll begin dragging the beds. We spy what we assume is the lighthouse on

Loggerhead Key, but as we get closer, it turns out to be Pulaski Shoals, and we jibe ninety degrees downwind to the Tortugas.

Just past sunset, we drop the anchor to windward of East Key and let the boat drift back to the surge line, a few feet from shore. We can see the silhouettes of the Loggerhead lighthouse in the twilight to the west, and the low geometric shadow of Fort Jefferson; the lights shine from a few lobster boats and a huge freighter anchored out in the Gulf Stream. A gibbous moon rises about 10:30, its cloud-diffused light forecasting its arrival so that we have anticipated it like the dawn. It comes up red with a smile, and I half expect to hear a commercial for Florida orange juice. We sleep on deck and wake in the night, feeling the hulls pounding in the surge. The anchor has slipped. We walk the boat around the island and moor it in the lee.

AT FIRST LIGHT I swim to East Key and watch the nearly transparent ghost crabs skittering over the beach, the white sand evenly patterned with star-shaped bird tracks. We drift downwind toward Garden Key, and after a day saturated with greens and blues, the first glimpse of the massive red-brick symmetry of Fort Jefferson is startling. It's the largest masonry fort in the Western Hemisphere, built prior to the Civil War to control Confederate shipping in the Florida Straits. It saw little action, became a prison following the war, and is most notable for its incarceration of Dr. Samuel Mudd, who was convicted of treason for having set the leg John Wilkes Booth fractured upon leaping to the stage of Ford's Theater.

From the subdued light of the cells and gun ports each view of the ultramarine water beyond the moat seems too dramatic to exist anywhere but in my childhood memories of pirate movies. White egrets are hunting insects beneath the mangrove trees of the parade grounds and a Canada goose seems oddly out of place on the brick path by the monument office. Sweat pours off my ribs and restores my faded T-shirt to its original navy blue.

After lunch and a siesta in the shade of the yellow tarp we've rigged across the boom, we drop down to an anchorage off Loggerhead Key, the southernmost point of U.S. land, and explore the reefs and the remains of the *Candelaria,* a sixty-five-foot messenger boat from the same fleet as the *Atocha.* Once Don diagrams them for me, I can discern her coral-encrusted ribs and the rectangular mast step. I lie on the surface, breathing through my snorkel, and watch Don, ten feet below, photograph and explore for almost three minutes before it occurs to me that he isn't wearing tanks. He surfaces for a breath and I dive to the bottom with him, startling a large hog snapper, which changes color from red to white as we approach. A jawfish pokes its head from the hole it's excavated in the bottom sand and then retreats. Don drops a pebble down the hole, and immediately the jawfish spits it back at us. We swim among the sea fans and coral heads. I follow a black French angelfish with periwinkle fins until my fingertips begin to shrivel.

Sailing back to Fort Jefferson, we leave Loggerhead a good half-hour behind a forty-one-foot ketch-rigged monohull, and are at anchor forty-five minutes before she arrives, a result of our greater speed and ability to cut across reefs that she is obliged to circumnavigate. There are waters and conditions the ketch could weather without difficulty that I wouldn't want to face in the Stiletto, but I love her quickness and ability to skim these shoals with relative impunity.

Listening to Dink's radio after dinner, we hear that the prime rate has risen to fourteen-and-a-half percent and that the first game of the World Series has been rained out—no doubt important events in the world of men, but here under the stars it sounds like local news from another planet. A few clouds blow in above us, black, like burned-out spaces in the Milky Way, and later there are a few showers. I dive down a forward hatch, bent like a pretzel among sailbags, swim fins, and anchor chain, but the storm passes quickly. I climb back out and fall asleep on the still-damp trampoline.

Just before sunset Dink had looked at the sky and recited the old sailor's axiom, "Mackerel skies and mares' tails,/Prudent sailors reef their sails," but in the morning there's hardly a breeze. We heat water for coffee and point northwest off Garden Key to gain latitude for crossing the channel, beginning the trip home. A light plane, probably the Drug Enforcement Administration, dives low enough to check our sail numbers and the depth of our waterline, circles, passes again, then heads out for the anchored freighter. We are making a little progress, flying the drifter in air so light it would becalm any boat with ballast in her keel. Each time I check my watch I'm chagrined at how rapidly the hour hand works off its increments and how little our points of reference have changed. I want to take some action to improve our speed, but there's nothing to be done. Sailors and fishermen learn that waiting can be an all-consuming activity. It's three o'clock in the afternoon, only four hours of daylight left, as we idle past Rebecca Shoals. We've been sailing for seven hours, barely a third of the way to our planned anchorage in the Marquesas. The sky becomes overcast and oily, the channel an eerie calm, and our wake disappears altogether. Joan Baez is singing "And I heard you were lost at sea. . . ."

Thunderheads have been building all afternoon, and we see the first flash of lightning to the northwest. Don scans the horizon, checks his watch, and I can detect a tinge of consternation in his sigh, and the way his eyes roll from the slack sails to the water and back. Dink's blank expression meets mine. He shrugs his shoulders and smiles, "Nobody said it was gonna be easy." I return his smile, but it comes from no deeper than my chin. I begin involuntarily composing a letter to my wife and children from the great beyond, and it goes something like this: "Well, here I am, drifting on the featureless sea. I have no control of my fate. I'm not sure I ever did; it's just more evident here. I can see the lights of freighters in the Gulf Stream. Their propellers are larger than this boat, and they won't even feel it when their bows suck us under. There's lightning in the west. Electricity is still magic to me, and I have no idea what will happen when it strikes us, or if our taste will be spoiled for the fish who'll come up to siphon the debris for singed meat. . . ."

A little melodramatic, you say? Of course it is, viewed from the relative security of a winter evening by the fire. It isn't like a duel with sabres or battling a storm in which you have no attention to spare. I may have overstated the case a trifle. None of us speak of our concern. We can't afford to indulge our apprehensions, but they're easy to detect in the tight edge of our voices, the lame quips and exaggerated politeness that often mask a sense of doom. Yet I wouldn't hesitate to take another chance on finding myself in these conditions. All in all, it's one of my finest memories, realizing what narrow margins we play on and how unexpectedly they can be called. It may seem absurd to speak of the beauty of it, but a ray of sun ghosting through the overcast, the glassy water, even the thunderheads, are beautiful to us in that moment in the way an eighty-year-old woman can be beautiful, truly beautiful as a woman, to an eighty-year-old man who sees her in the light of an understanding not available to others.

Two porpoises surface astern and break the spell. Almost as if they'd brought it to us, we pick up a zephyr and hear again the reassuring sound of our wake. We pass the Half Moon Shoal marker at the edge of the channel and, just after sunset, spot the mast of the *Arbutus,* which we know to be anchored on the edge of the Quicksands. In the dark, we navigate by dead reckoning on Cosgrove Light, an hour more on our easterly course before we change the drifter for the Genoa and tack northward, Dink and I on the bows, straining the night for the battery-powered road construction flasher, which, if the battery hasn't died, Don assures us will mark the *Arbutus* and water shallow enough to hold our anchor.

On the radio we hear that the Coast Guard has rescued 103 Haitian refugees who've been at sea forty-five days on a thirty-five-foot boat. The news relieves us and puts in perspective our apprehensions about running on a deadhead in the dark or missing the Quicksands altogether. What we at first imagine to be the flashing yellow light eventually becomes the *Arbutus.* We sail upwind of her a hundred yards, drop our hook, and find bottom in about fifteen feet of water. It's midnight. We polish off the remaining two-thirds of a bottle of rum and fall asleep on deck, exhausted and relieved at the reassuring glow of Key West, thirty miles to the east.

Strange to wake at anchor with no land in sight. A few terns calling, and the dawn a soft red. There's a line of thunderheads to the north, though we feel no tension about the day, knowing we'll spot the Marquesas in an hour's sail and be in sight of other islands all the way to Key West. Before getting underway, we make a brief dive near the site of the *Atocha,* and Don demonstrates the treasure-hunting technique of sweeping the bottom sand by fanning the water above it with his hand. In twenty minutes we find two fifty-eight-caliber musket balls, molded for firing in a Spanish arquebus. Back on deck I hold them in my hand, awed by the realization that they've lain there on the bottom since two years after the Pilgrims landed at Plymouth Rock.

This last day is a slow, sweltering sail, uneventful except for a manta ray, almost ten feet in diameter, who takes flight just off our stern and smacks down again with a report like a 30.06. Off the Marquesas a waterspout has descended from the line of thunderheads, the sun catching one edge, opalescent against the gunmetal stack of it. The DEA plane dives on us four more times. Near Sand Key, a Coast Guard cutter appears to be bearing down on us at full steam, but she veers off as we pass the channel buoy, and I wonder why it is that we feel like smugglers. We munch on turkey spread and crackers from the larder. It's pretty awful, but it's all there is. "Nothing is too disgusting for pirates," Dink says, rolling his Long John Silver eye. And we must look a little like pirates, with our four-day beards, and our clothes, skin, and gear permeated with sunscreen, salt grit, and sweat.

A low-flying osprey guides us into Key West harbor, past Mallory Pier and the locals assembled for their traditional observance of sunset. We get a round of cheers and handclapping from them as we sail by, then realize it's the setting sun they're applauding. A bearded man at the end of the pier cups his hands and hollers, "You guys give up on the Tortugas?"

"No."

"You gonna try again?"

"We've been there and back," I shout, feeling a little giddy over his incredulity. But he just shakes his head, turns, and walks into the crowd.

No Salt but Plenty of Pepper

$\mathbf{A}$ WANING MOON is reflected in the water astern and Taurus is rising to the east. It would be an excellent night for laying out the constellations of July, but I'm numb with the exhaustion of too many sail changes and too little sleep. I gulp soda from a can as if it were all that mattered. It is a mild evening, warm for any time of year on Lake Michigan, and the dry ice we took on in Chicago has made the aluminum can so cold it numbs the rope burns on my hands. I had held on to the spinnaker guy too long after the sheet was let go; then, gathering sail, burned my hands again on the sheet as the shifting wind carried the raging kite astern. My elbows ache from being rapped repeatedly by winch handles.

I had done a fair share of racing in small one-design-class boats that require advanced gymnastic ability, and had always regarded yacht racing as a genteel sport for those who had gotten either too old or too feeble to do backbends off the windward rail. It was, in my mind, a kind of *Better Homes and Gardens* cruise on which you set your sails, broke out the beer and suntan lotion, and hoped the wind might blow you to the finish faster than the other boats. Now, aboard the Islander 41

Osprey, my illusions are severely eroded. I keep telling myself I'm having fun.

I look up at the stars again and see our watch captain, George Stevens, at the helm. He has been manning it for more than three hours, sleighriding in a following sea, and the veins on his forehead are protruding like those of a weight lifter. We lose a wave, the stern sinks into a swell, and for a moment it feels almost as if we've stopped. The knotmeter falls to five-and-a-half, we hear the stern wake break as it catches us, then suddenly we rise as if cresting a hill and speed down the other side, our wake boiling and the bow lurching sharply to port. The needle of the knotmeter surges to nine. George spins the large destroyer wheel all the way to the lock, then backs off on it to bring the bow back on line with Point Betsie light.

We have been sailing for nearly thirty-three hours, and in another thirty minutes the watch will change and George, Jeff Fisher (the captain's brother), Steve Chambers, and I will have an opportunity to get some sleep. I find myself selfishly contriving to be the first below and to grab a leeward berth so I can sleep without having to cling to the mattress.

We have fallen below the rhumb line (the most direct course from Chicago to Mackinac Island) and are pointing hard, trying to clear Point Betsie, a rocky shoal on the Michigan shore. In half an hour it will be midnight Sunday, and ever since we took the starting gun at 2:30 Saturday afternoon the wind has been shifting steadily from east to southeast to south to southwest. The red glow of the relative wind dial now indicates that the wind is coming straight out of the west, almost eighty degrees off our port beam, and I realize we'll have to tack to make the point. The sleigh ride is over.

A line of thunderheads becomes visible as lightning flashes to the east and south. It occurs to me that the smaller boats we passed during the previous night are probably back there in the storm, surrounded by the thunder that we can only imagine with each pink flash through the clouds. I have been hoping that there wouldn't be any more sail changes before my watch went off duty at midnight, that I could just hold on, try to stay awake, and let the starboard watch tack around Point Betsie while I collapse in my berth. But I can see that it's not to be. *Meteor,* another Islander 41 and one of the boats closest to us in the complex handicap system that determines who has to finish when to beat whom, is almost within shouting distance off our stern to the east.

Our skipper, Mike Fisher, and Hank Burkhard, skipper of *Meteor,* have established a special race within the class they call the Winnebago Cup, since both Islander 41s have enough freeboard to be considered the seagoing equivalents of those slab-sided motor homes. Because of her extended spinnaker poles, *Meteor* has to give us two minutes, thirty-nine seconds, and at the moment, being slightly ahead and to windward, we estimate that we have about two minutes lead on her. I see her blooper, a cut-down spinnaker, collapse, and realize that she is making her tack for Point Betsie. Though it is his off-watch, Mike Fisher has been forward, watching the Point Betsie light and hollering information back to the helmsman. Every time our starcut starts to curl, Mike calls back, George falls off on the helm to keep it from collapsing, and I reach over the leeward rail to take up the slack. Several times I've been almost jerked overboard as the starcut has filled and the sheet has snapped taut.

Our boat beat *Meteor* in the Port Huron-Mackinac race, and Burkhard is trying to even the score. I call to Mike to let him know that *Meteor* is making her tack, but he tells George to keep steady on the helm and to work upwind in the lulls. With only her jib and mainsail, *Meteor* has lost some speed, but she's outpointing us and beginning to move across our wake.

Mike is opting to maintain our speed with the starcut and staysail and make a last-minute tack for the point. George argues that the wind may slack close to shore, but Mike has decided to take that risk. In the cabin below, Bill Carlson, Robert Ball, and Eric are sleeping away the last minutes of their off-watch before they take over the midwatch. Several times Mike has called them to help with sail changes, but he was able to stir only Robert, who stumbled up from the galley and cranked the halyard in a trance, then stumbled back below without saying a word. I find myself pitying the starboard watch for the rude awakening they will have, but at the same time I'm greedy for one of their berths and hoping that they won't be able to rouse me for any sail changes. At this point I know that even if I hear them calling, I'll pretend to be asleep.

The night before, I had had the midwatch, and the blackflies, which seem to come alive about dawn and are a hazard of yacht racing on the Great Lakes, had kept me from getting any sleep before I had to come back on at eight. I realize it would be foolish to total the sleep I've had in the last three days. The night before the race it was eighty-five degrees and muggy in Chicago. Revelers, sailors, and groupies ran over the decks like loquacious squirrels, the traffic streamed by a hundred feet away on Lake Shore Drive, and the whole harbor area smelled of stale beer, sweat, dead fish, and diesel oil. It was 4:30 the last time I'd looked at my watch, and 6 A.M. when the first sunlight flared through the starboard portholes. I laughed cynically to myself as I remembered the orders on the schedule sheet Mike had taped to the forward bulkhead: "5. Get plenty of rest prior to the race, as we will be driving *Osprey* as hard as possible. 6. Side advice . . . Don't be hung over Saturday morning! . . . Unless you are in training."

The afternoon before the race, the Chicago Yacht Club resembled the setting for the International Telephone Linemen's Pole Climbing Championships. An occasional sunburned sailor in a bosun's chair, freeing a halyard or tightening the screws on an aluminum spar, reinforced this image. Eric, a photographer who had spent several seasons on the Southern Ocean Racing Circuit and who had expected the Chicago-Mackinac to be a moderately small inland lake race, was amazed to see so many racing and quasi-racing yachts assembled in one place, 244 boats, ranging from former America's Cup contenders *Heritage* and *Weatherly* to a pair of twenty-seven-foot C&Cs.

The yacht club is in the heart of downtown Chicago, and the masts of the boats seemed emulations of the skyscrapers half circling the harbor. Brylcreemed men in business suits roamed the narrow docks, dodging barefoot, long-haired sailors in cut-off jeans balancing cases of beer on their shoulders. Models, wives, ancient commodores, and Coast Guard officers from the icebreaker *Mackinac*, which would escort the racing boats on the 333-mile voyage to the island, wandered among crews folding spinnakers a few feet from rush-hour traffic. City police-men patrolled the harbor area and paused to read such boat names as *Porcus Maximus* (the yacht bore the effigy of a pig in a Superman cos-tume on its transom), *Rub-a-Dub, Agape, Better Life, Uber Alles,* and *Overdraft II* (this boat's awning was a facsimile of a check stamped INSUFFICIENT FUNDS).

Four hours after the start, drifting in light to nonexistent winds, the tops of the skyscrapers had disappeared in the gray-black smog line that followed the curve of the lakeshore to the south and east toward Gary, Indiana. It was cooler, and breathing was noticeably easier out on the lake as the fleet spread out to the north along the Wisconsin shoreline.

Now we are less than half a mile from Point Betsie. I can see the individual lights in the cottages near Frankfort. *Meteor* is moving up off our port quarter. Being closer to the Point Betsie light, we should be able to maintain our lead on the broad reach from the point to the Manitou Passage, but an efficient tack here is critical. This is not to be. At one point a runaway sheet snaps Jeff halfway over the leeward rail. I dive across the cockpit and grab his legs just in time to keep him from going into the water.

The tack is sloppy at best, and because of the momentum lost luffing while we freed the fouled starcut, *Meteor* has fallen off the wind and slipped by our bow. As we settle back on course, we can hear the surge from her wake and see her white transom reflected in the moon-light as she beats down the shoreline toward Sleeping Bear Point. I'm so numb that I don't really care. All that occurs to me is that she looks quite majestic, my elbows ache, it's past midnight, and my watch is over. I stumble below, turn on the light, and fall into the leeward berth the minute Eric has fumbled his way out of it. I'm uncomfortable in my foul-weather gear, but can't raise myself to peel it off.

The flies are at work again. The forward hatch is closed and the sour stench of the head pervades the cabin. Eric is shaking me and I wake with a start. I've been dreaming of a cool, green, insect-free meadow where the ground is steady under my feet, and it takes an anx-ious moment for me to recall I'm in a race. Beneath my foul-weather gear I'm soaked with sweat, and my first thought is that Eric is trying to wake me for a sail change. It can't be four already; I've barely gotten to sleep. "How far to the Manitou Passage?" I ask. "We're there," he replies. He and Bill are stripping off their rubber suits, and I can see the first faint intimations of dawn through the companionway. I swing my legs over the edge of the berth and try to find a spot on the sole that isn't covered with sails, duffel bags, or bodies. My left foot lands on something soft that groans like Steve, and he wakes to find me standing on his stomach. I quickly grab the handrail that runs along the ceiling and swing clear.

On deck I can see the lights from Leland Harbor and Pyramid Point against the gray-pink sky, North Manitou Island to port and an ore boat moving up on us astern. The wind has fallen off considerably and we are making four-and-a-half knots on almost glassy water. Mike tells me that during the night we have put some "smooth moves" on *Meteor* and several other unidentified boats and left them behind and far inshore. He points back to where *Meteor's* lights were last seen. We are making excellent time and our only concern at the moment is whether the ore boat astern is going to take us to port and blanket our wind, or fall off and pass to starboard. Looking through the binoculars we can't see anyone on deck, but we are assuming that she has picked us up on her radar. She falls off, looking like a deserted city passing silently a hundred yards to starboard. I read U.S. STEEL on her stacks but can see no one on the bridge or brightly lighted decks.

Mike gives George a course of thirty degrees and goes below to get some sleep. He has stood three continuous watches, and if it is possible to inspire by example at 4:30 A.M., we are so inspired. There is also a certain sense of bleary-eyed elation at waking to find ourselves so far ahead of *Meteor*. We are well out in the lake, where the wind is, or should be, and all we have to do is maintain that advantage. I am also feeling a certain glow, knowing that I will be on Mackinac Island before nightfall, enjoying a hot shower, a shave, flush toilets, and a shore-cooked meal.

At 4:45 the spinnaker begins to collapse. George falls off to try and keep it filled, but there is nothing he can do. The wind is dying and our speed has fallen to two knots. A butterfly appears, carried on the remnants of the near-dawn southwest breeze. The wind dies altogether and the butterfly overtakes us. The sails fall slack and a dead alewife lingers interminably off our port beam.

George and Steve argue about how to capture a nonexistent wind, and during the next three hours we engage in a comic opera of sail changes; from starcut to blooper, blooper to drifter, drifter to tallboy, tallboy to drifter, drifter to blooper and staysail and back to starcut, but we might as well be changing our laundry. *Meteor* has picked up an inshore breeze as the sun warms the beach, and we watch her sail steadily past the pine-capped sand dunes and clear the point of land off Northport. Mackinac Island seems farther and farther away, and we all dread having to tell Mike that in the three-and-a-half hours since he went off watch we have moved forward less than one mile.

It's beginning to seem like a drifting race, more a test of patience than of sailing skill, not the kind of excitement I had pictured, and I know this isn't typical of Lake Michigan. Though they might be shocked to discover no salt in the taste of a wave breaking over the bow, few ocean sailors would dismiss the Great Lakes as a series of millponds or a safe harbor. In 1851, Herman Melville described them as "Swept by Borean and dismasting blasts as direful as any that lash the salted wave; they know what shipwrecks are, for out of sight of land, however inland, they have drowned full many a midnight ship with all its shrieking crew." I am reminded that forty-three boats dropped out of the race on this leg in 1970, but not from lack of wind. When the main body of the fleet had reached Frankfort, a warm front had begun to move through and a moderate west-southwest wind had shifted to the northwest and begun blowing at forty mph with gusts up to sixty. The lake had kicked up an eight-foot chop, not the roller-coaster effect of easy ocean swells but violent, short-interval, hull-jarring slaps, wrenching the boats laterally, straining the rigging, and making footing almost impossible. In the six hours it took the front to move through, five boats had been dismasted and thirty-eight others, many of them seasoned ocean racers, had sought safe harbors, suffering gear failure and crew fatigue.

A front is moving in from the south and as we drift helplessly more than one hundred smaller boats, which we had left out of sight the previous day, move up on us. I imagine how terrifying it must have been for a lone British merchantman sitting in a pocket of dead air, watching the Spanish Armada closing fast on a wind off the Azores. These racing yachts out of Chicago might as well be carrying cannon for all the dread and sense of futility their approach is causing us.

With the fleet still a mile astern, Jeff spots the dark water of a wind line moving in from the west. We position the spinnaker to starboard and the dead alewife drifts astern and disappears. Now we have the bubbles of our bow wake to gauge our progress, but I almost wish the calm had held till Mike came back on deck. It would have made it easier to explain our position.

The wind rises steadily during the morning, and by noon the second of two rain squalls hits. We are reaching at a steady seven-and-a-half knots as the water pours off the mainsail. We catch and pass several Section 3 boats (one class below ours), but it is no consolation for the three hours lost drifting in the Manitou Passage. By the time we approach the cut at Grays Reef, the race has taken on the quality of an idyll. The Coast Guard has broadcast that the first boat crossed the finish line at about 8:30 this morning, and we can't hope to make the island before 5:30 P.M. As we round the Grays Reef light, someone hollers down that we are the forty-seventh boat to pass. We have given up all hope. We round the last buoy, pull in the jib, set the spinnaker and staysail with remarkable smoothness, and start the last downwind leg under the Mackinac Bridge. Now that we have nothing to lose, we are simply enjoying the sun, the motion of the boat as she rides down the following sea, surging to nine-and-a-half knots, and the endless line of multicolored spinnakers spread out behind us.

From our angle on the water, it seems impossible that our spar will clear the bridge. The lower girders close on us and I look up through the grating at a lone car crossing with deliberate slowness. Then I see a telephoto lens protruding from the back window. I am feeling giddy and I wave to spoil the picture. We sail past the white colonnade of the Grand Hotel, which has the longest continuous porch in the world, and the ferryboat from Mackinaw City gives way to starboard as we take the gun in front of the Iroquois Hotel.

I walk down Main Street feeling I have sailed to a lost continent. The pavement rocks under my legs and I am surfeited with the mingling aromas of popcorn, fudge from the numerous fudgeries for which the island is famous, and the horse manure that supplants exhaust fumes on this carless oasis. I have had a shower and feel human again, if no less exhausted. I find Mike Fisher at the bar of the Chippewa and we celebrate the unexpected good news that we have finished eighth in a class of twenty-six. Though the race committee doesn't post overall positions, we figure we have finished forty-first in a field of 244 boats. I suppress a vague impulse to make an apologetic reference to the morning's three-hour lull and instead raise my glass of gin and tonic.

There is a burst of laughter from the table behind us. A drunken orthodontist with a striped shirt, white bell-bottoms, and a gold ring in his right ear is yelling at the barmaid to "make hard the larboard scuppers and moisten the mizzen halyards." Eventually nautical flummery overtakes everyone and I can see that the party that began three days ago in Chicago will continue through the night. I start to ask Mike about his plans for next year's race from Port Huron to Chicago, but the floor lurches under my feet and I have to grab the bar rail to steady myself. Maybe when I've had a week's rest I'll think about crewing another race. I finish my drink, thank Mike for signing me on, and wander across the street to my hotel and that uncertain country of sleep.

The Havana Wind

W<small>HEN</small> I <small>WAS</small> growing up on the eastern shore of Lake Michigan, there were hot summer days, given to mirage, when I thought I could make out the skyline of Milwaukee across the lake, ninety miles away. I probably just wanted a glimpse of something exotic, and for years wondered what a "Milwaukee" might look like.

Now I live in Key West, and there are nights when Havana, about as far away as Milwaukee is from Michigan, seems to shimmer in the moonless dark. You cannot see Cuba from Key West, of course, but it's always just over the horizon, enchanting yet remotely menacing. The one solemn note struck on the Conch Train, a trolley tour of the island, comes when it pauses at "the Southernmost Point in the Continental U.S." and the driver announces, "Ninety miles over the water there lies communist Cuba." People often squint, as if trying to catch a glimpse of a great shark cruising the edge of a reef.

Forty years ago, Cuba was a weekend getaway for wealthy Americans, who would fly down to Havana, and for not-so-wealthy Key Westers, who would take the family fishing boat across the Florida Straits. They went for the slightly illicit taste of gambling in the casinos or the aura of Latin debauchery. Then revolution, the Bay of Pigs, the Cuban Missile Crisis, the specter of communism, and two generations of isolation transformed the once-beautiful playground into a darkly shrouded satellite of the Evil Empire. And in 1961, the United States government, bowing to pressure from the Cuban American exile community and to a residual vendetta against Castro and communism in general, imposed a trade embargo against the island. It is off-limits to American companies, including airlines, so the best way to get there directly is by boat.

My friend A. D. Tinkham, a Key West artist, and his wife, Rebecca, own the thirty-eight-foot trimaran, *Restless Native,* and they often invite Debbie, my wife, and me along for sunset cruises. Debbie and I are experienced sailors, and A. D. and Rebecca enjoy the company of people who appreciate the workings of the boat as a break from their usual business of ferrying snorkelers and sightseers out to the reefs that surround the lower Keys.

It was on an evening junket in the summer of 1994 that the idea of sailing to Havana came up. What if, rather than turning back at sunset, as was our routine, we just kept going? There is nothing illegal about Americans going to Cuba, and therefore nothing for which we could be prosecuted—unless it was proved that we had spent money there. True, the government—specifically U.S. Customs—frowns on the idea of American citizens traveling to Cuba, but investigating every vessel headed south from Florida would be akin to the state highway patrol pulling over every car traveling sixty-six mph. As for the Cuban government, it welcomes visitors from Europe, even depends on them to sustain the tenuous economy. We didn't see any reason it wouldn't welcome Americans as well.

We knew of a dozen boats that had made the crossing in the past year, and, to our knowledge, none of their crews had been blown out of the water or thrown in jail. The only troubling incident had occurred last April, when John J. Young, the leader of Basta!, a movement dedicated to running supplies to Cuba, had been detained by U.S. Customs officials on his return to Key West from Havana. Agents had roughly searched his forty-four-foot fishing boat and confiscated two bottles of rum, eight Cohiba cigars, and two T-shirts. The search had won the government a good deal of adverse publicity of the "jack-booted thug" variety. We discounted the incident as a strictly political statement and set about planning our trip.

A. D., hoping to play according to Hoyle, inquired at the Customs office in Key West about forms and procedures. "I can clear you for Mexico or the Bahamas, but I can't clear you for Cuba," an agent warned him. "If you go there in a commercial vessel, it could be impounded." Then, with a wry smile, he added, "But I didn't ask you the name of your boat." A. D., whose boat is commercially registered, beat a hasty retreat.

We persevered over the next six months, discussing our plans with friends, some of whom had made the trip themselves. I was given the name of a man who had made several crossings, and I called to ask his advice. He was away, but the message on his answering machine was encouraging: "If you are thinking of going to Cuba, *go*. It's a beautiful country."

So at 4:30 on a clear May afternoon, after freeing up our schedules for a three-night journey, packing a few extra provisions and goodwill trade goods—soap, toothpaste, aspirin, Miami Dolphins and Grateful Dead T-shirts, and a few baseball caps from the Saltwater Angler, a friend's fly-fishing shop in Key West—we set out.

As we left the harbor, someone radioed to ask where we were going.

"Oh, just down to Woman Key," A. D. replied, referring to a remote island ten miles to the west.

"I heard a rumor you might be headed somewhere a bit south of that," the radio voice rejoined.

"No. We're just headed out toward Woman," A. D. dissembled.

He wasn't lying, exactly. Owing to the strong southeasterly flow of the Gulf Stream—sixty-five-miles wide and two-and-a-half knots, according to the last report we had gotten from NOAA Weather Radio—we had decided to tack west toward Woman Key and sail twenty-five miles past it until we paralleled the Marquesas, a group of islands near the entrance to the Gulf of Mexico. There we would catch the Gulf

Stream, the warm ocean current that flows around the tip of Florida and north along the east coast, and let it carry us toward Havana.

It was a beautiful evening with a fair breeze from the west. We were in high spirits as we passed the last navigational buoy at the end of Southwest Channel. Our home island was fading, and as the last trace of the outlying Keys dissolved into a chain of broken dots, the adventure became real for us. After a year of talking about it, our next landfall was actually going to be Cuba.

An hour beyond the channel, we passed a dead sea turtle—a large hawksbill, bloated and floating to our port side. At first I had taken it for a truck tire, though as we drew close, its tautly swollen skin glowed like burnished copper in the last red rays of the sun. "Not a very good start," said Rebecca. And for the next hour, nobody had much to say.

At eight o'clock we approached the Western Dry Rocks, nine miles from Key West. Heading southwest, we bisected the cobalt-colored Gulf Stream. I could feel its pull on the tiller like a sudden shift in the wind.

The Florida Strait is the main shipping route to the Panama Canal for vessels from Europe and the East Coast of North America. It's a big water, and a busy one for cargo carriers ten thousand times *Restless Native's* tonnage. One of these seaborne warehouses could unwittingly crush us like flotsam under its bow, so it was important to keep a close watch for silhouettes on the horizon and to closely track the progress of navigation lights during the night.

Around 9:30 we met the track of the *Gypsum Baron,* a mega-freighter we had spotted an hour earlier off our stern quarter. It looked as if we would cross her bow, but then she adjusted her course to the south, and as we saw her transom off toward Galveston, her shuddering wake crashed over our bow and put us in a confused, deck-sopping sea.

When we had regained our composure and changed into dry clothes, Rebecca fixed supper, which we capped off with tumblers of Haitian rum. As the moon rose, chasing away all but the brightest stars, the wind fell off to the point that we dropped our jib and fired up the diesel.

A. D. and I were sleeping below when the first call came from the Coast Guard. Debbie was at the helm, and Rebecca came down to wake us. It was 4:30 A.M., and we emerged like hibernating groundhogs.

"This is the United States Coast Guard calling the vessel four miles off our port bow at twenty-three degrees, twenty-three minutes north latitude and eighty-two degrees, eighteen minutes west longitude."

After a moment, I said, "Maybe they're calling someone else," and we decided not to respond, even though we could see the cutter's lights to the northeast. By their fourth call, we had booted up a handheld global positioning system and confirmed that they had us pinpointed.

A. D. responded, "Coast Guard, this is *Restless Native.*"

"What is your last port and intended destination?"

"Tell 'em the truth," I said. "What else can we do?"

A. D. shrugged and said, "*Restless Native* out of Key West and bound for Marina Hemingway." I held my breath, waiting for the ax to fall.

"What is the purpose of your trip?"

"Journalism."

They asked for our vessel numbers, boat length, and the number of people aboard, then told us to stand by. It was a long few minutes, protracted by a silent litany of imagined repercussions, before the voice returned.

"Have a safe trip."

We celebrated with a predawn sip of rum. We were making six knots to the southwest, compensating for the eastward pull of the Stream. At about 10:30, eighteen hours after we had left Key Wet, we began to wonder if we had gone too far west and missed Cuba. Then, suddenly, there was Havana, materializing through a blanket of heavy smog. Our arrival was heralded by a few dozen flying fish, at least ten inches long, the largest I had ever seen. We entered Marina Hemingway, the yacht basin just west of the city, through a narrow break in the reef a quarter-mile offshore.

In the outer harbor, we spotted the Cuban flag flying outside a small stucco building: Cuban Customs. We tied up along its pier.

For three hours, we visited with uniformed officials from

Agriculture, Immigration, Customs, and the Cuban Coast Guard. The protocol was the same with each: handshakes, soft drinks or coffee, forms to fill out. They spoke little or no English, and our collective Spanish was rudimentary at best. We consulted our English/Spanish dictionary frequently and used some creative sign language. The officials were friendly and welcoming. One, dressed in uniform and epaulets, left the boat wearing a Saltwater Angler hat.

We had landed during the annual Hemingway Sport Fishing Tournament. Dozens of fishing boats were lined up at the piers, along with sailboats from Sweden, Brazil, Germany, Britain, and France.

At the concierge desk of a hotel near the marina, we booked rooms for the night at the Inglaterra Hotel in Havana, made dinner reservations, and arranged for a car with an English-speaking driver to pick us up the next day. Then we called a taxi and headed into town.

The streets of Havana seemed oddly familiar, like cities in Florida I had visited as a child. Traffic was light, and almost all the cars were pre-1958. We entered on Fifth Avenue, a broad thoroughfare of palatial homes—Havana's Sunset Boulevard—that had, since the revolution, become the embassy row.

We arrived at the Inglaterra Hotel around 7:30. It had jury-rigged partitions for walls, and exposed wiring. From our balcony, Debbie and I heard a political rally going on in a baroque building across the narrow street. We couldn't pick up many of the words, but the tone of the rhetoric and the martial music of the brass band were unmistakable.

The plumbing in our room was out of order, as was the telephone, so I went down to the front desk to see when we might be able to shower. On my way back up, I met a man at the door of the elevator and, after we played a little "after you, Alphonse" about who might enter first, he smiled at me and said, "My *Ingles* is not so good."

"Nor is my Spanish."

"You are *Inglés?*" he asked.

"No. *Americano.*"

He pulled in his chin, widened his eyes, and, with a tone of incredulity, asked, *"Norte Americano?"*

"Si." I nodded.

"Norte *Americano?*" He smiled and shook his head slightly. "*Muy interasante,*" he said, and we bowed to each other before he got out on his floor.

The next morning the four of us wandered a bit through the streets of Havana, which were, by the turn of a corner, elegant or squalid, friendly or forbidding, redolent of diesel fumes or gardenias or human waste. The Cubans we encountered seemed surprised that we were Americans rather than Europeans. They said they were happier learning English than they had been struggling with Russian. We handed out goodwill items and were given one- and five-peso notes as gifts. Cuban money seems to be purely decorative: All the prices in the bars and shops were in American dollars. We paid for everything in cash, to avoid leaving a paper trail.

After lunch we met our driver, Umberto, who took us into the countryside. We drove past sugarcane fields, muddy streams, and forests, and often encountered horse- and ox-drawn carts. As it turned out, Umberto spoke no English, but he suffered our poor Spanish and drove us past his mother's house and the houses of several friends, pointing first out the window, then to himself, saying, "*Mi amigo, mi amigo.*"

Hoping to return to Key West early the next day, we decided to sleep on the boat. At five o'clock, we asked Umberto to drop us off at Marina Hemingway. After a drink at the Old Man and the Sea Hotel, we turned in.

What appeared to be apartment buildings were being built near the marina. As we were preparing for our departure the next morning, one of the construction workers wandered over. After standing and watching for a few minutes from the dock and making several attempts to help, he asked if we would take him back to Key West with us. He said he had friends in Miami with "*mucho dinero.*" We shook our heads and told him we were sorry. A few minutes later we were relieved we had.

At the Customs dock on our way out, a Cuban Coast Guard officer gave our boat a meticulous search, looking under every cushion and in every tiny drawer, presumably searching for stowaways. We had nothing Cuban aboard, not even a cigar.

We cleared the harbor on a brisk east wind. Heading northeast, we had the Gulf Stream working for us most of the way and made the crossing in thirteen hours. Except for a whale that rolled and spouted a few dozen times off to port, we had an uneventful trip. An hour out of Key West Harbor, I radioed U.S. Customs and, with some trepidation, announced, "This is *Restless Native,* inbound to Key West from Marina Hemingway."

The woman who responded seemed taken aback. "Marina Hemingway? That's in Cuba, isn't it?"

"Yes, it is," I replied.

"Hold on a minute."

A few seconds later a man's voice joined hers on the line, and she said, "There's a boat out there that says it's coming in from Cuba. What am I gonna do about that?"

"It's pretty late," he said. "Why don't you just tell them to hit the dock and go on home."

My guess is that they figured anyone ingenuous enough to announce they were sailing in from Cuba was unlikely to be a smuggler.

We arrived in Key West after midnight, a bit weary, and addled by what had seemed like an odyssey in time. We were happy we had made the crossing while Cuba is still what it is, while it still has some grit. A few years down the road, I suspect, it may be a port of call for the *Love Boat,* as homogenized as Key West and all the other formerly distinctive island cultures in the aquatic theme park that once was the Caribbean.

Icebreaker

I GREW UP watching the profiles of the long ships on Lake Michigan, their bridges rising over their bows like seaborne ziggurats, and later, after the opening of the St. Lawrence Seaway, the more conventional silhouettes of Liberian freighters passed on the horizon, nearly as little-noticed as clouds. "Ore boats," my father would murmur, looking over his paper to the west, squinting against the evening sun.

In the heat of late summer, I imagined this littoral as a Pacific island. It was always the Pacific because the sun set over the water, and I dug foxholes in the sand, waiting for the Japanese to storm the beach from their homeland across this imaginary ocean.

My fantasy was reinforced by the Navy Corsairs and Hellcats flying training missions along the shore, so low I could see the faces of the pilots, who waved at me, their cockpit canopies open. Of course it was a childhood conceit, though I didn't realize that Jean Nicolet, the first white man to gaze across this water, expected to find China on its western shore and even carried a damask robe to be properly attired for his arrival.

It's interesting to speculate what the Winnebagos of northern Wisconsin might have made of this vision.

Later, when we lived in a small farming town some twenty miles inland, there was the story of the German flier who escaped from the local POW camp and made his way cross-country to the coast. Believing he'd reached the Pacific, he watched for U-boats, hoping to be rescued.

To anyone seeing the Great Lakes for the first time, this story isn't so far-fetched. On a flight from Paris, I was seated among the members of a French film crew, bound for Chicago. It was a clear day, and as we circled over the southern end of Lake Michigan, one of the Frenchmen tugged at my sleeve and pointed to the water below. *"Quelle est cette mer?"*

"Lake Michigan," I replied with exaggerated enunciation.

"Lake? *Qu'est-ce que* lake?" He turned to one of his companions. *"Lac? No. Mer no.* What sea is this?"

The film crew remained unconvinced. This apparently infinite expanse of water didn't jibe with their conception of a lake, and I've encountered a similar incredulity among ocean sailors, who envision the Great Lakes as broad pastoral ponds.

THE POPULAR SONG on the sinking of the *Edmund Fitzgerald* spread some awareness that the Great Lakes could be great in devastation as well as in size. The song is misleading, however, in that it portrays Lake Superior alone as formidable. Lake Michigan, because of its unpredictable weather, lack of sea room in which to run out a storm, and scarcity of safe harbors in which to seek refuge, has claimed many more sizeable ships, like the 640-foot limestone carrier *Carl D. Bradley,* which broke in two in November 1958 and went to the bottom with thirty-three of its thirty-five-man crew.

Yet, apart from its legend in song, the sinking of the *Edmund Fitzgerald,* because of the suddenness with which it disappeared and the mysteries still surrounding it, remains the most horrifying and intriguing. A steel carrier and two saltwater ships were in contact with the *Fitzgerald,* which was reporting thirty-foot combers and some even higher. The captain's last words were, "Big sea, I've never seen anything like it." Minutes later her lights disappeared and she vanished from the radar screens; a 729-foot ship gone down without even a Mayday call.

There's a theory that she might have been raised, bow and stern, by two monstrous waves, causing her unsupported weight to collapse her amidships. One can imagine the scream of parting steel in the dark of that storm. Another theory, and the one considered more likely, is that she was simply battered, nose down, in the trough of a monster wave and driven, bow first, to the bottom by the sheer weight of water. But all that's certain is that the *Fitzgerald* lies broken in two on the bottom in 530 feet of water too cold to support the microorganisms that could cause the bodies of those drowned to surface.

Now, in late January, the ice floes extend lakeward as far as I can see, their ridged and slaggy surface peaked with ice volcanoes, geysers intermittently spraying from their cones in the surge of compressed waves below. The spray freezes and the cones mount in a frozen moonscape.

The ice reaches a mile from land, its curved edge mimicking the serpentine contours of the shore. The brash ice at its edge dissolves into the open water beyond, its somber steely blue crazed with whitecaps in a twenty-knot wind. In 1976, the ice pack extended eighty miles, all the way to the Wisconsin shore. It's a world quite unlike that of my barefoot childhood memories.

At Sturgeon Bay, I join the Coast Guard cutter *Mobile Bay,* one of the new class of small icebreakers commissioned for year-round search and rescue and clearing ice in the shipping channels. Its commanding officer, Lt. Erik Funk, explains the bubbler system of compressed air jettisoned below the waterline to help free the ship from locked ice, like that now imprisoning it at the pier. Water begins to boil around the hull and spread out over the ice, softening it with air from below, and collapsing it with the weight of water on its surface.

The twin diesel electrics are started and we begin the laborious process of rocking back and forth against the spring lines to break enough ice from around the hull so that we can clear the tugs moored off our bow and the two lake freighters, in for winter layover, astern. The ice clearing takes approximately an hour, and I'm standing on the bridge with Walter Moorland, the engineering officer. Moorland, a native of Washington, is telling me how he had underestimated the lakes when he was first transferred here from duty on Puget Sound. "I wasn't expecting anything like what they are," he muses. "The lakes can get a whole lot rougher. On the ocean you can have thirty-foot seas and the waves will come two hundred feet apart, but on the lakes the seas get just as big, and the waves might come every one hundred feet." It's the difference between a queasy but rhythmic ballet and a series of rock-shuddering jabs from a heavyweight. The lake waves blast you again and again while you're still reeling from the previous blow.

The *Mobile Bay* is 140-feet long with a single screw and two engines which, together, develop 25,000 horsepower. Horsepower-to-length ratio is perhaps the best gauge of a ship's capabilities in navigating ice. With a ratio of about seventeen-and-a-half, the *Mobile Bay*'s is about twice that of most freighters and about half that of the 290-foot cutter *Mackinaw*. In this age of austerity, ships like the *Mobile Bay* are the wave of the future. Two ships of its class, each with a crew of seventeen men and burning 200 gallons per hour of icebreaking operation can do the work of a cutter of the *Mackinaw* class which carries a crew of 127 men and burns 1,200 gallons per hour. The *Mackinaw* could just do the job a little faster.

Finally, we've freed enough ice to back clear of the ships astern, and as we maneuver to turn toward the channel I have a chance to look over the 770-foot freighter *St. Clair*. It seems a city afloat. When I drove into Sturgeon Bay and caught first sight of the icebound ore boats in the harbor, I was startled, as I have always been, by their immensity. They miniaturize every other object in their purview—boxcars, factories, bridges—as outlandishly as one of those gigantic plaster Xanadus on which a desperately isolated settlement along the interstate in say, South Dakota, pins its identity and hopes for survival.

In my childhood memories, these ships were like toys on the horizon, stable particulars of the seascape, so distant their movement was no more discernible than that of the sun. As I look up the black steel wall of its freeboard, perhaps forty feet to the rail, it seems inconceivable that this colossus could be fazed by the storms of any sea on Earth, and yet I recall that the *Fitzgerald,* in its time the largest freshwater ship afloat and, like the *Titanic,* thought to be unsinkable, was devoured by the raging waters of Lake Superior with "all her shrieking crew" in a matter of seconds.

Now we are clear and headed lakeward, and the roar of fracturing ice is impressive, a continuous rumbling explosion with no diminuendo. A single engine of the *Mobile Bay* will move her through clear water at thirteen knots, and engaging the second engine will increase that speed by only 1.7 knots. This minute gain in speed and the fact that it doubles the ship's fuel consumption to two hundred gallons an hour is a clear indication that it is used almost exclusively for breaking ice. The bow is three-inch steel at the stem and five-eighths of an inch along the ice-breaking belt. It's coated with something called "Inerta," a superslick Teflon-like paint.

We are reopening the track of approximately two-feet-thick brash ice like a serrated blade through stale bread, leaving a wake of wagon-sized slabs astern. To port, Lt. Funk points out two gunboats under construction for Saudi Arabia and a tuna trawler to be delivered to Ecuador. Strange progeny, it seems to me, for a boatyard in northern Wisconsin. After we clear the drawbridge to the outer harbor, we stop for lunch. There's no need to drop anchor, as the ice holds us firmly in place.

Though I hadn't been anticipating lunch aboard the *Mobile Bay* with enthusiasm, I am pleasantly surprised. In fact, I find the virtuosity of her cook more deeply impressive than her capacity for breaking ice. T-bone steaks, beautifully grilled to medium rare and smothered in mushrooms and onions, delicately braised new potatoes, mixed green salad, and the most delicious "Coast Guard"—not Navy, I am informed—bean soup I've ever tasted. In the officers' ward room, John Bechtle, the executive officer, is telling me how at first the wives of the crew were up in arms about the ship's cook because their husbands were regularly comparing their cooking, unfavorably, with his. "We've got a daily meal allowance of $4.17 per man, and it's amazing what a good cook can do with that. We have to hide him whenever the brass comes aboard or they'd steal him for their own mess. Nothing is more important for good morale than good chow."

What strikes me about the morale aboard the *Mobile Bay* is that it's not something that has to be consciously contended with. Though the ship appears spotless and efficiently run, the atmosphere is much less G.I. than I had anticipated. One gets the impression that this is a spectacular yacht in which each man has an equal share and equal pride.

While the galley is being secured after lunch, the executive officer obliges me by putting a Jacob's ladder over the side so that I might trudge out over the ice to get some photographs of the ship. The skipper has warned me to stay well clear of the bauchy ice around the ship's stern. The chill factor is well below zero and the footing difficult on the heaved and frozen surface of the bay. When I look up at the cutter's bow, I'm struck by the mass of ice coating it, which gives it the amorphous appearance of a slightly used figurine candle.

From the bridge, I notice that freeing the ship of ice is an almost continuous activity. Crewmen are constantly heaving chunks overboard. "We use baseball bats to break it free of the rails and superstructure," Lt. Funk tells me, "and we get about three cleanings per bat before they break. We've got some aluminum bats ordered. They're more expensive, but they'll last longer."

We're under way again, and Lt. Funk recites an old winter duty proverb, "If you break ice, you make ice," which refers to the fact that the ice in your track freezes harder and gets tougher to break each time. He explains that freshwater ice is harder than saltwater ice, tougher to break, but more stable. The broken ice comes together with the fast ice peaks and forms windows along our track.

Halfway up the channel leading out to Lake Michigan, we come into open water and suddenly there's a great stillness. The crunching roar of our bow against the ice pack had become the norm, and for a moment, the quiet is eerie, as if emerging into the silent sea. I can see "Christmas Trees" on the horizon, wave peaks which indicate rough seas, but in this twenty-knot offshore wind the waters in the immediate lee of the Wisconsin shore have only a moderate roll. Several crewmen take turns at the helm while we perform maneuvers to recalibrate a VHF direction finder, used to locate and track down the radio signals of ships in distress. "Everybody knows how to drive the boat," Lt. Funk comments. "My job as C.O. is just to keep it safe."

We spot several icebergs, their visible tops about the size of our ship, hazards to navigation which are noted and recorded. In the bitter wind and arctic landscapes of the shoreline, it's difficult to imagine that anyone will ever swim in these waters again or that, a few months from now, pleasure boats with scantily clad crews will be setting out from this bay for Mackinac or Detroit or up the St. Lawrence to the Atlantic and beyond.

Fishing

Sailfishing off Key West

W<small>E ARE FISHING</small> for sailfish off Key West and everything is as I imagined it: the roll and pitch of the deck, the whiteness of the transom upon which my bare feet are propped, the worn precision of the reels, the smell of bait and diesel. Then, at the edge of the Gulf Stream, the water abruptly darkens and our only connections with the land are the main channel markers along American Shoal.

The truth is that this kind of fishing is boring—boring enough to escalate the blood pressure and irritate the colon of a flagpole sitter. And, oddly enough, this propensity for boredom is the most fundamental aspect of its charm. Deep-sea fishing is more a meditation than an activity. After the first hour the novelty of its beauty wears off. The brilliantly variegated water becomes just brilliantly variegated water. The sun that bathed us in the warming and subtle hues of early morning becomes a brutal white light reflected in all directions, multiplying in intensity. If nothing else, I intend to get a good burn, a flushed face and bleached mustache as emblems of my patience.

The idling rumble of the engines becomes hypnotic, and watching four silver ballyhoo bait-fish and the "teaser" of rubber squids skipping over our wake hour after hour can become as tedious and as irritating to the eyes as adding an endless column of identical one-digit figures. Everything becomes an inducement to drift off, to adopt a glazed stare and rehearse old love affairs, to dredge up every conceivable worry, both real and imagined, I had come out here hoping to escape.

But there's something else to consider. I am not alone. There's a captain and a mate who do this every day. And I've made an arrangement with them: they drive the boat, take me where the fish are most likely to be, rig the baits, and help to keep the lines unfouled; and I pay attention to what's happening, watching those baits so that if the bill of a sailfish comes up through the wake I'm ready.

A sailfish will generally make a first pass, striking the bait with its bill as if to stun it. The fish will then fall off for a moment before hitting again, this time devouring the bait.

Paying attention becomes a point of honor that keeps me honest and awake. But as the time wears on I begin to break through the boredom, becoming aware of the life of the sea. The frigate birds to the east are circling because there's something moving under the surface that will keep them alive. And those needlefish skittering over the swells, trying to become birds, fleeing from something big beneath them.

As we turn to try and intercept whatever it is that's pursuing the needlefish, I watch them being attacked from above, and some of them, if not becoming birds, at least take flight for the first and last time. The big fish that chased them up to the waiting birds is not drawn to our lures, but for a little while we have felt something. Then the birds begin circling behind us, taking an interest in our baits, and we toss them a few bits of half-frozen fish to distract them.

This is the fourth day out, and nothing has happened. Not even one bait has been retrieved bearing teeth marks. By now we are all convinced, though we don't say it, that we could be just as profitably dragging our laundry. If I were fly-fishing on the Yellowstone I would at least be able to amuse myself by working out my line, spotting a pool just off the bank to test the accuracy and finesse of my cast, knowing that each time I set it down just right a four-pound brown trout might go for it. And if nothing happened, I would at least go home with the satisfaction of having *done* something. But here I just sit and listen to the surge of twin diesels as we ride off a swell, knowing that for these twenty-eight hours of fishing I have done little more than occupy space. And brood. It's a perilous moment. I'm on the ragged edge of lapsing into speculations about all the other places I could be, and all the things I could be doing.

I want the mate to jump over and grab one of the hooks.

Or I want the boat to sink so the Coast Guard will have to come and reel us up into the belly of a helicopter.

I want a story to tell.

And it's just at this point, just beyond hope, that the mystique comes back. "He was an old man . . ." Hemingway wrote, "and he had gone eighty-four days without taking a fish."

My eyes narrow to the baits again and I begin to feel wise, sagacious even. Everything looks right again. I'll maintain my composure. The others aboard won't be able to fault my performance even if it's no performance at all.

When the strike comes I'm not even thinking about fish anymore. I'm simply basking in my powers of endurance, and the first glimpse of that angry bill thrashing our teaser doesn't startle me. If it had happened the first day out I probably would have ripped the bait from the fish's jaws, snapping the delicate twelve-pound test line in my eagerness to land him, my mind fixed all the while on some winter night back in Michigan when I would stand beneath his plaster effigy and improve my virtuosity with each retelling.

But now, after three and a half days of waiting, it's almost an anticlimax. I grab one of the spinning rods from its holder and reel in the bait till it catches up to him. He turns from the teaser and takes the bait. He starts to run with it and I let him. When he stops, I reel in until he decides to run again. Meanwhile, the captain is backing down on him, playing him with the boat, closing the distance.

With twelve-pound test I can play him but I can't fight him. I just follow his lead and keep the pressure on. He comes out of the water, tail walks behind us, and I know that it would have been worth waiting eighty-four days for this. I'm in no hurry to bring him in. The ten or fifteen minutes during which I can feel him in my fingers goes by in a matter of seconds. And suddenly he is at the transom.

He is five or six feet long. He moves like nothing I have seen on earth, and his eye seems to roll for a glimpse of me. The mate has the leader in his hand and the gaff ready. He raises it for the kill. This is all like a movie I'm watching, and I hear my voice hollering:

"No!"

The gaff disappears and a long curved knife takes its place. The knife comes down on the leader. The skin of this fish would be the envy of every custom-body painter in the world. I can taste the blue of it, and suddenly it's a memory.

Now, months later, I wonder why I let him go, the only billfish I had, at that time, ever caught. It wasn't because I thought the sea would miss one fish or that I felt sentimental and simply didn't want to kill him. I've killed and eaten hundreds of fish.

When I was eighteen, I caught a forty-pound amberjack off Fort Lauderdale. It was nothing exceptional, but it had been a good hour-long fight and I felt it in my arms and shoulders for three days after. It was my first big fish, and I had it mounted. At that age I thought that a moment of fishing could be preserved in a trophy. It arrived by Railway Express a year later. It stayed in the box for another five, and I finally gave it away. I'm writing all this down now, not to preserve it, but so I can forget it. I'm going out to fly a kite this afternoon, and I don't want to think about anything but the sky.

The Marlin Misunderstanding

THE FIRST BIG fish I took on a fly was a tarpon that weighed somewhere between 140 and 160 pounds. I hooked her–tarpon above eighty pounds are almost always female–on a bright sandy flat on the ocean side of Key West, and she towed my skiff a mile up a channel through a flotilla of moored yachts before she finally gave up near a bridge on the Overseas Highway.

The last hour and twenty minutes of that fight was about as much fun as moving a piano. After a few screaming runs spiced with dazzling leaps, flips, and gill-rattling tail walks, the fish went for the bottom, and we settled into a grim tug-of-war in the ninety-degree heat. It wasn't very interesting for my twenty-six-year-old son, Frank, or our guide and fishing buddy, Simon Becker, to spend all that time watching a red-faced, middle-aged man sweating and grimacing with the butt of a fly rod buried in his navel. It ate up a good part of a June day when they could have been jumping fish of their own.

Later, during lunch with Simon and another guide, Michael Pollack, I learned that I probably could have boated that fish in twenty or thirty minutes if I'd known just how much pressure a twenty-pound test leader will take.

"With more big fish under your belt, you bring 'em in faster," Michael said, "because you don't really care if you break 'em off. It's easier on you and it's easier on the fish."

I verified this on subsequent tarpon and then on Pacific sailfish off Costa Rica. I put all the muscle I had into the fight and within fifteen minutes of the appearance of a bill at our teasers, I'd boated and released my first sailfish on fly.

Gee, this is easy, I thought. I bowed to the fish's gorgeous leaps, played it hard while the captain backed down on it, and it came to the boat with sails flared, lit up like blue neon.

The leaps of sailfish are spectacular and usually fairly predictable, alternating left and right, about forty-five degrees off the stern. Putting heavy pressure on them and backing down the boat at every opportunity, I was able to land one in only four minutes after setting the hook. The fish was hardly tired; still, we held it alongside at slow speed, forcing water through its gills to ensure it was fit before we let it go.

I was amazed how quickly I'd gotten comfortable with this kind of fishing. The drowsing Pacific swells nearly satisfied my innate human hunger for blue, a deep cobalt/indigo; maxi-blue, I called it. The teamwork was intricate, the encounters exciting though not too terribly demanding. I was feeling pleased and pretty confident.

AND THEN THE marlin showed up.

The thing was that, while I was fighting it, I knew only that it was big. I didn't realize it was a marlin, and I've spent a lot of time since wondering what I might have done differently, had I known. The largest sailfish we had taken weighed about one hundred pounds, but a blue marlin will commonly weigh three hundred pounds, and could reach a ton.

There was a bill at the teaser, the usual Chinese fire drill of getting the teaser out of its face and the fly in front of it, the strip, the hookup, and then all hell broke loose.

This fish, unlike any of the others, took off like a crazed skipping stone, greyhounding dead astern, a dozen and a half chain-lightning leaps in thirty seconds, ripping off my line and about three hundred yards of thirty-pound Dacron backing. All I could do was hang on, bowing to and recovering from the jumps like a yo-yo and keeping my right hand well clear of the screaming reel and its blurred handle, which could have scythed my fingers like a rotary lawn mower. One hell of a sailfish, I thought. The captain was backing on him, and I was winding up bright yellow Dacron as fast as I could.

Nobody bothered to tell me it was a marlin, and I think now that only the captain knew. The mate spoke no English and Simon was up on the bridge with the captain. Like me, he was inexperienced with billfish and, although the captain had said, "*Pez vela no brincon asi!*" ("No sailfish jumps like that!"), Simon didn't mention it.

I'd retrieved two or three hundred yards of Dacron by the time the boat stopped backing down, but the rest of the bright yellow line faded straight down toward the bottom through the peerless sun-streaked blue. That's when the lifting and cranking began.

I took in line steadily, if not easily, until I could see the Albright knot, which I knew to be about ten feet above the dark green of my one-hundred-foot fly line. And there the fish parked. From that point up, every rotation of the reel was like trying to lift a Winnebago, and I was beginning to regret having switched from a fourteen- to a twelve-weight rod for this fish. But gradually I worked it up until a satisfying dark green veneer of line covered the yellow backing.

At a depth of about fifty feet the cranking became even tougher and the recovery of line slowed to a stop. For a few seconds nothing happened. Then the rod began to shudder and suddenly my forearm was pulled down hard against the gunwhale. I eased my palm away from the reel as all that hard-earned fly line and far too much yellow backing followed the fish down.

This wasn't like any other fish I had seen or fought. Maybe I had foul-hooked it, I thought. It was beginning to look like a long afternoon.

Once more, with far greater effort than it takes to tell about it, I managed to wrench the fish back in close enough to recover the first fifty feet of fly line. Then it was off again and I had to repeat the process.

We did this laborious bargaining four or five times, until I thought the afternoon was pretty well shot. Glancing at my watch, I was amazed to discover it was only two o'clock. The fight had been going on for only an hour, but I was nearly exhausted. My legs were trembling, I had goose bumps, and I felt cold and was shivering in that ninety-degree sun. When I took a cup of water from the mate, my hand trembled as though I were shaking a martini.

I thought about breaking the fish off. I was anticipating terminal chest pains, and in any case I didn't want to monopolize the afternoon's fishing. Yet I figured that if the fish was anywhere near as tired as I was, it was going to need resuscitation before it resumed its life in the sea.

When the fish sounded for the sixth time, the rod suddenly snapped in two places and the severed sections quickly disappeared down the yellow backing–a primitive telegraph carrying news to the fish that it was winning. Well, maybe the shorter rod, about three feet long, would make a better lifting tool. Simon said he thought it did.

My pelvis and abdomen were bruised from the rod butt, and I was trying to keep it braced against the narrow leather belt on my shorts. The mate brought me a Styrofoam and nylon fighting belt, but the rod butt, with no gimbel, kept slipping off.

I decided to give the fish every chance to break free. I screwed the drag down hard, clamped the line against the grip, and cupped the reel firmly, but when the fish wanted line, it took it away. I felt near death, desperate and a bit apologetic toward Simon for monopolizing the day with another epic trudge.

Once more I slowly recovered line until I could see the Albright knot, with my broken rod tip hanging from it. At fifty feet we could see the blue and silver silhouette of the fish, but couldn't tell how big it was. There was another fish with it, its mate and/or cheerleader, I assumed. Maybe if that other fish deserted my quarry, it'd be disheartened.

Nearly a dozen times I thought I'd turned the fish and had a momentary sense of impending victory, or impending relief. But each time it was squelched at a distance of about fifty feet, when, once again, the fish said, "No."

The rod guides left on the surviving section were coated with a film like soap flakes or shaved wax where the Teflon coating had peeled off my line and backing. Then the guides themselves started going. First the top guide pinged off the ferrule and shot across the cockpit like a tiny piece of shrapnel. Then the Teflon rings pulled out of the stripping guides and became little red lifesavers dancing on the taut line.

I tried to convey a mental message down the line to the fish: "Give up, dammit! It's for your own good." Yet the fish was fighting a force that was threatening its existence, and I was supposedly doing this for fun. At least it had started out that way. Now this great being had become my responsibility, for I was certain it would die of exhaustion or fall prey to sharks if it didn't receive some resuscitation. Yet I also feared that if I persisted in this madness I might die from heart failure or be asphyxiated by the diesel fumes billowing up over the transom.

Brown boobies flew by. Frigate birds watched. Dolphin jumped off to the west toward Malaysia. Another charter boat, with our friends David Kesar and Tom Rowland aboard, passed several hundred feet astern.

"I've got them on the radio, Dan," Simon hollered down from the bridge, "and they're pulling for you." I wished they literally *could* pull for me.

I thought of Santiago in *The Old Man and the Sea,* but resisted the notion that I was doing something heroic. Nevertheless, I wanted to end the struggle with the fish by the boat, and I couldn't understand why I hadn't been able to break its will, if fish have a will.

"*Muerto,*" the mate said. "*La pez es muerto.*"

He was telling me the fish had died down there. I couldn't comprehend this immediately, and when it did begin to sink in, all I could think about was that other fish with him, how I had killed his buddy or mate with my stubbornness—and how I had almost let this stubbornness kill me.

Using all my remaining strength, I tried to lift the supposedly dead fish, but couldn't budge it, couldn't take up even half a turn of line. The mate reached over the transom and grabbed my fly line, and I let him do it. He pulled sharply, and the leader parted. Simon patted me on the back and called me an old tackle buster. "Three hours," he said, shaking his head.

I reeled in the limp line, discarded the stubby remnant of my rod, and lay down on the cushioned cover of the port engine. I was in pain and feeling utterly sad and defeated. The engine revved up for the hour-long run back to Quepos, and I fell asleep.

Later, as we were approaching the harbor, Simon told me the fish had been a marlin. The captain confirmed it and said he was quite certain it hadn't died. Of course, I don't know if he was saying that just to cheer me up, but if he was, it worked. I was, and still am, willing to believe him.

Yet, I still wonder. If I had known it was a blue marlin, would I have been willing to stay out there all night if I could have persuaded the captain to do it?

From the comfort of my writing desk, it's easy to say I think I might have. I wonder what the marlin thinks.

The Fascination of
What's Difficult

THERE IS A possibility of going crazy out here on the glassy water of this falling tide. And going crazy is part of the idea—crazy in the sense of getting lost and, more to the point, of losing ourselves. By the ways in which normal people think, we would *have* to be crazy to devote so much energy and so many precious hours to trying to fool one particular soft-lipped fish into believing a quarter-sized dollop of beige yarn and feathers with a couple of beady lead eyes, giving it the aghast expression of a thyroid patient, might be the succulent crab it's been seeking for lunch.

We are poling a broad flat on the west side of the Marquesas, zeroing in on a patch of nervous water where, a moment ago, we are almost certain, we saw the brief silver flash of a tailing permit. We know, however, from long experience, that what caught our attention may have simply been our desire to see a permit's tail, a filleting knife piercing the surface as the elusive fish angles down to the shallow bottom to eat.

Fly-fishing on the flats from a small skiff is a team sport. You can do it alone if you have enough skill and patience, but since you're trying to spot and hunt down an individual fish without letting him know you're there, the results are seldom satisfying. Especially for permit. It usually takes an experienced set of eyes to discern the shape and movement of your quarry through moving water against the dappled bottom of coral heads, sponges, sand, and turtle grass; it also takes a fine sense of geometry to pole the boat close enough to the fish so the angler, standing ready on the bow with ninety or one hundred feet of line stripped out, can present his fly without spooking the fish or snagging the poler off his perch on the backcast.

I had been at this game six years now, without success. In that time I'd boated and released dozens of magnificent tarpon, bonefish, and barracuda on flies and had taken a couple of spectacular permit on a spinning rod with live crabs. But fooling a permit with a fly is another matter. Taking a permit on a crab is a fine thing to do, like getting your bat on a good fastball, but taking one on a fly in the Florida Keys is akin to making solid contact off Nolan Ryan. In those six years I'd had maybe three dozen opportunities to put a permit on the other end of my flyline. A few of those I blew with sloppy casting, and a dozen more spooked before my guide and longtime co-conspirator, Simon Becker, could pole the boat close enough to give me the opportunity of scaring them off with great loops of white flyline waved over their heads like a semaphore of impending doom. But there were three dozen times at least when my imitation crab–for some wonderfully perverse reason called a Merkin–had settled down perfectly in front of a feeding permit and been twitched with the subtlest little strips of line, only to have this most finicky of the family *carangidae* brush it aside with its severely snubbed snout and turn away haughtily as if its intelligence had been insulted. Or maybe even its virtue.

There are many highly accomplished saltwater fly-fishermen who haven't had the pleasure of battling a permit, though there are a few obsessive types who have made a career of pursuing permit and, in an extreme case–like that of Del Brown, who spends upward of a hundred days a year at it–have enticed several hundred to take a fly. And there are places in the Caribbean and in the shoal waters of Mexico where–so my more widely experienced fishing friends tell me–permit are generally smaller and a good bit sillier than they are on the flats off Key West. There are also anglers who have claimed permit on flies offshore after bringing them to a feeding frenzy with chum, but that's a whole other order of experience, more like shooting a captive kudu on a game ranch and offering the trophy as evidence that one is a skillful hunter.

Fly-fishing for permit is the fortuitous coming together of a broad range of long-practiced skills to locate, stalk, mystify, outfence, capture, and safely release an idea clothed in intelligence, wariness, tenacity, and fins. It requires a knowledge of tides, currents, winds, temperature, and the behavior of birds and rays, as well as vigilance, instinct, muscular and delicate casting—maybe out to ninety feet in a bothering wind—timing and sensitivity in setting the hook, a lot of luck in clearing the line to the reel, and, from there on, the strength of your arms, an understanding of the fish, dexterity, readiness of wit, and, if it all works out, the grace not to gloat about it. It's really more akin to hunting than to trolling for dolphins, reef fishing, or even working a spring creek. Catching a permit on a fly is something to write home about, assuming, of course, that those at home have any idea of what's involved or even what a permit is.

To many, this kind of fishing seems pointlessly difficult and intimidating. A friend of mine calls it my "holier-than-thou" kind of fishing and tells me that when she goes fishing, she just wants to catch fish. And Woody Sexton, an old-time Keys flats guide with whom I first went tarpon fishing almost thirty years ago, used to say that fly-fishing for permit is really a spectator sport. It's true we set up a bunch of rules that give the fish all kinds of advantages, but I do want to catch them. Some of my fondest memories are of sitting on a channel pier connecting a small inland lake with "the big lake," as we called Lake Michigan, fishing for perch just off the bottom with live minnows. Perch fishing was something I loved to do when I was ten years old, and I could recommend it to almost anyone as a pleasant way to spend a summer afternoon. It's just that now there's something else I love to do and find infinitely challenging, and, more to the point, I love the places in which I can do it. When I'm out on the flats, I *become* that world, and I forget all about *me* and the baggage I carry. It's all that life of sea and sky where "mind chains cannot clink," as Thomas Hardy would say.

But catching fish is only one small part of why I like to go fishing. The possibility of catching fish and, in the case of permit, the improbability of it, is what keeps my adrenaline up and my attention focused. It's that quality of attention and my absorption in some of the most beautiful and abundantly fecund waters on earth that I'm seeking.

As it turns out, the nervous water we've been watching is in fact a tailing permit, but before we can sneak within casting range, the shadow of a low-flying cormorant crosses its feeding spot and the delicate ripple becomes a purposeful bulge, like that of a small nuclear submarine getting under way as it shoots off toward the safety of deeper water with alarming speed. I have seen fleeing permit more than a few times and continue to be awestruck by their power and acceleration. And as we watch this one, it's easy to envision how thrilling it might be to see a white flyline ripping its impressive wake and to hear the high-pitched scream of the reel.

It had been a good morning for permit. I'd had two well-placed shots refused at the edge of a channel on the south side of the Marquesas and two more blown with abysmal casts when I tried too hard to drive the fly into the wind and watched the leader collapse back on itself in a pathetic heap.

Textbook casts are fairly easy for me, until the fish show up. And when you've been in the gun seat as many times as I have, you ought to have learned to control the adrenaline. One morning the previous winter I had contained my excitement masterfully during three clearly observed, near-perfect presentations to the same huge permit off a shore called Palm Beach on the west side of this archipelago. That fish might've run about thirty-five pounds. And when it finally swam away after the third refusal, my right hand started shaking so violently I had to lay down my rod and eat a couple of chocolate-chip cookies to keep from fainting. I also had to remind myself that what I was doing here was supposed to be fun. And it is fun. But sometimes it feels as if you're endlessly laying your heart out for the same merciless woman. We watch the fleeing ridge of water dissolve in the rip of current where the Marquesas fall off into Rebecca Channel, and I seem to let out more breath than I remember taking in.

We decide to run around to the north side of the Marquesas and see what we can find. On our way we speed past a basking loggerhead and glance back to see him kick over and sink into the teal green depths. We see an eagle ray make a spectacular leap and crash with great sheets of spray off our port bow and agree that, with or without fish on, this has been a spectacular day.

We drop down off plane, idle up to the edge of the flat, and pole in to within about fifty feet of a shore that, if it weren't protected as a National Wildlife Sanctuary, would be a beachfront developer's dream. As we parallel the white sand edge, I half expect to see a rubber football or a pair of errant water wings drift by, so I'm startled when I hear Simon call out, "Two fish at two o'clock. They're permit, and they're coming right for us."

I glance over my shoulder and spot them instantly. They stand out like a couple of stainless-steel baking pans in this foot-and-a-half-deep water.

"No time to set up the boat," Simon whispers. There are two good-sized fish swimming side by side a hundred feet out and closing fast. I drop my fly to the water, make two false casts toward the beach to clear the shooting head, double-haul, and lay down my backcast about sixty feet behind me. It lands about six feet to the right of their approach. I'm about to pick it up and try again when Simon whispers, "Wait! They're turning on it."

I look again and can't believe what I'm seeing.

"She's going for it," Simon rasps. "She's going to eat it."

And so she does. After six years of my watching permit scrutinize and decline my presentations, this particular fish in this most improbable setting is going for it like a meteor being sucked into a black hole. I doubt I could have kept her away from it. I watch her close in on my faux crab, and suddenly my leader is trailing from her mouth as she turns and bolts off toward Texas. I grasp the line with my left hand and strike her lightly to set the hook. Instinctively I look down to make sure I'm not standing on the line and then realize, as it comes tight and the reel starts screaming, that since I've done little stripping, there isn't much line to clear.

"She's on. You've got a permit on," Simon screams. Simon has taken close to a dozen permit on fly himself, and yet he seems more excited about this one than I am.

The fish makes an initial run of about 150 yards in the direction from which she came, and her companion sticks right with her, streaking over the dark turtle grass, two fleeing spirits in their argentine brilliance. Then she turns and comes back at us, and I'm taking in line as fast as I can, trying to keep my hand rotating smoothly in the tight circumference of the reel. The other fish is gone now, having sensed something awry when her desperate companion suddenly reversed course and headed back toward the shallows. Fifty feet from the boat, the fish turns side to, and I feel the prodigious strength of her lateral swimming. I remember how, a few years back, in conversation with a friend, we designed the perfect fighting fish and decided it would be shaped just like the scrappy, slab-sided bluegill, only bigger, much bigger. What we had come up with, we realized, was the permit.

I bend the rod low to the water and turn her to the right. Then, when she tries to swim off toward the Dry Tortugas, I work her back toward Key West. Simon positions the skiff to keep me facing her and calls to me from the poling tower, "I hope you're remembering to breathe down there."

And I do remember to breathe. I'm savoring this brief affair with the fish of my dreams, though, after all these rehearsals, it seems almost anticlimactic. But only a little. Pound for pound, permit are the most tenacious of fighters. I haven't gotten her to the boat yet, and I realize it could be a long time before I have another opportunity like this. She makes three more heroic runs for the open sea, a couple of last-ditch turns around the bow, and then she's lolling at the gunwale.

SIMON GRASPS THE leader, takes her gently by the tail, lifts her over the deck, and cradles her like a baby in both hands. I hold her for a photograph, then kiss her conch-pink lips, kneel to the waterline, and let her go.

Last Words

Last Words

$\mathbf{H}$E MOTIONED ME down to the pillow where he lay in the intensive care unit. "I just want you to know I don't give a damn how this turns out," he whispered.

"I know you don't." I started to reach for his hand, then hesitated. It occurred to me that in his mind this wasn't one of the major events of his life but rather a sort of messy inconvenience that was happening very near the end of it. I had never seen my father lying in bed before, except perhaps very early on a Christmas morning when my sisters and I would barge into our parents' bedroom to awaken them to our frenzy of yuletide avarice.

There were tubes in his nose, and a heart monitor strapped to his chest, and yet I had to restrain him from trying to rise in deference each time a nurse entered the room. Other than being treated for a shrapnel wound in France in 1918, my father had never been in a hospital or even in a doctor's office, and didn't understand the protocol.

Several hours earlier my mother had called. "I think your father is dying. He's turned blue," she said. I raced the five or six miles to their house and arrived just ahead of the ambulance I had called before leaving home. He *had* turned blue. Congestive heart failure, the doctor said. His resistance to treatment, to having anyone inconvenienced by his condition, had been precluded by the fluid strangling his heart and, with a look that seemed to beg forgiveness, he surrendered to me and to the ambulance driver and allowed us to strap him onto the gurney. At the bend in the staircase his breathing stopped, and while the ambulance driver and I balanced him over the banister, the doctor plunged a needle into his chest and shot adrenaline directly into his heart.

THE OSCILLOSCOPE WAS the brightest thing in the room. Every few seconds an incandescent green arrow erupted and skittered off the northeast sector of the screen. My father and I were having one of those awkward silences we'd shared so often before when we found ourselves alone together, the same laconic spell I have since experienced with my son, like trying to make conversation on your first date with a girl you can't believe would actually deign to go out with you. I've never been able to figure out exactly why it's so hard to think of what to say, but I suspect it's because nothing can be taken back and because you respect and admire this person so much that you're always a little afraid of muddying the water between you. Or maybe it isn't that at all.

Once when my mother had taken up one of her self-imposed exiles in a Chicago hotel and my father had reluctantly followed her there, I took the opportunity, in a letter, to say some things I never seemed to be able to say in person. I simply told him that I loved him and that it had occurred to me that if my son ended up feeling about me the way I felt about him, that whatever else I did or didn't do in my life, I would consider it to have been a success.

A few days later he called, and through the interminable pauses he characteristically took in his speech, often waiting a full thirty seconds for the wanted word to occur to him, he thanked me for my letter and told me how it had made him think of all the men he had loved and how he wished he had taken the opportunity to tell them rather than telling someone else at their funerals.

I began to remember all the things I had said to my father, the things I had regretted because I feared, in retrospect, they would make him think less of me, things that caused him to sputter and flounder for a response, like the morning when I was twelve and told him that I thought it was time I acquired some sexual experience and suggested he should take me to a prostitute. I read a lot as a child, stored up ideas from books, and believed they ought to be tested on life.

The nurse returned to try to find a vein in his already needle-ravaged arms. He attempted to rise and I restrained him with a hand on his shoulder. "It's okay, she works here," I said, glad for the excuse to say something even so obvious.

He looked down at his bloodstained, perforated arm. The nurse was taking up her tools again to try and torment him back toward life. For a moment he had the imploring look of a child, and I wanted to protect him. But from what? I'm not fond of needles myself, though I'd have offered my arm if I could have. A Zen master I once knew told me that the really tough thing about compassion, what makes it so important, is that in actual experience we can't take on even so much as a fart for somebody else. My father would have appreciated that. It's the sort of thing he might have said.

The nurse made several more futile attempts with her needle and surgical tube, and then her heart won out. "Okay," she said, "we'll give it a rest."

I once had a conversation with a friend about last words. "Do you ever worry that the last thing you say on earth might be something really stupid," he asked, "really inane, and that you'll see your life floating away and think, 'Oh no! I can't believe I actually said *that!*'?" He told me the story of a famous restaurateur who raised his head feebly from the pillow and croaked, "Slice the ham thinner." And he told me how his father's last words to him came in the form of a precept: "Never eat a hamburger in a drug store," something Laertes might have heard before leaving Denmark.

My friend, Simon Rosenbaum, told me of his eighty-six-year-old father dying in the hospital. A nurse was trying to place an oxygen mask over his nose and mouth but Simon's father kept pushing it away.

Finally the nurse gave a deep sigh and said, "Well, Mr. Rosenbaum, are you comfortable?"

Mr. Rosenbaum rolled his head to face her. "I make a living," he said.

I ONCE HEARD someone say that many last words concern food. Eating is a pleasure—or should be a pleasure—we engage in several times a day, and if you don't take enjoyment in it, you don't enjoy your life. My father loved food. His letters to my grandparents from the trenches in France were mostly about food and the lack of it. He speculated about the pea crop in Michigan that summer, quipped that the only real danger he faced was from starvation, as they had the Germans on the run and it often took four days for their mess to catch up with them, and, as an afterthought, remarked that he had forgotten to mention in his previous letters that he had been awarded the *Croix de Guerre* several months earlier.

My father's last words were also about food. They came after another of those long silent spells and come back to me whenever I catch myself taking things a little too seriously. He motioned me down close again and whispered, "You know the only thing I'm going to miss?"

"No. What's that?"

"That spaghetti sauce your mother was cooking," he said. He looked off toward the foot of the bed and smiled as if he could see it floating there in all its heaped and steaming splendor. Well, those weren't really his last words. I remember now that he did say one more thing, something that made me think of Orson Welles saying "Rosebud" at the beginning of *Citizen Kane,* something I will never understand. He said, "You know, I think this is a blessing."

I knew what he meant, that it was a blessing he was going out like this rather than lingering on and becoming a burden. But, just to prolong the conversation, I asked, "What's that?"

His eyes swept across the ceiling and he smiled broadly, almost laughing, as if he'd seen something that pleased and amused him. "The Sky Raiders," he said. And then he closed his eyes.

I held his hand, feeling a little stunned by his inside joke. The Sky Raiders. I wanted to see this vision that he had found so entertaining. Maybe in time I will. I held his hand until it turned cold, and once the self-consciousness of life had fled, the self-consciousness of my life, I spoke freely. I said things like, "Well, what else is there to miss?" and "I love you, Dad," and "Don't worry, I'll take care of everything," and other things that didn't really need to be said, but that I needed to say, things I'm saying still.

A Few Thoughts
on Adam's Curse

As THE SUN begins to burn through the morning fog my eye is drawn to a curious movement in the grass. Two quail, in their odd, pizzicato gait, scurry past my window, and I see them simultaneously as divine fellow creatures and succulent roasted delights. I won't kill these lovely neighbors to put them on my plate—those days are over for me—though I'd be delighted to join any one of my still predatory friends to savor them with a little foie gras, garlic-roasted potatoes, and a bottle of Di Bruno Sangiovese. I know that this imagined feast, to which I seek an invitation, will be a sacrament, and that my friends will not have taken these lives without an awareness of their own mortality, and also without a touch of regret.

Killing, too, is a form of our ancient wandering affliction, to borrow from Rilke, a form of Adam's curse, as is the language through which I must labor to discover what I am trying to say here. The birthright of Esau, the hunter, has been usurped by Jacob, the herdsman, yet both would kill to court favor with their father.

There's a wonderful passage in *The Upanishads:*

Oh wonderful, oh wonderful, oh wonderful.
I am food, I am food, I am food.
I am an eater of food. I am an eater of food. I am an eater of food.

Joseph Campbell suggests that clinging to yourself and not letting yourself become food is the primary life-denying act that runs counter to the great mystery experience of thanking the animal one is about to eat for having given itself. For we realize that in the realm of *real* time, it is always ourselves we are eating.

I wonder how many hunters today, how many so-called sportsmen, carry this kind of awareness about what they are doing, let alone how many would kill a being—a lion, a wolf, or a trophy bull—they have no intention of eating? How many kill with empathy for the animal? How many see themselves as food? We are life feeding on life, the most fundamental fact of our existence, and if we're not aware of and grateful to the various spirits who give up their lives to sustain us, mere existence, not life, is our portion. *And whoever walks a furlong without sympathy*—Whitman warns us—*walks to his own funeral dressed in his shroud.*

On a sultry afternoon in Key West almost twenty-five years ago, Truman Capote told me about all the mass murderers he had interviewed. He told me that the one thing they all had in common was that they broke into uncontrollable laughter when they told him, in detail, about the actual acts of killing they had performed. Tears streamed down their cheeks as they tried to contain themselves to finish their stories. And, without exception, they apologized to him, saying, "I'm sorry. I know this isn't funny to you, but it was funny to me when I did it."

THIS IS SOMETHING we learned—or should have—from *Macbeth,* that what distinguishes the cold-blooded killer is his, or her, lack of imagination, his utter lack of empathy, that he is able to kill without ever imagining himself on the receiving end, that he is incapable of imagining himself as a victim.

My father was passionate about bird hunting, and so I grew up as a hunter. I have cherished memories of the sonar-like conversations by which we would keep track of each other's whereabouts as we stalked pheasants through a field of tall corn, and of time spent together—time we probably wouldn't have otherwise shared—as the predawn mist rose from the water surrounding our duck blind while we shivered indistinguishably through the chill and our anticipation of the first pass of canvas backs.

Later, in my teens, I'd often get up at 4:00 A.M. on late fall mornings and paddle through the marsh with my friend Bob VandenBerg to spend an hour or two before Mr. Cooper's economics class watching over our decoys while we broke football training rules with our furtive pack of Mapleton cigarettes. And I have other, less fond, memories, of mornings when the ducks never appeared and we exorcised our boredom and our idle lust blasting inedible coots simply because they were within range. Their blood darkened the bilge of our boat and their limp bodies condemned me—I can't speak for my friend Bob—like the albatross of *The Ancient Mariner,* long after we pitched them into the cattails as we paddled home.

Though I miss the camaraderie of upland hunting, the intricate work with the dogs, and the satisfactions of weariness and well-earned appetite at the end of a long day in the field, I never hunted without feeling a little bit conflicted, never enjoyed it without a mild accompanying sense of dread and a touch of regret each time the rules of the game required me to take a life. There was always that sobering moment. Maybe I'm a more blatant hypocrite now. Maybe we all are, to some degree. But there finally came that day when I held the warm, still-fluttering body of a downed wookcock in my hand and saw for a moment my own eye reflected in his before I put his lights out against the butt of my gun. And I knew then that I didn't want to do this anymore. Maybe I'd gotten soft. Maybe it was a heightened sense of my own mortality. Maybe age. Maybe all of these.

OFTEN, WHEN WE look very closely at any given realm of life what we see is a world of terror, as in the ultimate dominion of decay, the terror of the pewit about to be impaled by the jaeger, of whatever creature my fly may at the moment be imitating as it's devoured by the trout, and of the trout itself, being bulled inevitably in its struggle toward the shore to be beheaded and stripped of its meat. And yet when we step back to a more encompassing window, even now to see the earth itself from the point of view of the moon, we see all these minute tyrannies as the finely woven threads of a complete and flourishing fabric. What ruthless hoard of microbes may, at this moment, be scourging the plains of my hand?

I'M STILL A meat eater, and I'm still a fly-fisher. Last night I killed a two-pound rainbow trout for my supper and savored it both as a delicacy and as a sacrament of the interdependent nature of our existence, while at the same time having serious second thoughts even about the undeniable pain and distress I cause the trout or tarpon I catch and release for my pleasure.

Recently, my oldest and dearest friend, a man who keeps October sacrosanct and will brook no interference whatsoever with grouse season, confessed that he'd been having second thoughts. "Hunting is so final," he mused, "so Wagnerian, while fishing seems to have an almost Mozartian lightness about it. In fishing, at least, most of the time, you have the option of returning the fish to its life. There is no catch-and-release hunting."

Just now I lay down my pen to swat a yellow jacket my dog was worrying against the window glass. I did it to prevent my dog from getting stung and to protect myself as well. The minor threat is past, and the yellow jacket lies curled in death on the windowsill. What the answer is, I don't know. With Rilke, I'm resolved to live the questions.

Notebook of an
Arctic Explorer

I WOKE THIS morning to the clattering call of sandhill cranes and lay for a moment trying to make sense of the beamed ceiling of my bedroom. A week earlier I had awakened to this same unmusical song in a tent on a nameless lake scarcely two hundred miles from the Magnetic North Pole. Why, I wondered, are these cranes here now in this abundance, on a hot summer morning just west of the Teton range in eastern Idaho, while those other cranes were standing on the thin tundra soil, a few inches above the permanent ice shelf, where, already now, in late August, winter is earnestly presenting its card. The movements of animals and the reasons behind them are matters of conjecture, even for scientists. These cranes are here and those cranes were there.

JUST BEFORE I left, somewhat reluctantly, for my ten-day trip to the Arctic, I told my wife that I envied her the time she would spend there at home without me. Though maybe what I was really up to in going was trying to take a vacation from me. We see the world by the light of our own moon, someone said. The shadow it casts is no one else's. Though the Arctic moon was too pale for shadows, above a land that, in August, never gets dark. And in the low sun along the horizon, my shadow was the longest I've ever seen, all legs, with no head at all.

I WAS WATCHING the shadow of our 737 as it dropped down to meet us on the runway at Kaluktutiak, more commonly known as Cambridge Bay. And suddenly our shadow, the runway, the entire Arctic coastline disappeared in a cloud of smoke, which turned out to be a cloud of dust. I'd never before landed on a gravel runway in a commercial jet, and it alerted me to the fact that, with the possible exception of the Kaisut Desert, I'd never been quite this far off the beaten path. Just below the gravel is the permafrost, so you could, I suppose, say we were landing on ice. I'd also never flown in a commercial jet with moveable bulkheads, sectioning off most of fuselage for cargo, ahead of the six or eight rows of seats provided for passengers. Cambridge Bay (population 1,400, mostly Inuit) is the demographic center of an Arctic island the size of Texas.

I HAD HOPED to see what Polaris might look like this close to the pole and to see the Great Bear, directly overhead, revolving around it, but between prevailing cloud cover and the absence, this time of year, of anything resembling what I think of as night, apart from the sun, I saw no stars at all.

OSTENSIBLY, I CAME here at the invitation of my son Frank to fly-fish for arctic char. This expedition is my sixtieth birthday present, and since I will have my birthday above the Arctic Circle on a day on which night will never really fall, I'm wondering if, technically, I remain fifty-nine.

The arctic char is most closely related to the Dolly Varden trout, though, the char's greater size notwithstanding, due to the lower light conditions and the greater density of colder water, as Barry Lopez points out,* arctic fish species tend to have larger eyes and be stronger swimmers than their more southerly counterparts.

Except in desert country, fishing is always a good excuse for travel and a ligature around which to build an adventure. We have no concrete information about fly-fishing for char, no guides to tell us what sorts of arrangements of feathers and fur might appeal to a char, so our fishing will be largely experimental. But then everything about this trip, into country so unlike anything we've experienced, will be largely experimental. We've brought just about every imaginable kind of streamer and dry fly, but find, oddly, that flies designed to attract tropical bonefish are the most effective. And I discover that the closest analogy I can make to fishing for char is to the bonefish. You present the fly in clear water over a frequently sandy bottom and strip it in slow retreat, as to a bonefish. And when the char takes it, he makes a long, streaking run, like a bonefish, and then, again like a bonefish, turns and runs right back at you so that you are reeling in line almost as rapidly as the fish has taken it out in order not to give him the slack with which to throw the barbless hook. We had enough success with our bonefishing techniques to make char the staple of our diet: boiled char, fried char, char sashimi, and char-salad-sandwiches.

THE FLOAT PLANE, which met us at an inlet near Cambridge Bay, took us to our base camp and from there to our outpost camps, all the way up to the Arctic Ocean. We seldom flew at an altitude of more than one hundred feet, and in the course of our time there we flew over hundreds of miles of tundra, with lakes and rivers everywhere, reflecting each brief appearance of the sun, like fragments of fallen sky. And it occurred to me that this wasn't really a land at all, at least in these

*Barry Lopez, *Arctic Dreams* (New York: Charles Scribner's Sons, 1986).

precious few weeks of summer, but rather a great water with some land running through it.

Hiking up the Nanook River to a place I imagine I might be holding in the current if I were an arctic char, I splash through rocky pools in my waders and trudge lightly along the sedgy meadows as if I were walking on a great sponge. And, in fact, I am walking on a sort of sponge. Since the ice moved out–the ice as in the last Ice Age–there are places in this region that have been rising, like a decompressing sponge, as much as thirty centimeters a year.

I'm struck by just how dramatically my mood changes with the slightest appearance of sunlight on and above this barren landscape–from that of glowering awe and implied threat to one of deep contentment. A brief breakthrough, glorying the river rocks and the stippled water itself, brings an instant of complete clarity to the entirety of my life and death below the tree line. I can't say more about it than that. It's a rare moment without metaphor. Or finally, it's all metaphor.

THERE ARE CAIRNS everywhere on the tundra. Is it simple loneliness, I wonder, the desire to create some artificial being, some point of human reference in this daunting and almost featureless landscape that causes these structures to be built? Maybe, because even the slightest protrusion can be seen from a great distance, they are personal aids to navigation, a way of finding one's way back. Maybe they are built to assuage boredom near a campsite, maybe to say "I was here," though no personal "I" is identified. Maybe they are built because the rocks themselves asked someone to arrange them that way, though we, or even the person who arranged them, didn't understand the request in terms of language. Maybe they are vertical petroglyphs built by another form of the Anasazi. Maybe someone like me built them simply to make another someone like me wonder.

THE LACK OF discernable color variation in any large-scale view of the terrain and the preternaturally clear arctic air conspire to make a joke of my judgments of scale and distance. What turned out to be the antlers of a caribou I at first took to be a set of radio antennas towering over the horizon. After a very few steps, a distant mesa or butte often turned into a ridge of small rocks I could easily step over.

Canada geese are whooping it up somewhere behind me, and a seagull, perfectly white, hovers to see if I might be edible. I spot an igloo-like structure with a tall antenna on a rise to the north, but when I arrive it has shrunk to become another cairn, not more than a foot high, and the antenna a plain piece of lath. I wanted it to be a tomb on this almost imperceptible hill.

THE ARCTIC IS a place without wood, as we think of it, the largest plant being the ground-hugging willow with roots and branches about the diameter of a finger. The willows sometimes reach a height of a foot and a half and are the tallest plant that can survive here. One might imagine a log cabin in this wilderness setting, but if there were one, the logs, along with all the other supplies that support life, would have had to be imported from that abundant country below the tree line. What wood one sees is almost entirely plywood. Cambridge Bay is a plywood settlement, and the few cabins at our base camp, ninety miles to the north, are made of plywood.

The Arctic's abrupt growing season isn't limited to plant life. Musk oxen grow very slowly because they gain weight only during the relative (though still meager) luxuriance of July and August and are in a "neutral balance" or even in a weight losing mode for the remainder of the year.* I think of Janis Joplin's "Get It While You Can." At first I thought of musk oxen as a sort of shaggy, northern Cape buffalo, though, up close, I see that they are very much smaller, a big bull weighing only seven hundred pounds to the buffalo's ton.

*Barry Lopez, *Arctic Dreams* (New York: Charles Scribner's Sons, 1986).

Sparse though it seems to me, this landscape is in its flowering now. I try to imagine it in winter. I try to imagine the life of the musk ox through three months of solid, unrelieved darkness and unvarying cold. Here is an animal who has mastered patience and acceptance, I think. But then it occurs to me that acceptance is a human idea. The musk ox simply *is* acceptance given form in the field of time. There is nothing he longs for beyond the endless polar day and the endless polar night. I will endeavor to be alert enough to embrace him as my teacher whenever I'm tempted to feel inconvenienced or put upon.

I observe the superabundance of water here, now in late summer, and think of how barren it will be, and for how long, a few months from now. There's little snow in the Arctic winter because there's so little moisture to draw upon. Just how musk oxen manage to survive year-round in country this barren, this harsh, even in the rare feeding areas, is still a mystery to scientists. They browse on the low, sedgy grass and gain concentrated energy from the tenuous willows.

There's a man at our base camp who has come up here to shoot a musk ox—a challenge akin to shooting a cow in a pasture—primarily because he's never shot a musk ox. Like some violent and acquisitive birder, he wants to fill out his life list.

I HAVE SUCH a blissful sense of personal insignificance here. I'm, at most, a curiosity to the musk ox and the caribou, and also, most probably, to Jimmy Haniliak, our Inuit guide. On our first day of fishing, having been dropped off by float plane at a lake, perhaps ten miles from our base camp, Jimmy and Frank and I had traveled a good two hours by seven-horse outboard toward the mouth of a nameless river. I'd been taking photographs of the shoreline, and it occurred to me how difficult it is to capture anything of the grandeur of this country on film as it is its very absence of features, the vast nothingness itself, that makes it dramatic. It was cold and empty whenever the sun was shrouded, and I motioned toward our lunch pack and asked if we'd brought along any water. Jimmy looked at me as if I'd asked him if my nose was still in the center of my face, and then, with politely suppressed mirth, he pointed to the lake. He slowed and took a cup and, after clearing a bit of foam and feather from the surface, dipped the cup into the water and handed it to me. When I was thirteen, at summer camp in the Tetons in western Wyoming, we carried no canteens and drank with impunity from the rivers and streams. But, having been so much a creature of the industrialized world, the idea of drinking surface water hadn't occurred to me in almost half a century. In this regard, this water, which is water such a brief portion of the year, must be among the last pure water on earth.

As FRANK AND I were about to depart for one of the outpost camps, Jimmy asked me how big my finger was. I held out my hand. He took off his wedding ring, and it fit my ring finger perfectly. "I want to make you something for your birthday," he said, "now you are one of the old ones." He smiled at me, and when we returned, three days later, he gave me a signet ring, beautifully carved from a musk ox horn with only a knife and a file. I've never worn rings, but I'll treasure this one. I like being one of the old ones.

A MERE WEEK in this remoteness suggests to me how minute and tenuous a presence man is and how the earth might appear to some disembodied observer if man were suddenly absent from it. I realize that the preceding sentence has the specious logic of an Escher drawing, but then so does the very life of the Arctic. No one discrete element or being within it would make any sense at all without the entire supporting cast which makes its part possible. In this sense the Arctic is the quintessential metaphor, a demonstration laboratory for the interdependence of all life's beings. Life feeding on life.

HERE, WHERE THE Hamilton River, through Hadley Bay, enters the Viscount Melville Sound, we are well above the northernmost point of Alaska at a north latitude of seventy-four degrees, in a line with Baffin Bay and northern Greenland. We are scarcely two hundred miles from the present location of the Magnetic North Pole—which is said to have moved more than four hundred miles north in the past two hundred years—though still one thousand miles south of the top of the world. I pull out my pocket compass to investigate our exact relationship to the MNP, and the compass laughs at me. Its needle wanders forty degrees east and west and never settles down. "Would you ask Boreas, god of the north wind, which way the north wind is blowing?" it chuckles. "Would you ask the source where it came from? You are here," it says dismissively. "You are here now."

Due to the prevailing southerly winds this summer the sea ice has moved out to the northern edge of the sound, leaving only scattered icebergs. Their submerged portions have taken on a deep cerulean blue in the light of this cloudy afternoon, and their exposed tops have been sculpted into Henry Moore-like shapes by the sun and wind. We had hoped for a glimpse of polar bears, which would have been a good possibility if the sea ice hadn't been displaced by this year's remarkably mild temperatures during late July and August. Melville Bay, just beyond the sound, is also known as "the breaking up yard," as it is a place along the Northwest Passage where ships have often been trapped and crushed by the sea ice.

Frank and I are wading, chest-deep, in the Hamilton, several hundred yards apart at the edge of the drop-off. I'm stripping a rather large orange streamer across the current, hoping, with each retrieve, to feel my line come tight. Frank has given me this fly, with which he has taken and released several "torpedoes," one- to two-foot-long silver lake trout. But I seem to be fooling no fish into believing this streamer might be a fleeing fingerling char.

Jack, our pilot, who has been flying this country since 1959, is waiting with the float plane, which we have beached just off a pool closer to the river mouth. I have mixed feelings about the northward migration of the sea ice. I had been thrilled by the prospect of seeing polar bears but also thrilled less pleasantly by my imagining what our adventure might be if we should experience engine trouble over the ice-packed bay and find ourselves down there with our fly rods and those chillingly white bears on their turfless turf. So I'm content to be holding against the flow of the river and the rapidly incoming tide, fooling nothing, not even myself, knowing finally that no expedition could be an adventure without the spice of imagined possibilities.

The wind is a raw forty miles per hour, and, looking downstream, I can see the tight, persistent loops of Frank's fly line against the dark sky. I was fly-fishing while Frank was learning to walk, and I'm both pleased and peeved that he has become a better caster than I am, though, due perhaps to youthful impatience, he breaks off more of the fish he's hooked. Since he first pinned me in an impromptu wrestling match when he was nineteen, I've watched myself being incrementally surpassed in almost every arena, though I console myself with the knowledge—or perhaps it's only a trope—that one garners more wisdom in defeat. If this is true, he is making me wise indeed.

FINALLY THERE'S AN enlivening sense of mystery in simply being in so remote a place, engulfed in all this emptiness. The primordial quietness and space can, at moments, blot *you* out completely; the experiencer is gone, and there is only the experience. I've had such moments of bliss here as I've often had in a trout stream, absorbed in my imagining the worldview of the trout. As my friend Jim Harrison has pointed out, fly-fishing is the most hypnotic of sports, and, apart from the pure pleasure of casting a fly line, its value to me is, like this landscape, a white ground of attention against which memory and imagination can do their work, unimpeded by the normally abiding governor of *me*. I can actually feel poems beginning to grow, like geometric shapes. The char is my ally, not in catching her, but in simply realizing there is that possibility.

In our northernmost camp, near Hadley Bay, I drift in and out of my dreams to the thundering flap of a large Canadian flag being flailed by a forty-knot wind. The whir of the flag becomes a constant, alternately a sea, a storm, a helicopter searching for me on the ice floe. Now, as I lie awake in my cold tent, it is exactly the ripping sound of a flag at the South Pole I heard once in a television drama, the Norwegian flag which Robert Falcon Scott found on his arrival after losing his race with Amundsen by only a few days. The sound of defeat. It may well have been the last sound Scott heard as he perished with his men on their journey back. And now it's the sound of this very flag on this very morning in this very place that I am but can't begin to conceive.

Barry Lopez posits the fascinating idea that, after an arctic river has frozen, one could cut through the ice and walk around on the dry river bottom, since the river's headwaters are also frozen, and that this tunnel of the dried-up river is a favorite haunt of the polar bear.

My walk up the empty corridor of the frozen riverbed under a translucent ceiling of ice will have to be in early spring, when sunlight has returned to this end of the earth. There is a dim fluorescent glow along the dark, meandering hallway. I am sheltered from the wind and the extreme cold, and at every dark bend in the riverbed I face the fatal possibility of disturbing a bivouacked polar bear. I listen for the sound of his breathing, magnified in this serpentine echo chamber, and know that each of my footfalls on the river floor is being carried to him, perhaps miles ahead, up this immense auditory canal. The bear will, of course, eat only my choice parts, finding me not nearly as tasty as a ringed seal, and will leave the lion's share of me strewn along the river bottom, where, in the brief season of flow next summer, my spleen will provide unusual fare for the returning sea run char. Or perhaps the bear isn't there at all, and I trudge on till I'm engulfed in the cascade of melting headwaters, lifted on their roiling crests until I'm thrust up through the now thinning ice and returned to the Arctic summer.

WHAT I HAVE discovered, now that I've returned to the tree line, is that I've spent more hours in reflection on my time in the Arctic than I actually spent on the tundra. And I suspect I left something there, some confusion I'm richer without.

Now, in September, while the aspens are just beginning to yellow in Wyoming, I know that if the country I flew out of a scant month ago remained as watery and fecund as it was when I left it, it would hold little magic. It's the mystery of a summer place all boarded up, the lakes already freezing, devoid of human presence and human observation, unchanged, for the next ten months, more or less, from the way it was before humans crossed the Bering land bridge at least 14,000 years ago.

There are rings of caribou antlers I saw. A blind built by ancient hunters? And I saw a circle of stones which once probably anchored the skirts of a seal-skin tent. In the middle of the circle there reposed a human skull. Who knows for how long, one hundred, five hundred, or one thousand years, in this place almost too cold for decay? And there are those few plywood cabins at our outfitter's permanent camp that undoubtedly give the winter wind a more haunting pitch, which only the musk ox will hear. Though in truth, I'm still there too, for my discovery is that the Arctic isn't so much a place as a state of mind. I brought some of that dramatic, unphotographable emptiness back with me. I keep it, as in a shaman's pouch, and parcel it out over my little daily life when I forget who it is that I am.

An Interview

conducted by Greg Rappleye

D AN GERBER WAS born and raised in Fremont, Michigan, and graduated from Michigan State University in 1962. He has traveled widely and currently divides his time between the central coast of California and a ranch in southeastern Idaho. For five years he lived in Key West.

This interview was conducted in a hotel room in downtown Grand Rapids, Michigan, in the summer of 1998, where Gerber had come to read with Stuart Dybek at the Urban Institute for Contemporary Art. Over Gerber's shoulder and seven floors below, the Grand River could be seen, and the dam which slows the river, to no apparent purpose, creating a waterfall across the river's width.

It was a hot day. In the distance, north of the city, thunderstorms formed and dissipated, the lightning occasionally igniting the sky to startling effect.

Interviewer: You are considered, at least by those of us here in Michigan, as a Michigan writer. Now you are living in California and Idaho. In what way is it fair to consider you a Michigan writer, a writer of the Upper Great Lakes?

Gerber: Well, I think it's fair in the same way it's fair to consider T. S. Eliot an American poet. He spent the first twenty-six years of his life in the United States. He later became a British subject and an Anglophile, but an Englishman can't become an Anglophile; an Englishman is just an Englishman. I think this is given away when he writes of "that delightful custom of taking tea." I mean, an Englishman wouldn't say that. This is someone from the outside, an observer. Michigan is in me. It's been there and still is my frame of reference. I lived here for fifty years. I'm certainly not a California poet. I'm not an Idaho poet.

It's funny; I've been introduced elsewhere as a Michigan poet. I did a reading twenty-five years ago in Minneapolis with James Welch. It was the first time I'd met him, and he was introduced as a Blackfeet Indian poet. And Welch said, "I'm not a Blackfeet Indian poet. I'm a poet who also happens to be a Blackfeet Indian, or I'm a Blackfeet Indian who also happens to be a poet."

I'm a poet who happens to be from Michigan.

Interviewer: How important is landscape in your work?

Gerber: Landscape is that, through which, if not out of which, my poems emerge. Just lately, the landscape of Idaho has taken on considerable importance in my work. And it's seen through the eyes of someone who grew up in the Midwest, in a landscape somewhat similar to Idaho, but still quite different. I only realized that from reading and re-reading the poems, and seeing words like "prairie" and "coulee." We don't have those things here in Michigan, at least not in the same sense. There was a place called "Big Prairie Desert" where I grew up. It resembled a prairie after the big fires went through in the late 1800s and took all the trees.

California is different in that it is, in its own way, exotic. It will always be a little exotic for me, in the same way England was always exotic for Eliot.

Interviewer: Do you think being away from Michigan gives you a different perspective on the Midwest or the Upper Great Lakes as a setting for your work?

Gerber: Oh, yes. I've found that I often write about the ocean when I'm in the desert and the desert when I'm by the sea. There's a kind of homesickness or nostalgia that generates the poem; Robert Frost said that's where it begins. I was thinking of Sarah Orne Jewett, a distinctly New England writer, who said that you have to know the world before you can appreciate the parish.

Interviewer: Has being well-traveled made you more adaptable as a writer to different locations?

Gerber: Thoreau said that a writer is a traveler who stays at home. Travel enlarges one's field of reference and probably, though not always, one's vision. It can also simply be a distraction.

I view Michigan differently now that I've lived away from it. But I think I've written as well about landscapes I've never visited. In *A Voice From the River* I wrote about New Guinea, a place I've never been. . . .

Interviewer: Really? I went back and re-read that novel and I was certain that you'd been there. You really seemed to have that landscape down. I had the sense that you had been there and had spent some time researching it. That's not true?

Gerber: No, it was all reading and imagining. But since there are 701 cultures in New Guinea, it wasn't too hard to take parts from many and create one. People who have been to New Guinea said they thought it was pretty accurate.

It may be the hazards of travel and the "giving up" that accompanies traveling that makes it a benefit for a writer; the leaving of a safe place.

Interviewer: As I understand it, you have dyslexia, or a touch of it.

Gerber: Yes. Of course, I didn't know that until I was in my thirties because they didn't have the term when I was a kid. I just couldn't spell very well, and I didn't know right from left. I was thought to be a little bit stupid. I couldn't get spelling because I developed my ear instead of my eye. A good speller, so I have learned, sees the word in front of him and then spells it out. With me it's all hearing. I don't know how much a part that particular syndrome played in it, but my teachers always said that I was better at talking than I was on tests. When I got to college it was easier, because we wrote essay exams, and I could spin out a good line. I remember one of the first tests in college was for a survey course in American literature, Whitman to the present. The professor had given quotes from five poets and asked us to identify the poets and discuss the quotes. I got it back with a "D" and a note that I'd written wonderful essays but unfortunately about the wrong poets. So I brought the test back and asked the professor if he would take another look at it. I was sure the essays were about the right poets, and it came back to me with an A+. The professor, or whoever had corrected it, had been in a hurry, I guess. It was one time I was glad that I pressed the point.

Interviewer: To what extent do you rely on third-party readers of early drafts of your work?

Gerber: I have several friends with whom I exchange manuscripts, most notably Jim Harrison over a long period of time, and more recently Judith Minty and Robert VanderMolen. The value of doing that is in getting a more objective look at the work, and it can speed up the process. It might take months to see the work in a way in which a friend might see it fresh. Often people who read my work have quite different tastes and perspectives, but being aware of those differences can lend clarity and perspective to the process of revision. I often read movie critics with whom I almost always disagree, but I know by their reaction to the movie whether or not I want to see it. These contrary reviews might even be more useful to me than those of a critic whose taste I almost always find in line with my own. For example, if I were to send the same poem to you, to Judith, and to Robert, I would probably get quite differing reactions. Maybe Judith loves the poem and VanderMolen thinks it's off. But knowing them, I know where their statements are coming from; I realize what's behind what they're saying. It wouldn't be that useful if I didn't know their work and their proclivities. That's sometimes the danger of a young writer showing his or her work to a so-called established writer and wanting feedback. When I'm asked to comment, I'm concerned that the person asking is going to take what I tell him or her too seriously. I have to tell them that I have to be honest, but I don't want to crush them. But the process is useful. It can save a lot of time, and sometimes it saves a poem. Sometimes a reader will have a perception about something I didn't see at all. After a reading at the University of Michigan a woman came up and pointed out that one of my poems was built around a pun. I hadn't thought of it that way because the pun was unintentional, but there it was.

Interviewer: Do you write for a particular audience?

Gerber: Keats said that he wrote for the spirit of poetry, the all-being and the memory of great men. That's good enough for me. I write for a few friends, both living and no-longer-living, whom I love. And I'm one of those people. If a poem doesn't satisfy me, I don't care what anybody else thinks of it. And if I write something that I don't like and others do, it makes me uncomfortable. The idea of an audience separate and apart from the standards I set for myself isn't a very useful notion. You have to keep the critic out of your work-room when you're writing. He can't be looking over your shoulder all the time. You just have to be the artist and then later you have to put on the other hat. I care what you think—I care what everybody thinks. I want everybody to like what I do, but I realize that's probably not going to happen. If I wrote a poem that none of my friends liked, I'd have to think seriously that there might be something wrong with it. But if everyone liked it and I didn't, I'd have to think that there might be something wrong with me.

Interviewer: Is there an audience, in the age of the Internet, blockbuster-special-effects-driven movies, and videos, for serious literary fiction and poetry?

Gerber: Yes, there is. It's a small audience, but I think that in this country that audience has always been small. And it does matter. Literature makes us human. Pound says that its function is to nurture our desire to go on living. I think we're in danger of losing what makes us human through a popular culture which desensitizes us to human suffering. Children kill vicariously through films and video games, and in doing so they kill something in themselves. I find myself, oddly enough, thinking of the First Amendment. I'm still against externally imposed censorship, but we've got moviemakers making brilliant movies pandering to an audience they themselves have created, movies in which it becomes funny to blow someone's head off. In many ways *Pulp Fiction* was a brilliant film, but at the same time I detest it. I think that artists have to take responsibility for their work. I've gotten off on a tangent here. But yes, there is an audience.

Jim Harrison published a novella called *A Woman Lit by Fireflies* in *The New Yorker*. He told me he received a letter from a woman in Nebraska who got up in the middle of the night, contemplating suicide, and went downstairs, picked up the magazine, and read his story. And instead of killing herself she wrote to tell him she'd changed her mind. If I got a letter like that, I'd consider my work to have been worthwhile. That story changed someone. I write for the effect the work will have on me, and I hope that, by extension, it will have a similar effect on others.

Interviewer: You're a writer who is identified with a community of writers such as Jim Harrison, Tom McGuane, and the artist and writer Russell Chatham. What's the history of those friendships, and how important was a sense of community in your development as a writer?

Gerber: Well, Harrison and McGuane and I went to school together, although we knew each other only vaguely. We got to know each other later through our writing and through correspondence. A sense of community wasn't terribly important to my work, except in the case of a few writers who were contemporaries and a few older writers like George Oppen. I think more than anything, a young writer wants the value of his work to be recognized by other writers. If there is an "out there" seal of approval, that's it; to be taken seriously by one's peers. There is no authority that says you are a bona fide poet. You've got one to certify you're a doctor or a lawyer but you haven't got one that says you're an artist. It's something you just know, and you'd like to have it confirmed by other artists whose work you admire.

Interviewer: On a panel several years ago, I recall you saying that the so-called Michigan State Writers—Richard Ford, Jim Harrison, yourself, Tom McGuane, Ted Weesner—are always talked about as early products of a creative writing program which never existed.

Gerber: It's funny how those things happen in retrospect. That statement was in the university newspaper when I was teaching at Michigan State back in 1970. It amused me because there *was* no writing program when we were students. I've had a number of inquiries from grad students about the "Five Blind Men School" of American poetry. *Five Blind Men* was an anthology that Charles Simic, George Quasha, J. D. Reed, Jim Harrison, and I were in, back in 1969. There was no "school" or agreed upon aesthetic. We were just five poets whose work appeared in a book together. Thirty years ago I got to know Basil Bunting, George Oppen, and Carl Rakosi, who along with Louis Zukovsky, Charles Reznikoff, Ezra Pound, and several others were grouped together as "The Objectivists." But the amazing thing to me in talking with these men was that often they had little knowledge of or regard for each other's work. They appeared in an anthology together and became known as a movement.

Interviewer: Is it still useful today for to you to think of a community of writers of which you are a member?

Gerber: Not in any concrete sense. There are writers I read from time to time, writers with whom I correspond, and there are writers, both living and dead, with whose work I feel in accord. I have writers as friends who remain very important to me. In Key West I was surrounded by writers, many of whom are friends and very stimulating people. I loved to talk with them and found their company informing and invigorating. But what they did on paper might or might not make a connection with me.

I'm quite isolated in Idaho, and that's nice too. One of my closest neighbors in Key West was Annie Dillard. Annie and I corresponded for twenty-five years before we ever met. I was in the offices of *Sports Illustrated* when they were publishing an excerpt from my second novel, and my editor handed me the manuscript of *Pilgrim at Tinker Creek,* from which they were also publishing an excerpt, and said, "Here, I think this might interest you." Well, it knocked me out. I wrote to Annie before the book came out, and we've corresponded ever since. I hadn't actually met her when she gave me that wonderful quote for *A Last Bridge Home,* and when we did meet, by chance at a dinner party in Key West, we went off in a corner and talked about old times. I still have writer-friends I know only by correspondence. William Heyen and I have corresponded for years, though we've never actually met.

It can be deadly though, for a writer to live among other writers, in that thinking of yourself as a part of that community can become your credential for being an artist, and you may feel you don't have to revalidate it through your work. I have a friend who went to the artist's and writer's colony at Deya on Majorca and wrote a very amusing piece about all the good poetry not being written in Spain that summer.

Interviewer: Much of your development as a writer occurred during the late 1960s and early 1970s. To what extent were the distractions, excesses, and issues of the day—the war in Vietnam, the civil rights movement—important in your writing?

Gerber: Everything—causes, distractions, and excesses included—go into making a life. What comes out of life is experience and imagination. The 1960s and early 1970s took me over. I was, for a time, a walking, talking cause. I had bleeding ulcers and astronomical blood pressure. The courts informed me that the Michigan State Police had compiled a subversive activities dossier on me. I was an antiwar activist who might punch you in the nose if you disagreed with me. It wasn't that I was a pacifist, but I was against the Vietnam War. I was about to become engaged in an act of violence against someone because he was for the war and I was against it when I had an epiphany, and it occurred to me that peace comes from something far more fundamental than any cause. I thought of Yeats's "These times when the best lack all conviction and the worst are filled with passionate intensity." It's easy, as a zealot, to become the very thing that you oppose. The most important thing for me as a writer was realizing this and consequently discovering and clarifying my own sense of injustice. When I met Carl Rakosi in Minneapolis I asked him why he had stopped writing for twenty years, and he said, "Because I became convinced there was no place for the artist in a Marxist world." When I asked why he started writing again, he said, "Because I became convinced there was no place for Marxism in the life of an artist."

Interviewer: Has your involvement with social issues changed over time? I know that you are involved with Amnesty International. To what extent is an artist or a writer obligated to speak out on the issues of social justice, peace, economic justice, and the other larger issues of the day?

Gerber: A writer is obliged to discover his vocation and the truth and fact of his work, and he or she is obliged to speak out about what he or she feels obliged to speak out about. But that doesn't mean falling into some politically correct lock-step of the stupid. Our responsibility as writers and as human beings is to discover our lives and the world around us and to pour all the ardor of our lives back into those things. The image comes from the thing and in turn makes the thing more than it originally was, by virtue of having allowed itself to be so vividly perceived. Rilke learned that from Rodin. Through art we can make things more intimately our own. We can live more passionately and fully. We can give more life back to our lives, and whether we're the maker or the perceiver ultimately doesn't matter.

I sometimes feel now that I have less personal ambition as a writer. I don't mean less ambition for the work itself, but less ambition for what comes of it. And I think I have more patience. Sometimes you think you've come to a dead end, but in fact it's just a stopping place along the road. The time spent there may be measured in years. But if the work is going to come, it will come in its own time. In *The Writing Life*, Annie Dillard says, "You'll know tomorrow or this time next year." I think now I have a greater willingness to take risks and probably less concern for what the world makes of my work. Though I still care a great deal about that particular individual James Wright called "the intelligent reader of good will," or Dylan Thomas "the lovers with their arms round the griefs of the ages."

You asked what shaped the evolution of my work. I would say, loss, divorce, death, displacement, estrangement, grief, discovery, new love supporting the old, regeneration, old truths in new clothes, reality, the fallacy of age, and my dog. She's been successively reincarnated.

Interviewer: Was that age of turmoil, the late 1960s, and early 1970s—a useful time for your work, a necessary time, or was it something that just happened?

Gerber: It was both useful *and* necessary, and it happened as it had to, to rectify everything that led up to it. It was a tremendously vital and hopeful time, and it was also very disillusioning and destructive—sounds like *The Tale of Two Cities*, doesn't it? It was a rich time, in which I felt torn apart. I felt both energized and enervated. I got very sick and discovered I couldn't live my life as a zealot. I couldn't live my life as a cause.

Interviewer: Is excess useful to a writer? I mean, to what extent can it be a liberating force, and to what extent can it be a destructive force? Where do you draw the line?

Gerber: Blake said that the road of excess leads to the palace of wisdom. I think excess is vital to a young writer if he's going to learn to take risks, and it's probably fatal to him if he doesn't learn to control it. I think you must take your work too far before you know how to take it to the right place. William Kittredge said a wonderful thing. I think he might have been paraphrasing Richard Hugo. "If the work doesn't risk sentimentality, it doesn't stand a chance of getting at the depth of things." Now if it just becomes sentimental work, then it's embarrassing. But if you're *not* willing to take that risk, you're going to produce possibly brilliant but ultimately shallow work. You have to risk being bad in order to have a chance of being good. And maybe that's where that third-party question comes in. You ask, "Gee, have I gone too far? Have I flipped out?" Your friend looks at it and says, "No. Not at all. I think it's perfect." Or she may say, "Well, it's all right in itself, but it doesn't sound like *your* work." And that may or may not be a good thing.

Interviewer: Who were your early influences? Whose work had an impact on you?

Gerber: Early influences for me were Poe, Alfred Noyes, Walter de la Mare, Paul Gallico, García Lorca, the Brothers Grimm, and Sherwood Anderson. Robert Frost was a very early influence and continues to be. I learned to write by learning to read, which seems to me two sides of the same coin. I felt compelled to try to make something with words that would create a new sense of mystery out of that which I received from the work of others. I learned by imitation.

Interviewer: So growing up you were a reader and spent a lot of time in the library?

Gerber: I read a lot, and as a child I built up an extensive library on three particular subjects: bullfighting, mountain climbing, and motor-racing. Those three things fascinated me, and I lived in the stories of the people who did them. They became my stories. Those people became my heroes and, as Kierkegaard's Johannes de Silento suggested, they became my better nature, with which I was in love. I did read a lot, and I remember my teachers being surprised that I didn't do better on tests because in class I seemed to have a breadth of general knowledge. I knew a lot of stuff, but I didn't learn it in the programmatic sense I needed to apply it to academic work.

Interviewer: What sorts of books do you read?

Gerber: I read voraciously, widely, and arcanely. Friends who are serious readers will ask me what I'm reading, and it's not what they're reading. I may be more likely reading some obscure biography than the latest novel, though I may read that too. I jump around a lot, but about sixty percent of the reading I do is re-reading. I go back and read something I've read at a different time in my life, and it's a different book. It tells me what's happened to me in the interim. To me, a book read only once is hardly read at all. And that may have to do with being dyslexic as a child and having to read everything twice to comprehend it. I read very slowly. I can quote from just about every book I've read. But I can't read that many of them. It's a greater pleasure for me to *absorb* a book if it's worth reading in the first place.

Interviewer: You sound like an attentive reader, in the sense that if we went into your library we'd find things pretty well annotated.

Gerber: I write all over everything I read. If I love a passage, I go back and read it again and again. I've re-read Rilke every year for about thirty years now, the poems, the letters, and the stories. When I first encountered his work I knew there was something big there. I just wasn't getting it, but I knew it was worth going after. And I think that that feeling points the way to good work. Something remains mysterious, no matter how many times you read it. Carl Sandburg said the experience of a good poem is like sitting at one end of a room. Someone comes in the door on one side, walks quickly through, and goes out the other, and you're left wondering, "Well, just what exactly did I see here?" So you go back to it again, but it retains that sense of mystery. A work of art occurs when the elements of a poem, or a painting, or a song, come together as something greater than their sum and remain indefinable. Was it Pound who said that poetry is news that stays news? I guess that's why I'm not a big fan of mystery novels. I wouldn't want to re-read them.

Interviewer: Who's doing good work today? Whose books do you look forward to? Whose work do you really admire?

Gerber: I never like to answer that question because I know that I'll overlook the most obvious people. Well, obviously, Jim Harrison, particularly his poems, though his novels receive so much more attention. I just read his wonderful new poem called "Geo-Bestiary." I always look forward to any new work by Robert Bly, as quirky as he can be. When I look at all of his work, it's magnificent. His translations of Neruda ,Vallejo, Jiménez, Machado, and Rilke have meant the world to me. Sometimes his perceptions get way out there, but there's a core of truth around which he works all the time. James Salter is an incomparable stylist, and I find almost everything William Gass writes fascinating and enlarging. Last year *Cold Mountain* by Charles Frazier just knocked my socks off. A novelist named Mildred Walker who wrote back in the 1930s. I discovered her a few years ago and think she's wonderful. Robert Richardson's biographies of Thoreau and Emerson, Annie Dillard, Roger Shattuck, Paul Fussell, Richard Nelson, Barry Lopez, Frederick Turner, James Welch, the Swedish poet Tomas Tranströmer, and Jack Gilbert, when he writes. I'm overlooking some of the most obvious living writers whose work I love—Peter

Matthiessen, especially *The Far Tortuga*—though most of the writers I read regularly are no longer writing: Rilke, Whitman, Blake, Wordsworth, Gaston Bachelard, Jiménez, Neruda, Hamsun, Thoreau, Homer, Herodotus, Jane Kenyon, Wallace Stevens, Yeats, Lorca, Rimbaud, Sherwood Anderson, Jens Peter Jacobson, James Wright, Hui Neng, Keats, Thomas Hardy, Shinkichi Takahashi, Su Tung-P'o, *The Secret of the Golden Flower* (the best source book for poets I know), Willa Cather, Shakespeare always, and on forever. I think that's enough.

Interviewer: Do you read in a particular field when you're writing in that field, for example, read fiction when you're writing fiction, or poetry when you're writing poetry?

Gerber: I read poetry when I'm writing poetry, though I'm much less likely to read fiction when I'm writing fiction. It's too easy to confuse the voice in which you are writing with the voice you're reading. And also, when I'm writing a novel I'm so lost in that world I probably couldn't comprehend another situation. But poetry begets poetry. I often think I've never written anything original in my life. Everything comes from something else. I've been really taken with the great Spanish poet Juan Ramón Jiménez, who won the Nobel Prize in 1956. Jiménez said, "When I don't understand a poem or part of it I don't insist. I try to be satisfied with what I understand, and I'm sure that another time under other conditions I'll understand more and understand something else. The understanding of a poem comes in successive surprises." In my experience this certainly has been true. As I said, it took me years to begin to penetrate Rilke and some of the other poets I now live by. And this notion of "successive surprises" is as true in my writing as it is in reading. Jiménez says, "If my work were to make itself without any effort on my part, I would like it very little. But if I were to make it alone, without any effort on its part, I would like it even less." You can't worry the poem into existence, he's saying; you can't make it as an act of will. You have to tap some deeper place.

Interviewer: Is it a fair statement about your fiction to say that you get a voice who's telling you a story, and you are, in effect, translating that voice to the page?

Gerber: Every piece of fiction I've written has started that way. I've had ideas for short stories that never come to fruition because they're just ideas or because I've learned too much and by the time I get ready to write, there's no mystery. Every successful story, and by successful I mean in the sense of completion and fruition, begins with a line, just the way a poem does, begins with somebody talking, somebody saying something. Who would say something like that? Who is this person? What's their story? And certainly that's where all the stories in *Grass Fires* came from. They all start with a voice, somebody talking or telling a story. And they may end up telling quite a different story than the one I thought, or even they thought, they were telling.

Interviewer: To what extent is what you write *received,* and to what extent is it *work?* Can you separate the two?

Gerber: If a poem or a story was just something I was conscious of having made up, it wouldn't be very effective. I like Randall Jarrell's idea that a good poet is a person who, in a lifetime of standing out in thunderstorms, manages to get struck by lightning a half-dozen times. You do the hard work of finding the thunderstorms, polishing the lightning rod, and going out and waving it over your head, but you can't make the lightning strike. You can create the conditions. You keep yourself tuned to the language. You pay attention to the experience of your life and the tradition you come from and how it smells right after a rain.

Paul Celan said that poems are also gifts to the attentive. And I believe Celan meant to include the reader when he said it. Real attention is rare, and that, I believe, is the reason the audience for true poems is likely to be small. Most people aren't capable of paying attention. Their world and their practice is distraction. They want interpreted experience, i.e., entertainment.

Interviewer: With regard to your books of poems and your short story collection, it seems to me you have a sense of pacing in organizing the structure of a book. The way you put these short, lyric, meditative poems and then these more narrative poems together is stunning, not only in the poems themselves but in the synthesis they make.

Gerber: Now you're speaking of the poems?

Interviewer: I am speaking of poems but I think the same is true of the way the short story collection, *Grass Fires,* is organized. The pacing of everything just seems so right. Is that deliberate? Do you deliberately arrange the poems and stories to create that effect that I can't exactly articulate?

Gerber: Well, I can't articulate it either. I do spend a lot of time thinking about the arrangement of poems in a volume, but I don't think I could shed any light on the process. It's intuitive. "This one here and maybe that one there, because it feels right." I don't have any kind of template; I have no sense that, "Okay now, we need a longer narrative piece here." Sometimes it seems arbitrary. Finally it seems that I just get all the poems together and put them where they tell me they want to go. I had this experience with the novel when I finished *A Voice from the River.* I cleared a big space and laid out all forty-four chapters on the floor. I was familiar enough with each chapter so that I could see it whole at a glance, and I stood above them on a tall stool and arranged them as if I were directing children on a playground, "You there, and you, over there."

Interviewer: In an increasingly specialized age, you are a diverse writer. You're a poet, an essayist, a short story writer, and a novelist. And you've been an editor as well. Is there a form in which you prefer to work?

Gerber: Well, the poem is primary for me and most necessary. It's where I began, and it's what I always come back to. It seems to me the most demanding form and at the same time, maybe because it's so demanding, the easiest one to indulge if the writer is content to rest on poor work. I mean that in the same way that it's probably easier to fake it as an abstract painter than it is as a realist because there's less comparison to the objects of the world and to tradition. There's plenty of tradition in poetry, of course, but I think it's possible to get away with things in a poem that you couldn't in prose, because in prose the reader has more specific expectations.

Interviewer: But it's a difficult form to do well?

Gerber: The most difficult. There's a lot of gibberish out there. I remember once in a conversation with George Oppen he told me that somebody handed him a poem and asked, "Is this a poem?" and he said, "Yes, it's a poem, because it looks like a poem. But that doesn't have anything to do with the question of whether or not it's any good. If it looks like a poem, it's a poem."

For me the short story comes from an impulse closer to the lyric poem than to the novel. Maybe I'm not really a short story writer at all, though I am naturally and probably even sometimes obsessively a storyteller. In his book *Winter Count,* Barry Lopez has a character who, at the end of the story, muses, "Everything is held together with stories, he thought. That is all that is holding us together, stories and compassion." I love that. Sometimes I want a larger, more narrative form to absorb me, though often when I've been working on a novel I've felt torn, missing the poem, and I wonder how many poems I might be sacrificing since all my energy is going into the writing of the novel. The poem is like air to me; I can't imagine living without it. When the language of a novel takes over and writes itself, it's as satisfying as a poem. And I think it almost is a poem. I think of Joyce more as a poet than as a novelist. I guess I've just come to realize that I'm better at making what I have to make in the form of a poem. And finally, I believe that I'm only interested in that prose which at least approaches the concision and intensity of a poem. This may be another way of saying that I think there's an awful lot of narrative prose out there with a very low power-to-weight ratio.

Interviewer: You said some interesting things about short stories and the lyric impulse. Last night I re-read several of the stories in *Grass Fires* and was struck, looking at "Crop Duster" and "Hardball," for example, by how finely cut they were, how well tuned. There was not a wasted line in either of them, no unnecessary narrative. Every line was telling. To what extent does your experience as a poet, writing the short, pointed lyric as you sometimes do, influence the way you write a short story like "Hardball" or "Crop Duster?"

Gerber: I think that those stories came from a lyric impulse. Each of those stories began with a first line or a first sentence that was somebody speaking, and I discovered who that person was in the writing of the story. Sometimes I didn't even know their gender. I would get into the story a little way and then realize it was a woman speaking. The first line engenders the second line. Somebody asked Faulkner if he planned his stories in advance, and he said, "No, a disorderly writer like me can't do that. Characters appear and start doing and saying things, and I follow them around with a pencil and try to get down what they do and say, and at some point a policeman comes in and blows the whistle and says, 'Look, you've got to make something coherent out of this,' and that's where the discipline comes in."

I've worked very hard to try to learn to say what I can say in as few words as possible. I remember the one creative writing course I took in college, which didn't do me a whole lot of good as a writer. Ultimately it did make me a better *reader,* but as far as writing goes, at the time it made me too analytical. I remember the instructor told a story about nailing some boards up on the side of his garage. He was up there on the ladder and he saw this old guy on the sidewalk watching him, and he kept on watching and finally he turned around and said to the man, "Speak!" And the old guy said, "Seven'll do it." And the nailer said, "What do you mean?" "You're just driving the twelfth nail into that board there, and it's not going to hold it any better than seven nails would hold it." And so he made a messier job of it and wasted a lot of nails, time, and energy. And I guess when you're a writer you're